READERS' GUIDES TO ESSENTIAL CRITICISM

CONSULTANT EDITOR: NICOLAS TREDELL

Published

Nicholas Potter	Shakespeare: *Othello*
Berthold Schoene–Harwood	Mary Shelley: *Frankenstein*
Nick Selby	T. S. Eliot: *The Waste Land*
Nick Selby	Herman Melville: *Moby Dick*
Nick Selby	The Poetry of Walt Whitman
David Smale	Salman Rushdie: *Midnight's Children – The Satanic Verses*
Patsy Stoneman	Emily Brontë: *Wuthering Heights*
Susie Thomas	Hanif Kureishi
Nicolas Tredell	F. Scott Fitzgerald: *The Great Gatsby*
Nicolas Tredell	Joseph Conrad: *Heart of Darkness*
Nicolas Tredell	Charles Dickens: *Great Expectations*
Nicolas Tredell	William Faulkner: *The Sound and the Fury – As I Lay Dying*
Nicolas Tredell	Shakespeare: *Macbeth*
Nicolas Tredell	The Fiction of Martin Amis
Angela Wright	Gothic Fiction

Forthcoming

Pascale Aebischer	Jacobean Drama
Simon Avery	Thomas Hardy: *The Mayor of Casterbridge – Jude the Obscure*
Annika Bautz	Jane Austen: *Sense and Sensibility – Pride and Prejudice – Emma*
Matthew Beedham	The Novels of Kazuo Ishiguro
Justin Edwards	Postcolonial Literature
Jodi–Anne George	*Beowulf*
William Hughes	Bram Stoker: *Dracula*
Matthew Jordan	Milton: *Paradise Lost*
Sara Lodge	Charlotte Brontë: *Jane Eyre*
Aaron Kelly	Twentieth–Century Irish Literature
Matthew McGuire	Contemporary Scottish Literature
Timothy Milnes	Wordsworth: *The Prelude*
Steven Price	The Plays, Screenplays and Films of David Mamet
Stephen Regan	The Poetry of Philip Larkin
Michael Whitworth	Virginia Woolf: *Mrs Dalloway*
Gina Wisker	The Fiction of Margaret Atwood
Matthew Woodcock	Shakespeare: *Henry V*

Readers' Guides to Essential Criticism
Series Standing Order
ISBN 1–4039–0108–2
(outside North America only)

You can receive future titles in this series as they are published by placing a standing order. Please contact your bookseller or, in the case of difficulty, write to us at the address below with your name and address, the title of the series and the ISBN quoted above.

Customer Services Department, Macmillan Distribution Ltd
Houndmills, Basingstoke, Hampshire RG21 6XS, England

The Fiction of A. S. Byatt

LOUISA HADLEY

Consultant editor: Nicolas Tredell

palgrave
macmillan

First published in 2008 by
PALGRAVE MACMILLAN
Houndmills, Basingstoke, Hampshire RG21 6XS and
175 Fifth Avenue, New York, N.Y. 10010
Companies and representatives throughout the world

PALGRAVE MACMILLAN is the global academic imprint of the Palgrave Macmillan division of St. Martin's Press, LLC and of Palgrave Macmillan Ltd. Macmillan® is a registered trademark in the United States, United Kingdom and other countries. Palgrave is a registered trademark in the European Union and other countries.

ISBN-13: 978-0-230-51791-2 hardback
ISBN-10: 0-230-51791-9 hardback
ISBN-13: 978-0-230-51792-9 paperback
ISBN-10: 0-230-51792-7 paperback

This book is printed on paper suitable for recycling and made from fully managed and sustained forest sources. Logging, pulping and manufacturing processes are expected to conform to the environmental regulations of the country of origin.

A catalogue record for this book is available from the British Library.

A catalog record for this book is available from the Library of Congress.

10 9 8 7 6 5 4 3 2 1
17 16 15 14 13 12 11 10 09 08

Printed and bound in China

Contents

Continues with critical accounts of the position of painting in *Still Life*; both Michael Worton and Sue Sorensen explore the tension between verbal and visual art in Byatt's novel by analysing its connections to Vincent van Gogh. Moves on to consider responses to Stephanie's death, most of which find no meaning or comfort in it. Sue Sorensen's essay presents a more sustained engagement with the issue of death, arguing that Byatt deliberately tries to capture this meaninglessness. This focus on death is balanced by Tess Cosslett's feminist account of the depiction of childbirth in *Still Life*. Chapter concludes with a brief consideration of Byatt's article 'Still Life/Nature morte' where she discusses the stylistic approach of *Still Life*.

Examines key review responses to Byatt's most successful novel, *Possession*, drawing out the recurrent concern with its position in relation to realism and postmodernism which continues to dominate critical accounts of the novel. Jackie Buxton and Bo Lundén both distance *Possession* from postmodern discourses, claiming that it contains elements that remain unaccounted for by postmodernism. By contrast, Chris Walsh designates *Possession* a postmodern text because of its self-conscious concern with reading. Elisabeth Bronfen similarly prioritizes the postmodern elements of *Possession* although she sees the romance genre as giving Byatt a way to incorporate a moral view into postmodernism. For Susanne Becker, however, *Possession* suggests a movement beyond postmodernism in its incorporation of the gothic genre. Chapter concludes with a discussion of the Postscript; again critics who see it as a Victorian element of the novel (Buxton, Frederick M. Holmes) are juxtaposed with those who see it as postmodern (Shiller, Walsh).

Focuses on *Possession*'s position as a historical novel. Traces the accounts of Del Ivan Janik and Frederick M. Holmes who find it combines a self-reflexive awareness about history with a commitment to depicting the past. For Dana Shiller, however, Byatt's novel more properly belongs to the subgenre of neo-Victorian fiction, which is distanced from accounts of postmodern historical fiction. Moves on to critical accounts of the method of connecting with the past in *Possession*, its incorporation of textual remains. Suzanne Keen's account of 'romances of the archive' posits *Possession* as the exemplar of the subgenre and hints at the political uses of the past. Similarly, John J. Su suggests that the past can be used for political purposes, to reimagine social identities, as long as this begins from an engagement with the textual remains of the past. Both Louise Yelin and Richard Todd examine the politics of Byatt's representation of the Victorian era, suggesting that, despite some criticism of its gender politics, the Victorian era is prioritized over the twentieth century. Chapter concludes with Sue Sorensen's account of the 2000 film version of *Possession*, which she views as simplifying many of the concerns of the novel, particularly its feminist politics and its engagement with postmodernism.

Opens with the review response to *Angels and Insects*, which often judged it superior to *Possession*, then moves on to more sustained analyses of the novellas. Sally Shuttleworth positions 'Morpho Eugenia' as part of a subgenre of 'retro-Victorian fiction' nostalgically concerned with the Darwinian moment. Hilary M. Schor considers both novellas in terms of their strategy of 'ghost-writing', which incorporates the intertextual echoes of Victorian texts as well as Byatt's concern with 'reanimating' realism. Susan Poznar and Louisa Hadley focus on 'The Conjugial Angel''s engagement with spiritualism. For Poznar, the séances are a metaphor for Byatt's' engagement with metaphoric language. Hadley draws out the connections between spiritualism and reading, suggesting that 'The Conjugial Angel' provides a model of the relationship to the past. Discussion then turns to Byatt's third neo-Victorian text, *The Biographer's Tale* which was also often judged against *Possession*, and generally found wanting. Chapter closes with Celia Wallhead's examination of the relationship between writing and self-identity in *The Biographer's Tale*.

Begins with the review response to *Babel Tower*, which often saw it as marking a departure from the previous two novels in the quartet. The intellectualism that was felt to mar the first two novels is generally thought to dominate *Babel Tower*. Criticism of *Babel Tower* focuses on similar issues to accounts of *Virgin* and *Still Life*. Celia Wallhead examines *Babel Tower*'s treatment of language, especially the relationship between language and truth, concluding that Byatt's work maintains a commitment to truth despite her awareness of postmodern scepticism. Wallhead's analysis of the multiple openings in *Babel Tower* provides a transition to Michael Noble on the nature of memory in the novel. Noble interprets the various openings as sites of memory, connecting them to the prologues in *Virgin* and *Still Life*.

Opens with the reviews of *A Whistling Woman*, which generally judged it less successful than the first two novels. Some reviewers comment on the feminist concerns of the quartet, but most find the novel oddly lacking in its engagement with feminist issues. Chapter then turns to responses to the quartet as a whole. It begins with Byatt's article on the relationship between science and literature in the quartet; she suggests a shift from a focus on literature and language in the first two novels to a more overt concern with science in the latter two. Peter Preston draws out the connections, problematic for a female author, between the quartet and D. H. Lawrence. Ultimately, he claims that Lawrence provides a means for Byatt to connect with a tradition of Victorian women writers. Chapter concludes by discussing various approaches to the quartet as a whole and drawing out the recurring view that there is a split, both thematic and stylistic, between its first two and last two novels.

Fiction-Making, Fairy-Tales and Feminism: Short Stories

Examines criticism of Byatt's five short-story collections, starting with *Sugar and Other Stories* (1987), which was often seen in autobiographical terms. Explores three critical responses to the collection: Claude Maisonnat on the issue of mourning in 'The July Ghost'; Charlotte Sturgess on the nature of story-telling in the collection; and Jane Campbell on the relationship between art and life in 'Precipice-Encurled'. Reviews of Byatt's second collection, *The Matisse Stories* (1993), often considered its engagement with art. Sarah Fishwick analyses the relationship between art, space and feminist concerns in the stories. Byatt's third collection, *The Djinn in the Nightingale's Eye* (1994), was generally reviewed in terms of its relationship to fairytales. Annegret Maack explores the functions of story-telling in the title story, seeing it as both a story and a metafictional comment on story-telling. Jane Campbell is similarly concerned with story-telling, although she presents an explicitly feminist account of the collection's engagement with the fairytale genre. Since *Elementals: Stories of Fire and Ice* (1999) and *The Little Black Book of Stories* (2003) have received little critical attention, the focus is on the review response to these collections. Reviews of *Elementals* often suggest that the short-story form gives Byatt more freedom which permits a wit and vivacity absent from the densely intellectual novels. Similarly, *Little Black Book* is seen to mark a departure from Byatt's novelistic style in the transition to darker territories. Chapter concludes by summarizing the response to the short stories, suggesting that they share the thematic concerns of Byatt's novels but are marked by a difference in style.

Draws out the main areas of criticism with which the Guide has been concerned: the role of the artist; the postmodernism versus realism debate; and Byatt's position in relation to feminism. Proposes that Byatt's novelistic output can be divided into three broad phases: her early fiction, the quartet and her neo-Victorian texts. It indicates some possible future directions for Byatt criticism.

Acknowledgements

I would like to thank my publishers for supporting this project, particularly Sonya Barker and Felicity Noble who have demonstrated considerable patience when dealing with my numerous enquiries. Also I would like to thank the consultant editor for this series, Nicolas Tredell, for his advice and encouragement at various stages in this project. The University of Edinburgh Library and the National Library of Scotland have proved invaluable resources during the researching of this book and, as usual, their staff have been extremely helpful and patient. Finally, a special thanks is owed to Gary Stewart for his patience and technical support at the critical junctures of this project.

The author and publishers wish to thank the following for permission to reproduce copyright material:

From *Passions of the Mind* by A. S. Byatt, published by Chatto & Windus. Reprinted by permission of The Random House Group Ltd.
From *The Shadow of the Sun* by A. S. Byatt, published by Chatto & Windus. Reprinted by permission of The Random House Group Ltd.
From *On Histories and Stories and The Matisse Stories* by A. S. Byatt, published by Chatto & Windus. Reprinted by permission of The Random House Group Ltd.
Excerpts from *The Shadow of the Sun: A Novel*, copyright © 1964 and renewed 1992 by A. S. Byatt, reprinted by permission of Harcourt, Inc.

Every effort has been made to trace the copyright holders, but if any have been inadvertently overlooked the publishers would be pleased to make the necessary arrangements at the first opportunity.

Introduction

A S. Byatt was born Antonia Susan Drabble in 1936 in Sheffield.
. Her mother, a Cambridge graduate who had given up teaching
to raise her family, insisted that her children gain a good education
and placed huge emphasis on the importance of going to Cambridge.
Byatt attended Newnham College, Cambridge, in the 1950s, study-
ing English Literature in an atmosphere dominated by the famous
literary critic F. R. Leavis (1895–1978). Leavis's views on the moral
import of literature deeply affected Byatt and her subsequent writing:
'my early novels are in one aspect a sort of questioning quarrel with
Leavis' vision and values, which nevertheless I inherit and share'.[1] After
graduating from Cambridge Byatt began a PhD on religious imagery
in seventeenth-century poetry; however, when she married Ian Byatt
in 1959 she had to abandon her studies, as married women were not
eligible for grants. Although Byatt divorced her first husband and married Peter Duffy in 1969, she has kept the name with which she began
her literary career.[2] Richard Todd sees in the 'manly initials' of Byatt's
pseudonym a connection to the similarly masculine pseudonym of
George Eliot (1819–80). Byatt herself, however, relates her choice of
name to another Eliot, T. S. Eliot (1888–1965), and his notion that
writers should remain anonymous.[3]

In 1964, Byatt entered the literary scene with her first novel, *Shadow
of a Sun*, which she wrote while still an undergraduate. This was
followed, in 1967, by a second novel, *The Game*. Although these novels
did receive some attention in the press, Byatt's success was not sufficient
for her to give up her teaching jobs. Indeed, both of these novels were
followed up by critical works: *Degrees of Freedom* (1965) and *Wordsworth
and Coleridge in the Their Time* (1970). During this period, Byatt's life
was hit by personal tragedy as her eleven-year-old son, Charles, was
killed in a drink-driving accident in 1972. Byatt is particularly resistant to autobiographical readings of her work and avoids discussing
her personal life in interviews. Yet, since critics continue to engage
in autobiographical readings, it is important to provide some relevant
details. As will be seen in Chapter 9, several critics draw on the death
of Byatt's son in their analysis of the story 'The July Ghost'. This strand

of autobiographical criticism is also apparent in accounts of Byatt's early novels, especially the sibling relationship in *The Game*. Byatt's relationship with her own sister, the novelist Margaret Drabble (born 1939), has been the subject of much speculation and is often depicted in the media as being characterized by jealousy and competition. Although she denies this, Byatt does resent the constant comparisons made by critics and the media. In an interview with Mervyn Rothstein, Byatt expresses her dislike with people comparing her to her sister and reading her works as 'written by somebody who happens to be the sister of another novelist', which she claims is 'very annoying if you've wanted to be a novelist since you were five'.[4]

Despite Byatt's intense dislike of comparisons with her sister, it is true that for the early part of her career Byatt's work was overshadowed by her sister's success. With the publication of *The Virgin in the Garden* in 1978, however, Byatt came out from under her sister's shadow and began to establish a reputation on her own terms. This novel marked the beginning of an ambitious project, a quartet that would not be completed until the publication of *A Whistling Woman* in 2002. The second in the series, *Still Life*, appeared in 1985 and confirmed Byatt's position as a serious novelist, winning her the PEN/Macmillan Silver Pen Award in 1986. Byatt followed up this success by bringing out her first collection of short stories, *Sugar and Other Stories* in 1987. Although she had been working as a full-time novelist since 1983, Byatt continued to produce critical works, editing a collection of George Eliot's essays in 1989. Byatt herself recognizes the necessary interaction between her critical and creative projects: 'Novelists sometimes claim that their fiction is a quite separate thing from their other written work. ... I have never felt such a separation, nor wanted to make such claims.'[5] Instead, she conceives of writing and reading as 'points on a circle'.[6] This dual role as critic and novelist has often led to Byatt being positioned with other 'academic-novelists' of her generation such as David Lodge (born 1935) and Malcolm Bradbury (1932–2000). Despite her continued role as a critic, Byatt defines herself as primarily a novelist: 'I am not an academic who happens to have written a novel ... I am a novelist who happens to be quite good academically.'[7] Consequently, this Guide focuses on Byatt's fictional works, although it will include brief considerations of her critical writings where relevant.

The publication of *Possession: A Romance* in 1990 marked the turning point in A. S. Byatt's career. Although she had enjoyed some critical success with *Still Life* Byatt was considered to be primarily an 'intellectual' writer whose novels necessarily had a limited readership. All that changed with the publication of *Possession*; the novel won both the Booker Prize and the Irish Times-Aer Lingus International Fiction Prize, with prize money totalling £45,000. As one American reporter commented 'Not a bad week for a novelist.'[8] But *Possession* earnt more than prize money for Byatt, it also earnt her a place on the bestsellers list and won her a new group of readers. As the then managing director of Waterstone's said: 'Winning [the Booker Prize] makes the difference between being a very good author that people who read a lot know to becoming an author with a national name.'[9] While *Possession* did not forsake the intellectual qualities that had become the hallmark of Byatt's fiction it also had a popular appeal, bringing together as it did a contemporary interest in the Victorians, a return towards plot and characterization and a narrative curiosity akin to that of detective fiction. In an interview Byatt explained that she had intended *Possession* to have this popular appeal, 'I actually paced it for the first time with the reader's attention span in mind.'[10]

The publication history of *Possession* was not all plain sailing however. Byatt struggled to find a publisher in America until Susan Kamil of Turtle Bay offered to publish it, providing the author made significant changes, mostly involving cutting the nineteenth-century letters and poems. Byatt recounts the incident in an interview with John F. Baker: 'when she started talking about what would have to go, I fainted dead away. It was very dramatic. She took me up to her room, and when I came round I said I couldn't agree to any of it.'[11] Byatt stuck to her guns and the book remained unpublished in America until it had proved its worth with its British sales. Byatt's novel was an instant hit with British readers and this success guaranteed its publication in America by Random House, where it sold more than 100,000 copies within a year of its publication.[12] *Possession* has continued to retain high sales figures over the decade and a half since its first appearance, making it the most popular and successful of Byatt's novels to date. Consequently, *Possession* occupies a central place in this Guide, with two chapters dedicated to the critical responses to it. The popular appeal of *Possession* was recognized by Warner Bros. who released a film version in 2002 starring Gwyneth Paltrow and Jeremy Northam. Since the film is both a product of and a contributing factor to the continued popularity of Byatt's novel Chapter 5 will conclude with a brief consideration of critical responses to it.

The success of *Possession* has had a lasting impact on the critical and popular perception of Byatt's fiction. Prior to *Possession* Byatt's work had received little critical attention and although it was generally admired by reviewers it was often considered too dry and intellectual to achieve any success with the general reader. Consequently some of her works had gone out of print by the time *Possession* hit the shelves. After her Booker success, reprints of Byatt's earlier novels were issued, bringing them to the attention of a wider reading audience. In the case of *Shadow of a Sun*, the reprint enabled Byatt to add a foreword explaining its genesis and to restore her original choice of title.

Byatt followed up the success of *Possession* with another foray into the Victorian world, the two novellas published as *Angels and Insects* in 1992. After this came the short-story collections, *The Matisse Stories* (1993) and *The Djinn in the Nightingale's Eye* (1994). In 1996, after a break of more than a decade, Byatt returned to her quartet, publishing the third volume, *Babel Tower*. She did not finish the quartet until 2002 though, with the publication of *A Whistling Woman*. In the intervening period, Byatt published another collection of short stories, *Elementals: Stories of Fire and Ice* (1998), and *The Biographer's Tale* (2000), which continues many of the concerns of *Possession*. Her most recent publication was another collection of short stories, *The Little Black Book of Stories* in 2003. Byatt's contribution to literature was recognized with a CBE (Commander of the British Empire) in 1990 and a DBE (Dame Commander of the British Empire) in 1999.

Since her writing career began over 30 years ago, Byatt's output has been steady, and has covered a range of genres, not only in the continuation of her critical writings but also in her alternation between short stories and novels. In tracing the various critical responses to Byatt's fictional works, this Guide considers both the responses to individual texts as well as the wider critical debates surrounding Byatt's oeuvre as a whole. The subsequent chapters will be primarily chronological and will each focus on one or two of Byatt's fictional works, considering both the initial review responses to the texts and, later, more sustained critical engagements. Although published a decade apart, *Angels and Insects* and *The Biographer's Tale* are considered in Chapter 6 since they, along with *Possession*, represent Byatt's contribution to the genre of neo-Victorian fiction. The other exception to the chronological organization is Chapter 9, which examines the critical responses to Byatt's short-story collections. Although Byatt's reputation as a writer is based mostly on her novelistic output, her five short-story collections represent a significant part of her oeuvre and deal with many of the same themes and concerns that are treated in the novels.

Although this Guide will concentrate on Byatt's fictional output, her critical works will be discussed when they shed light on her fictional preoccupations. Byatt's critical writings fall into two separate categories: her literary criticism of other writers and her more general critical writings. Of the first type, there are two key publications: *Degrees of Freedom* and *Wordsworth and Coleridge in Their Time*. In addition, Byatt has edited several works such as selections of George Eliot's essays and of the dramatic monologues of Robert Browning (1812–89). More interesting for the purposes of this Guide, however, are the critical writings of the second type: *Passions of the Mind* (1991) and *On Histories and Stories* (2000). While these texts are ostensibly general musings on the nature of art and literature they spring from a consideration of Byatt's own interests and so invariably relate to her fictional texts. Indeed, the overriding concerns in these texts are those that are identified in her fictional works: realism; history; artistic vision; the place of the woman writer; and literature of the past. In some cases, Byatt explicitly discusses her own fictions, as in the essay 'Still Life/Nature Morte', which will be briefly examined in Chapter 3.

Although this Guide considers each of the novels in isolation it will also draw out the overriding concerns within criticism of Byatt's work. The chapters that follow will trace three key areas of criticism that recur in considerations of all of Byatt's works: the relationship to literary traditions, the role of the artist and women's issues. The impulse to determine where Byatt fits within existing literary traditions is evident in critical responses to all her works. In terms of influences, she is more often aligned with earlier writers, such as Iris Murdoch (1919–99) and George Eliot, than with her contemporaries. This association is evident in Byatt's own critical writings. In *Passions of the Mind*, Byatt identifies the quality of Murdoch's writing that she values. Talking of Murdoch's 1961 essay 'Against Dryness', Byatt remarks that it 'defends, on moral grounds, the Tolstoyan "old-fashioned naturalistic idea of character"'.[13] This view of character belongs to the realist tradition of literature, of which both Murdoch and Eliot are proponents. Byatt's relationship to realism, however, is not as straightforward; her work sits on the boundaries between Victorian, Modernist and postmodernist narrative strategies and as such cannot be easily limited to any one category. Byatt herself rejects any attempt to confine her fiction to a single category, saying 'my temperament is agnostic, and I am a non-believer and a non-belonger to schools of thought'.[14] She does, however, concede that she is a defender of realism or rather what she sees as 'self-conscious realism', an idea which usefully encapsulates both postmodernist and realist approaches to narrative, as indeed do her novels.[15]

Byatt's relationship to feminism and women's concerns is equally ambivalent. Her recurring concern with the position of the female artist and the limitations surrounding their vision has not gone unnoticed and there is a growing body of feminist criticism of Byatt's work. She concedes that '[a]ll my books are about the woman artist – in that sense, they're terribly feminist books', yet elsewhere she is resistant to attempts to delimit her fictions as 'women's fiction'.[16] Indeed, she claims that *The Game* is 'about the fear of the "woman's novel" as an immoral devouring force'.[17] Part of Byatt's reluctance to being labelled a feminist writer comes from her insistence that she is concerned with the position of the artist in general, not just that of the female artist. As we shall see in the chapters that follow, Byatt's depiction of the artist figure is identified as a key feature of her works and is frequently connected to her fiction's overriding concern with the possibilities and limitations of representation, both verbal and visual. As the first chapter shows, these concerns with the nature of artistic visions and the position of the female artist were apparent from the very outset of Byatt's career in the figures of Henry and Anna in *Shadow of a Sun* and Julia and Cassandra in *The Game*.

CHAPTER ONE

Autobiography, Art and Gender: *Shadow of a Sun* (1964) and *The Game* (1967)

In 1964, A. S. Byatt published her first novel *Shadow of a Sun*. Written during her time as an undergraduate at Cambridge, the novel tells of the coming of age of Anna Severell, daughter of a famous writer and supposed literary genius. Given the novel's plot, it is unsurprising that many critics of the novel interpreted it as stemming from Byatt's own struggles to become a writer in the shadow of her novelist sister, Margaret Drabble, whose first novel *A Summer Bird-Cage* had appeared in 1963.

Started before the first novel had been completed, Byatt's second novel, *The Game*, appeared in 1967 and received more attention in the reviews. In particular reviewers began to comment on the family connections between Drabble and Byatt, not surprisingly considering this novel centres around two sisters, one of whom is a successful novelist while the other is an academic.

These two novels have received less critical attention than Byatt's later works, which may be, in part, due to their publication history. Both novels were unavailable for some time after their first printing and it was not until Byatt's reputation as a novelist was assured with the commercially and critically successful *Possession* that they were reprinted. The reprint of Byatt's first novel was particularly significant since when it was initially published she had been overridden on the issue of the title. The 1991 reprint restored Byatt's original title, *The Shadow of the Sun*. As she explains in the foreword to that edition: 'It is more what I meant, and I prefer its grittiness.... The sun has no shadow, that is the point. You have to be the sun or nothing.'[1] Indeed, the inclusion of a foreword explaining the novel's genesis and its connections to her subsequent work, as we shall see, also had an impact on critical responses to the novel. These reprints have made the texts more widely available and as such there has been an increase in critical analyses of them. They remain, however, among the least discussed texts of Byatt's oeuvre.

REVIEWS

As a first novel from an unknown author *Shadow of a Sun* did not receive much attention in the press. Reviews of Byatt's first novel were usually incorporated into overviews of the week's new fiction and were often limited to a paragraph at most. While reviewers were keen to present their opinion of the novel itself, they also often judged the novel in terms of what it indicated for Byatt's future writing career.

In his review of new fiction for *The Sunday Times*, the novelist Frederic Raphael (born 1931) was full of praise for the 'generosity of treatment' and 'degree of intelligence' of *Shadow of a Sun*, which he felt marked it out as both 'entertaining in itself and promising for the future'.[2] Despite the overall positive tone of this review, however, Raphael criticized Byatt's characterization, claiming that it was not always successful. While he felt that Anna was 'excellently achieved' he found the other protagonists, Oliver Canning and Henry Severell, less convincing.[3] For Raphael, Severell was 'too neatly tailored', a criticism of Byatt's characterization that, as we shall see, resurfaces in reviews of her second novel, *The Game*.[4]

The dislike of Byatt's main characters was a recurring feature of the initial reviews of the novel. Forsyth Hardy's comments in *The Scotsman Weekend Magazine*'s review of new fiction points out that none of the characters are 'wholly likeable or convincing', yet he commends Byatt's conscientious approach to their characterization, which at least renders them 'consistent in their oddness'.[5] Overall, Hardy judges the novel favourably; the reserved praise of the novel as having 'undoubted merit' is overridden by his confidence that it bodes well for her future works.[6] While some reviewers saw merit in the novel in spite of the characterization, Julian Maynahan's brief mention of *Shadow of a Sun* in his review of new fiction for *The Observer Weekend Review* was entirely negative, judging it to be 'mannered and over-written'.[7] Although he does recognize some promise for Byatt's future work in his reference to her as 'a woman writer of marked talent', the unnecessary reference to Byatt's gender implies that her work will never match up to that produced by male writers.[8]

While most reviews of Byatt's first novel were limited in space and scope it did receive more attention and more detailed criticism from some reviewers. *The Times Literary Supplement* was one of the few sources to present a substantial review of Byatt's first novel in its own terms, free of any discussion of other new fiction of the time. Although the review does devote a large portion of its space to plot summary, it also presents a sustained critique of the novel. The anonymous reviewer, identified by *The Times Literary Supplement Centenary Archive* as Marigold Johnson, judges Byatt to be a 'very feminine writer' because of her 'earnest sensibility' and the care with which she presents the 'emotional convolutions' of her characters' motivations.[9] The implicit criticism in these comments becomes more overt in the conclusion that 'a tougher, more experienced writer' would have cut these passages from the novel.[10] As we have seen, most of the reviews of this novel viewed the characterization negatively and *The Times Literary Supplement* review is no different. The presentation of the characters, in particular that of Henry Severell, is deemed unconvincing, although the reviewer forgives this fault on the grounds that Byatt 'feels deeply for her characters'.[11] The reviewer's comments on Byatt's style are implicitly critical, claiming that she 'luxuriates in tentative similes and asides' which disrupt the flow of the dialogue.[12] The implied criticism that runs throughout this review seems to be based on the reviewer's dislike of 'feminine novels'; yet even judging it within these terms the reviewer finds it wanting. The review concludes that Byatt's *Shadow of a Sun* is like an Elizabeth Bowen (1899–1973) novel, only not as successful. Despite the dominant negative tone of this review, it does end on a more positive note, suggesting that Byatt's first novel hints at powers yet to be fully realized, which may soon earn her 'a considerable reputation'.[13] *The Times'* review similarly aligns Byatt's novel with the supposedly feminine genre of romance. Although the reviewer sees *Shadow of a Sun* as belonging to that unfashionable mode of literature, Byatt is praised for managing to produce 'something genuinely fresh'.[14]

Although Byatt's first novel was largely ignored in the American literary press it did receive a brief review in *The New York Times* in August 1964. Martin Levin's review relies mostly on plot summary and when it does venture a judgement on the novel it is not particularly favourable. Levin concludes that despite expending a great deal of time, and words, in defining her characters Byatt fails to bring them to life. Of Anna, in particular, he laments that Byatt's 'ornamental rhetoric' forestalls any true revelation of character.[15] As we shall see in the following chapters, the criticism that Byatt's intellectual style hinders her characterization recurs in reviews of several of the later novels.

Three years later, the publication of Byatt's second novel, *The Game*, received slightly more attention, although it was still largely ignored in the American literary press. Generally, reviewers judged Byatt's second novel more favourably than her first. For instance, in *The Observer Review*, Irving Wardle views *The Game* as a 'work of great richness and precision', comparing the 'complex moral image' it presents to a 'many-faceted precious stone'.[16] Wardle's review is also noticeable for its comparison of Byatt with her novelist sister Margaret Drabble. For Wardle, Drabble and Byatt adopt a similar approach in 'using academic literary knowledge as a creative tool'.[17] As we shall see, this approach was to become a feature of subsequent critical analyses of *The Game*.

The reviews in *The Times* and *The Sunday Times* were more reserved in their praise than Wardle's review. Montague Haltrecht, in his review for *The Sunday Times*, remarks on the 'intellectual seriousness' of Byatt, which he connects to another contemporary novelist, Nicholas Mosley (born 1923).[18] Haltrecht praises Byatt's attempt to do justice to her 'strikingly true' perceptions but feels that her prose suffers under 'the strain of her struggle to pin down truth'.[19] Similarly, *The Times'* reviewer praises *The Game* as a 'sometimes intelligent novel' but feels that it is spoilt by Byatt's writing style, which is described as 'rather too coyly neat and unlively'.[20] In addition, this review raises an issue that is to recur in responses to later Byatt novels; for *The Times'* reviewer, Byatt's philosophizing is 'very often tedious'.[21]

In contrast, the comments on *The Game* by novelist Robert Nye (born 1939) in his overview of 'Books of the Day' for *The Guardian* were unequivocally negative. He views *The Game* as evidence of Byatt's 'potentially distinguished talent' going to waste.[22] Nye compares Byatt to Iris Murdoch, a comparison which many reviewers and critics have continued to make; in this instance, however, it is not a favourable comparison. It is clear that Nye disapproves of Murdoch's style and so *The Game* suffers by association since it is 'fairly saturated' with Murdoch, 'right through to the plain bad writing'.[23] Nye's final assessment of the novel is damning in its criticism: 'the depth is all too plausibly on the surface and you can't see the wood for the symbols'.[24]

A longer review of *The Game* appeared in *The Times Literary Supplement*. As in many of the reviews of *Shadow of a Sun*, the anonymous reviewer, identified by *The Times Literary Supplement Centenary Archive* as Mary-Kay Wilmers, criticizes Byatt's characterization, stating that the main characters 'have not enough substance to carry their philosophical load'.[25] Like *The Times* reviewer, this reviewer judges the philosophical aspects of *The Game* as hindering its literary and dramatic qualities. The reviewer continues in this vein, arguing that the novel 'suffers from a suffocating design'.[26] As we shall see in later chapters, Byatt's work is often criticized for being more interested in developing ideas than presenting characters. As Nye did in his review for *The Guardian*, this reviewer draws out the connections between Byatt and Murdoch, or more specifically Murdoch's later novels. Indeed, the claim that in the works of both 'one is frequently dazzled, less often convinced' is reminiscent of Nye's criticism that Byatt's novel is too much on the surface.[27] Despite these criticisms, Byatt's novel is praised as a 'work of intelligence, full of illuminating comment and perceptive observation'.[28] Ultimately, *The Game* is judged to be a 'more sophisticated' novel than *Shadow of a Sun* but 'lack[ing] its vitality'; here again, then, we have the implicit criticism that ideas are prioritized over characters.[29]

Malcolm Bradbury's review of *The Game* for *Encounter* presents a sustained critical analysis of the novel in terms of its place within the genre of 'novels of sensibility'.[30] Interestingly, in her foreword to the 1991 reprint of *The Shadow of the Sun*, Byatt rejects the models of Elizabeth Bowen, E. M. Forster (1879–1970) and Virginia Woolf (1882–1941) as 'too suffused with "sensibility"'.[31] Bradbury describes *The Game* as a 'deep and able book' which is 'deeply sympathetic to … sensitive personal relations'.[32] As his title 'On From Murdoch' suggests, Bradbury traces the connections between Byatt and Murdoch; unlike previous reviewers, however, Bradbury sees the connection in a positive light. He implicitly commends the revival of the novel of sensibility that he sees in both Murdoch and Byatt and claims Byatt as the better writer of this type of novel. Although Bradbury's review is generally positive, he is aware of some flaws. As previous reviewers had noted, Bradbury accepts that sometimes 'the literariness of the novel makes it lumpish' but diverges from prior opinion in his assessment of Byatt's characterization, which he claims is 'capable of real and intense achievement'.[33] Overall, Bradbury's review admires *The Game* in its own right and for the promise it suggests for Byatt's later career.

Bradbury's review draws out several features that are also prominent in subsequent critical analyses of *The Game*. He implicitly designates the novel as a 'woman's novel' in his assertions that '[t]he domestic-familial is the root experience' and the explorations of character focus on the anxieties of adolescence for women.[34] Bradbury's comments recall those of *The Times Literary Supplement* reviewer who described Byatt as a 'very feminine writer'. This focus on the gender of the author, and her supposedly gendered way of writing, comes out in critical commentaries of the novel, which focus on the depiction of the female artist. Moreover, it is also evident in the autobiographical readings of both *The Game* and *Shadow of a Sun*, which present the novels as accounts of the problems and anxieties encountered by Byatt as a female artist.

AUTOBIOGRAPHICAL READINGS

As we saw in the reviews discussed above, Byatt was often compared to her novelist sister, Margaret Drabble, in the early stages of her career. With its focus on the rivalry between the two Corbett sisters, it is not surprising that *The Game* is most often analysed in autobiographical terms. Joanne V. Creighton's essay, 'Sisterly Symbiosis: Margaret Drabble's *The Waterfall* [1969] and A. S. Byatt's *The Game*' (1987), is the most obvious example of this autobiographical approach to *The Game*. Creighton's essay is based on the belief that the 'creative tension' in Byatt and Drabble's work derives, at least in part, from 'the complexity of [their] sisterly bond'.[35] The autobiographical basis of Creighton's approach is evident in the fact that she devotes the first few pages of her essay to a biographical account of Drabble and Byatt. She comments that, like the sisters in *The Game*, Drabble and Byatt constructed their own fantasy world in childhood. Indeed, she connects both the Drabble sisters and the Corbett sisters to those other famous literary sisters, Charlotte (1816–55), Emily (1818–48) and Anne Brontë (1820–49), whose juvenilia reveals a richly imagined fantasy world constructed through childhood games.

Despite its autobiographical focus, Creighton's essay does attempt a more theoretical reading of *The Game*, linking it to feminist theories about creativity. Sandra M. Gilbert (born 1936) and Susan Gubar (born 1944) wrote an important and influential work of feminist literary criticism in the 1970s entitled *The Madwoman in the Attic: The Woman Writer and the Nineteenth-Century Literary Imagination* (1979). This wide-ranging text argued that whereas male writers suffered from an 'anxiety of influence' women writers suffered from an 'anxiety of authorship'. That is, while male writers had to break away from their predecessors in order to write anything original, women writers had no such predecessors and as such had to fight for the right to write anything at all:

■ the 'anxiety of influence' that a male poet experiences is felt by a female poet as an even more primary 'anxiety of authorship' – a radical fear that she cannot create, that because she can never become a 'precursor' the act of writing will isolate or destroy her.[36] □

With no 'foremothers' to turn to, women writers had only the portraits of women in literature written by men and, according to Gilbert and Gubar, these portraits tended to depict women as one of two extremes, either 'angel' or 'demon'. Gilbert and Gubar argue that for women to become writers they must first reject the image of the 'angelic' woman and instead embrace the monstrous side of womanhood. Creighton argues that, in their depiction of two sisters, Drabble's *The Waterfall* and Byatt's *The Game* dramatize this split within women:

■ For both Byatt and Drabble the sisterly paradigm functions as a fictional construct, schematizing not exactly an angel/monster polarity but a schizoid split between the social and the reclusive, the sexually experienced and the innocent, the gregarious and the contemplative, and ultimately between the real and the imagined.[37] □

What Creighton leaves out of this list is the split between the woman as artist and the woman as wife and mother, the split between the mind and the body. As we shall see in the later chapters, the Potter sisters in Byatt's quartet are often discussed in terms of this conflict between the life of the mind and the life of the body that faced many women writers at the time. Ultimately, for Creighton, *The Waterfall* and *The Game* reveal that 'a certain amount of "monstrous" appropriation of others is essential for the artist, including the female artist who has been taught that such aggression is "unfeminine"'.[38] Although Creighton's essay does present an interesting reading of *The Game*, Byatt herself has denounced autobiographical readings of her work, and in particular those that foreground her relationship with her sister. Moreover, in adopting an autobiographical approach there is a danger of reducing the novel to nothing more than a direct representation of the author's life. Such reduction of a complicated novel is apparent in Creighton's comment that despite Byatt's protests, 'it is impossible not to think of Julia Corbett as an unflattering and hostile portrait of Drabble'.[39] It is interesting that in an essay that implicitly asserts the dominance of the author, and their life, in a text, Creighton chooses to disregard Byatt's explicit statements about the novel.

Guiliana Giobbi's essay 'Sisters Beware of Sisters: Sisterhood As a Literary Motif in Jane Austen, A. S. Byatt and I. Bossi Fedrigottti' (1992) equally examines the sisterly relationship in Byatt's *The Game*, yet it does so without recourse to an autobiographical reading of the text. Rather than comparing Byatt's novel to the work of her sister, Giobbi draws on a much longer literary heritage analysing the relationship between sisters in *Sense and Sensibility* (1811) by Jane Austen (1775–1817). For Giobbi, Marian and Elinor depict 'equally possible and plausible female attitudes' for women at any time.[40] She does slide into autobiographical analysis when she remarks that the relationship between Elinor and Marianne can be read as a 'fictional transformation' of Jane Austen's relationship with her sister Cassandra.[41] Moreover, she hints at an autobiographical reading of Byatt's novel when she, like Creighton, relates *The Game* to the Brontë sisters' juvenilia.

For Giobbi, the connections between *The Game* and *Sense and Sensibility* mark Byatt's novel out as a postmodern text since 'the most frequent form of Post-modern fiction is a "rewriting" of an older story'.[42] She claims that Byatt's novel addresses the 'central dilemma between Art and Life' that occupies much Modernist and postmodernist fiction.[43] This opposition is explicitly explored in relation to the problems for women artists: 'By means of focusing her attention on the sibling relationship, the woman writer can explore the relation of self to other [and] illustrate the possibility of a divided self.'[44] Ultimately, Giobbi concludes that by focusing her story on two sisters who are both engaged in the world of literature Byatt constructs 'a whole debate on imagination, art and feeling'.[45]

Although *The Game* is more often read in autobiographical terms there is also a tendency among critics to read *Shadow of a Sun* in relation to Byatt's life. This may be in part a response to Byatt's decision to reprint the novel in 1991 with a foreword explaining the genesis and production of the novel. Despite her fear of writing a 'me-novel', Byatt's summary of the novel implicitly connects the character of Anna to herself:

> ■ It is the novel of a very young woman, a novel written by someone who *had* to write but was very unsure whether she should admit to wanting to write, unsure even whether she ought, being a woman, to want to write.[46] □

Moreover, Byatt identifies the problems surrounding female authorship as a key concern in the novel, which as we shall see is a dominant theme in critical accounts of both *Shadow of a Sun* and Byatt's work more generally. However, Byatt prevents a too easy identification of Anna with herself in her later comments that 'Henry Severell is partly simply my secret self' and Oliver Canning 'represents a kind of public vision of what I was about, a scholar, a critic, a user of literature, not a maker, a natural judge'.[47] Writing this foreword places Byatt in a difficult position; she is aware that readers and critics often want to connect a literary work with the living, breathing person that created it and yet she seems suspicious of such a project. Consequently, her prose is often quite defensive: 'if I'm seeing the novel as an allegory of my own life, which it isn't, of course, it has its own'.[48]

Interestingly, Christien Franken's study *A. S. Byatt: Art, Authorship, Creativity* (2001) analyses this foreword both for the light it throws on the theme of artistic vision in *Shadow of a Sun* and on its own terms. Franken notes that while Byatt is keen to deny allegiance to any critical school, particularly feminism, in her critical writings, the foreword presents an explicitly feminist analysis of the process of writing her first novel. As we shall see, Franken focuses on the treatment of artistic vision and the problems of being a woman artist within Byatt's first two novels and her most famous work, *Possession*. Franken points out the conditions surrounding the writing of the foreword; it was written almost 30 years after the novel on which it comments, by which time, thanks to the prize-winning *Possession*, Byatt had become established as a successful novelist. According to Franken, these conditions created 'a position which seems to allow for an untroubled distance from which to assess the genesis of one's writing career'.[49] It is interesting that Franken should comment on the 'untroubled distance' the foreword creates since her study claims that Byatt's first two novels explore the possibilities and problems of such objective distance.

ARTISTIC VISIONS

Moving on from autobiographical accounts, there are two dominant, and indeed interrelated, areas of criticism of Byatt's early novels: the portrayal of the artist and the position of women. Although not explicitly autobiographical, critical accounts that deal with these issues do presume a correlation between the situation of Byatt as author and the thematic concerns of her first two novels.

Kuno Schuhmann's article 'In Search of Self and Self-Fulfilment: Themes and Strategies in A. S. Byatt's Early Novels' (2001) recognizes the implicit autobiographical approach often adopted in response to the early works of authors. Similarly, his article implicitly adopts an autobiographical approach to *Shadow of a Sun* and *The Game* in its focus on the themes of 'self-fulfilment' and the search for self. He categorizes these novels as 'quest novels' and seems to conflate Byatt and the characters in his description of them as about 'a young author's search for her own identity and for possible ways of realising her artistic desires and ambitions'.[50] For Schuhmann, Byatt's concern with the notion of self-fulfilment is in part a response to the social situation in which she was writing, specifically the intellectual climate which led to the student movement of 1968.

Schuhmann's analysis of *Shadow of a Sun* moves away from this implicit autobiographical stance, declaring that Byatt has managed to distance herself from her protagonist, Anna, and so has 'resisted the temptation ... to write a "me-novel" '.[51] As we saw in the discussion of Byatt's foreword to the 1991 reprint of this novel, the desire to avoid writing a 'me-novel' was an explicit part of Byatt's writing process. Going against the opinion of critics such as Franken, Schuhmann does not see Byatt's first novel as a 'coming-of-age' story. Rather, he sees it as an attempt to probe what it means to be an artist, an issue that resurfaces throughout Byatt's writing career. This is aided by the fact that Byatt incorporates two stories into this novel, that of Anna and that of her father, Henry Severell. Schuhmann claims that through these two stories Byatt explores two contradictory ideas: Anna's story concerns 'the search for self and self-fulfilment' while Henry's addresses 'the oblivion of the self for the sake of creativity'.[52] Schuhmann also hints at a feminist approach to the novel when he deals with the character of Caroline, whose relationship with Henry is 'neither "self-actualising" ... nor is it "self-fulfilment" '.[53] Rather, it is 'a selfless actualising, enforced by social conventions', which is rejected by the more modern Anna and Byatt.[54]

Turning to *The Game*, Schuhmann claims that it is 'more complex' than *Shadow of a Sun*.[55] While it maintains an interest in the search for self, it explores the theme of self-fulfilment through 'various irritations of identity' rather than simply following the central character.[56] Interestingly, Schuhmann seems to have reduced the complexity he earlier ascribed to *Shadow of a Sun* in its dual focus on Anna and Henry. Moreover, despite claiming that the treatment of self-fulfilment is more complex in this second novel, Schuhmann barely deals with it, except to comment that for all the central characters social obligations are 'an infringement of their potential for self-fulfilment'.[57] Gone too is the implicit feminist analysis applied to the first novel; rather, Schuhmann focuses on the theme of vision or perception in *The Game*. He connects this concern to the issue of 'sense perception' in *Shadow of a Sun* but claims that whereas that novel is concerned with the subjective aspects of vision, the second novel focuses on the viewed object.[58] In this analysis, Schuhmann prioritizes the medium of representation, drawing on the novel's treatment of television. He argues that the novel constructs a difference between 'telling' and 'tellying' in terms of the nature of the illusion they create. While story-telling 'creates a momentary illusion, suspending the reader's disbelief', television 'depends on constant illusion'.[59] Consequently, Schuhmann implies that *The Game* is pessimistic about the possibilities of vision where *Shadow of a Sun* is optimistic. Whilst Byatt's first novel suggests that the imagination has the power to transform the viewed object, *The Game* warns that 'a "vision" that starts from a distorted version of reality can never achieve a reliable insight'.[60]

Other critics of Byatt's first two novels have similarly addressed the possibilities and limitations inherent in both subjective and objective perception. This issue links to wider debates about Byatt's engagement with various modes of representation, which, as we shall see in the subsequent chapters, dominate discussions of Byatt's later works.

Jane Campbell implicitly rejects autobiographical readings in her article 'The Hunger of the Imagination in A. S. Byatt's *The Game*' (1988). She argues that while the novel explores sibling rivalry, it is more than that; 'it is also an exploration of the imagination and of the activity of perception'.[61] This thematic focus is also evident at a structural level since the novel is 'patterned on [the structure] of a game with two players, alternating between Cassandra's and Julia's perceptions and between retrospective and present narrative'.[62] Campbell argues that the novel reveals the limitations of the imagination; both in terms of the restrictions the imagination places on life and the fact that the imagination 'can never be contained within any of our linguistic forms'.[63] The first of these relates to the relationship between Cassandra and Julia; a relationship that Campbell conceives of in terms of the myth of the Lady of Shalott. Campbell claims that while this myth obviously 'charts the course of Cassandra's entrapment by Julia, it also represents Julia's imprisonment by Cassandra'.[64] Thus, it works in a dual way to suggest both the possibilities and the limitations of the imagination. The second element in Byatt's exploration of the limitations of the imagination is the suggestion that it cannot be contained within language. The problem of capturing the world within language is a recurring concern in Byatt's work and, as we shall see in Chapter 3, is particularly fraught when it deals with the possibilities of incorporating visual representations into verbal art. Campbell suggests that the self-reflexive elements of the novel allow Byatt to examine 'the perils of fiction'.[65] In particular, the incorporation of a novelist within her novel allows Byatt to explore 'the moral problems of art and [show] herself to be a better novelist than Julia'.[66] By focusing on the two sisters, Campbell implicitly addresses the question of female creativity in *The Game*, yet she recognizes that Byatt's interest in the life of the imagination is not confined to the female imagination and so does not prevent her from dealing with 'the suffering of the male'.[67] Campbell does not further explore this aspect of Byatt's novel, however, except to state that the novel evokes sympathy towards Simon.

Kathleen Coyne Kelly interprets Byatt's first two novels as an early expression of what, in her later works, was to become a persistent interest in the artist and the nature of the imagination. She aligns *Shadow of a Sun* with the Romantic poet and critic Samuel Taylor Coleridge (1772–1834) in its exploration of the 'opposition of the demands of the world and the demands of the creative imagination'.[68] Kelly sees in Henry a 'terrible clarity of vision' which she claims recurs in other artist figures in Byatt's later texts, particularly Marcus in *The Virgin in the Garden* and Cassandra in *The Game*.[69] Kelly seems to go against most critics in her suggestion that Anna 'does share in Henry's overabundance of feeling and sensation' but she fails really to address the question of Anna's position in relation to art in the novel.[70]

While *The Game* similarly explores the nature of the imagination it does so through the metafictional device of incorporating texts within texts; a device which Kelly claims is the 'defining stamp of the postmodern'.[71] As we shall see in later chapters, the question of Byatt's status as a postmodern novelist frequently occupies critics of her fiction, especially as regards *Possession: A Romance*. Kelly, however, does not really address the question of whether *The Game* is a postmodern novel, but rather examines its metafictional aspects in terms of what they reveal about Byatt's interest in 'the position of the writer both outside and inside the text'.[72] Kelly contends that Byatt uses television as a parallel for literature, with the camera as a parallel for the narrator: 'both may seem "invisible" at times, but then each may reveal its presence at certain crucial points in order to remind the reader/viewer of the artifice behind the art'.[73] As we shall see, Christien Franken's study presents a more sustained engagement with the notion of 'vision' in *The Game* as indeed she presents a more sustained analysis of the connections between imagination and gender that Kelly only hints at.

Christien Franken's study *A. S. Byatt: Art, Authorship, Creativity* (2001) analyses the conception of the artistic imagination depicted in *Shadow of a Sun*, *The Game* and *Possession: A Romance*. Franken contends that Byatt's first two novels present ideas about 'art, creativity and authorship' which recur in her bestselling novel *Possession*.[74] I will return to Franken's discussion of creative identity in *Possession* in Chapter 4 but for now I want to focus on her analysis of *Shadow of a Sun* and *The Game*. Franken claims that in her first novel Byatt explores the notion of the writer as 'a visionary genius who creates through a "sublime" experience'; an idea that gained force during the Romantic era (about 1780–1848).[75] The sublime is a complicated term that has had many different applications in aesthetic theory. In this context, however, it is derived from the eighteenth-century theory of the sublime put forward by the philosopher Edmund Burke (1729–97) in his major work *A Philosophical Enquiry into the Origins of Our Ideas of the Sublime and Beautiful* (1757). Franken explains the sublime as having three stages. The first stage is the state of normal vision, 'a state of balance' between the mind and the object. The second stage is the effect of encountering an object that is almost beyond comprehension, usually because of its immensity. As a consequence of the attempt to perceive and comprehend this object the subject experiences fear and terror and has 'a violent aesthetic experience which threatens to overwhelm him'.[76] In the final stage the subject conquers the feelings of awe and terror evoked by the object and returns to the previous equilibrium of the first stage. Franken claims that Henry's visions are conceived of in terms of a sublime experience, and it is this access to the sublime that Anna is supposedly denied in the novel. Franken connects the sublime to Byatt's concern with the position of the female artist by way of Hélène Cixous (born 1937), a French feminist theorist much influenced by post-structuralist theories about the instability of language. Franken summarizes Cixous' theory that Western philosophy is grounded in oppositional thinking; that is, it constructs pairs of oppositional terms, one of which is usually associated with Man and the other with Woman. Cixous takes this observation further to claim that these oppositions are hierarchical, that whenever the two poles are linked the first term (that associated with the male) is prioritized over the second, feminine term. Franken argues that in Burke's theory the sublime is masculine while the beautiful is feminine and that, ultimately, Burke favours the sublime over the beautiful. It is not surprising, then, that Anna is denied access to such a masculine version of artistic vision. Yet, Franken contends that although Anna 'may not be an artist in the sublime sense' her experience in the bathroom, when she has a vision prompted by the light reflected in the mirror, 'does create this margin of singleness for her creative self'.[77]

Franken argues that *Shadow of a Sun* challenges the conception of the artist as a visionary in two ways: '[it] not only contains a feminist critique of the male artist as visionary genius but also criticizes the lack of women's access to artistic subjectivity in a feminist way'.[78] The first critique is forwarded through the character of Caroline, Henry's wife, since it reveals that 'the sublime is not as autonomous as it appears'; Henry is only able to be an 'artistic genius' because of the supportive role performed by Caroline.[79] The second criticism is proposed through the figure of Anna. In her 1991 foreword to the novel Byatt described Anna as 'a portrait of the artist with the artist left out', and it is in these terms that Franken analyses Anna's character.[80] Franken argues that Anna's approach presents a critique of the view that art 'transcends moral and emotional obligations'.[81] Franken implicitly suggests that, despite not producing any art, Anna's is the best artistic vision in the novel since it 'is not impersonal and does not distort, but is balanced and patient'.[82] This approach is connected to the conception of art presented in the short story 'The Djinn in the Nightingale's Eye'; in that story glass operates as a metaphor for art, suggesting that art should 'provide both "a way of seeing" and " a thing seen"'.[83]

While *Shadow of a Sun* seems to criticize the notion that art is created through subjective vision, *The Game* explores the possibilities of objective vision. Franken analyses *The Game* through its discussion of 'vision', which she claims in this novel 'refers [both] to observation...as well as to the objectifying "camera eye" mediated through (our watching of) television'.[84] This notion of vision is connected to the theory of the relationship between visual perception and knowledge presented by the feminist scientist Fox Keller (born 1936) in her article 'The Mind's Eye' (1996). Franken summarizes Keller's argument about the 'dissociative function of the visual metaphor as a model of knowledge': 'In Western science, vision came to be seen as creating a distance between subject and object, between the subject's eye and the object of his vision.'[85] Simon is the character that most embodies this notion of objective distance as '[h]e seeks to maintain clear-cut and well defined boundaries between himself and the object of his vision'.[86] However, Simon's attempts at objectivity are undermined since the narrator reveals them to be 'the result of fear and the denial of fear'.[87] Consequently, the novel remains ambivalent about the varying approaches to vision – that of the novelist Julia, the visionary Cassandra and the scientist Simon. Franken identifies a similar ambivalence in Byatt's critical work which both 'affirms and criticizes a concept of...art as the effect of "impersonality" and "transcendence"'.[88] She sees this ambivalence as a result of the combination of Leavisite and post-structuralist approaches that have influenced Byatt; Leavis's ideas about the moral responsibilities of fiction are at odds with post-structuralist theories about the impossibility of expressing truth in language. Franken claims that *The Game*, and implicitly *Shadow of a Sun*, present an alternative vision of art: 'one which neither assumes that art is a product of a totally free imagination, unrestricted by ethics, gender, personal histories and family identities, nor views art as completely determined by them'.[89]

WOMEN ARTISTS

Despite this, Franken analyses the ways in which Byatt's first two novels reveal the limitations of artistic vision that are experienced by women artists. In Franken's study, it is almost impossible to separate her discussion of artistic vision from her discussion of Byatt's examination of the relationship between gender and creativity. Indeed, she states in the preface that '[a]dequate readings of Byatt's novels...are impossible without a discussion of the work's relationship to "gender" and "feminism"...'.[90] As we have seen, Franken argues that Byatt's ambivalence towards the artist's visions is necessarily inflected with feminist concerns. She explicitly draws out these concerns by connecting the novels to three dominant myths of female creativity: the Lady of Shalott for *Shadow of a Sun*; Cassandra for *The Game*; and Melusine for *Possession*. Indeed, in her foreword to *The Shadow of the Sun* Byatt identifies this connection between her interest in artistic visions and the role of the woman artist: 'Female visionaries are poor mad exploited sibyls and pythonesses. Male ones are prophets and poets. Or so I thought. There was a feminine mystique but no tradition of female mysticism that wasn't hopelessly self-abnegating.'[91] Although I have already discussed Franken's study in some detail I want to briefly examine the connections she proposes between these myths and Byatt's first two novels.

Franken connects the figure of Anna in *Shadow of a Sun* with the myth of The Lady of Shalott, as presented in the poem of that name (1832) by Alfred, Lord Tennyson (1809–92). She reads Tennyson's poem as 'a portrait of failed female artisthood', suggesting that Anna and the Lady of Shalott are connected by their 'inability to experience direct unmediated visions and recreate them into art'.[92] However, her analysis assumes that *Shadow of a Sun* presents a positive version of 'The Lady of Shalott'. As indicated above, Franken believes that while Anna is not an artist in 'the sublime sense' that her father is, she does demonstrate creative potential. This analysis is problematized by the fact that Anna does not actually create anything in the novel. For Franken, Byatt's use of 'The Lady of Shalott' is part of her feminist critique of artistic subjectivity and so represents a 'counter-figuration of creative women'.[93] The notion of the creative woman that Franken connects with *The Game* is the figure of Cassandra who, according to Greek mythology, was given the gift of prophecy but was denied the power to make people believe her. As with her reading of 'The Lady of Shalott', Franken sees the mythical figure of Cassandra as representing the futility of female vision, which relates to Cassandra Corbett's self-image as 'a failed visionary and artist'.[94] Unlike *Shadow of a Sun*, Franken does not see *The Game* as transforming the mythical stories it draws from. Rather, she recognizes that Cassandra Corbett fails to achieve artistic vision in part because 'she lacks the kind of female support' that Henry Severell has.[95] It is the inability to distinguish between subject and object, between reality and imagination, that ultimately leads to Cassandra's death. Franken concludes that through the figure of Cassandra, Byatt is implying that 'women need to achieve a certain amount of "impersonality" and "autonomy" in order to prevent (self-)effacement'.[96]

In her foreword to *The Shadow of the Sun*, Byatt states that 'My subsequent novels all think about the problem of female vision, female art and thought...[but] not without interest in the male too.'[97] In the subsequent chapters we will encounter many critical responses to Byatt's depictions of artists, both male and female.

CHAPTER TWO

The Past, Language and Reality: *The Virgin in the Garden* (1978)

In 1978 Byatt published her third novel, *The Virgin in the Garden*, which marked the beginning of a planned quartet. This project spanned several decades, in both its setting and its production, and came to comprise *The Virgin in the Garden*, *Still Life* (1985), *Babel Tower* (1996) and *A Whistling Woman* (2002). So, reviewers of this initial novel had to deal with it as a novel in its own right and as the first of a yet-to-be written series. Although this was Byatt's third novel, it still received relatively little attention in terms of review space. However, it was to mark a change in opinion towards Byatt, as after its publication she came to be widely recognized as an important writer and acquired a growing readership.

REVIEWS

As the title of his *Times Literary Supplement* review, 'Growing up in 1953', suggests, Michael Irwin considers *The Virgin in the Garden* as belonging to the genre of 'Bildungsroman', that is, a novel which charts the education and emotional development of its hero. He sees the novel as focusing on three pairs of characters: Stephanie and Daniel; Frederica and Alexander; and Marcus and his schoolteacher Lucas Simmonds. For Irwin, each of these characters is caught up in an emotional drama that requires a process of growing up, of maturation. Irwin's review of *Virgin* focuses more on Byatt's style and method of characterization than on plot. He recognizes that Byatt's novel is ambitious and intelligent yet he suggests that this intelligence is both a 'weakness' and a 'strength'.[1] Irwin asserts that the display of intelligence in *Virgin* hinders the depiction of characters; he sees the novel as marred by a 'recurrent emotional and psychological insipidity' which he claims is a result of the literary sensibilities of the main characters.[2] Yet the fault is not only with the intelligence of the characters; rather, he sees it as a consequence of Byatt's own intelligence. He feels that the novel's reliance on literary allusion 'diminish[es] the characters, ... mak[ing] them seem mere agents of the author's own very academic intelligence'.[3] Byatt's novels are often charged with being too intelligent and more interested in exploring ideas rather than characters. For Irwin, *Virgin* only escapes this fault in the presentation of Marcus, who is 'mercifully inarticulate'.[4] Irwin concludes his review with yet another criticism of Byatt's style, claiming that in the passages of indirect narration the novel 'thicken[s] into heaviness'.[5] He sees this as indicating Byatt's 'comparative lack of interest in the routine chores of realistic fiction'.[6]

Rosemary Dinnage's review for *The New York Times*, 'England in the 50's' similarly comments on the novel's intelligence and density of allusion, seeing the novel as '[l]oaded, often overloaded' with symbols relating to Queen Elizabeth I (1533–1603, reigned 1558–1603).[7] Dinnage does not see this as a flaw, however, but rather as part of Byatt's personal style and, where Irwin saw it as hindering the depiction of character, Dinnage sees it as contributing to it. Indeed, Dinnage judges Byatt's characterization as one of the novel's best qualities, claiming that the characters 'live on in the mind'.[8] In contrast to Irwin, then, Dinnage implicitly aligns Byatt with the realist tradition in praising the reality of her characters and in her final assessment of Byatt as 'essentially a fine, careful and very traditional storyteller'.[9]

Iris Murdoch's review for the *New Statesman* similarly comments on the densely intellectual quality of Byatt's novel, yet she does not necessarily see this as a failing. While she recognizes that the novel can be criticized on the grounds of its extensive use of literary allusion and quotation, she declares that she 'would not wish that fault undone'.[10] In contrast to Irwin, Murdoch does not believe that Byatt's intellectual interests hinder her presentation of character; instead, Murdoch claims that the characters have an 'innate energy' which allows them to 'survive their creator's cleverness'.[11] Murdoch's review examines another important element of *The Virgin in the Garden*, its status as a historical novel. Interestingly, Murdoch feels that the historical period in which the novel is set 'never feels remote' and that the observation of social life is neatly integrated into the plot and thus is 'never obtrusive'.[12] Murdoch is ultimately favourable about *Virgin*; she sees it as 'a remarkable achievement' in its own right and asserts that the 'extensive and deep foundations' it lays set up high expectations for the rest of the projected series, which she believes will prove to be 'increasingly rewarding'.[13]

Although limited in length, Anthony Thwaite's review of *The Virgin in the Garden* for *The Observer* addresses similar features of the novel to those encountered in the reviews discussed above: Byatt's style, the literary allusions and the novel's historical setting. In contrast to Murdoch, Thwaite feels that the novel is less concerned with history than with allegory. He claims that the 'allegorical pageant' occupies the foreground of the novel and consequently the public events of the Coronation year in which the novel is set disappear into the background to the point that they 'are hardly there at all'.[14] Thwaite's comment draws on the assumption that historical fiction should present important, public events of the past through their impact on the personal lives of a group of fictional characters. Despite this criticism, Thwaite's review is mainly approving in tone and his most positive comments are to do with Byatt's style, which he compares to that of Iris Murdoch. He concludes that Byatt is a 'more elegant and assured stylist, and her human understanding [is] deeper and richer' than in the novels Murdoch was publishing at that time.[15]

As we saw in the previous chapter, Robert Nye's review of *The Game* was entirely negative, viewing it as an unfortunate waste of Byatt's promise. By contrast, his review of her third novel is wholly positive. He sees it as a 'considerable achievement' which demonstrates the skills in 'sensitive reporting' that he felt had been obscured in Byatt's previous novel.[16] His conclusion is unrestrained in its praise of *Virgin*: 'This is a beautifully *constructed* book,...a pleasure to read, but even more rewarding to reread.'[17] Nye's assessment of *Virgin* focuses on its position as a historical novel; he believes that the book's 'real purpose' is to express 'the extraordinary texture' of the early 1950s.[18] Byatt's novel is not merely rooted in the 1950s, though; through its complex time-frames it constantly juxtaposes the time the novel is set with the time in which it was written. Nye praises Byatt's use of such complex time-frames, saying that it shows a 'mastery...as clever as George Eliot's'.[19] As we shall see in the next section, the engagement with history is one of the focal points for critical analyses of *Virgin*.

Although initially reserved in its praise, John Naughton's review for *The Listener* ultimately judges *The Virgin in the Garden* favourably. In 'Leavisites in Yorkshire', he claims that the seriousness of both Byatt's characters and her treatment of them 'makes for a long, tortuous...read' but one that leaves the reader both 'exhausted and exhilarated'.[20] Naughton praises Byatt's style as 'austere, moving, intriguing by turns'.[21] As Naughton's title suggests, he believes that *The Virgin in the Garden* needs to be understood in relation to F. R. Leavis's attitudes towards English literature and its moral imperatives. He claims that Byatt's characters, all of whom are either teachers or related to teachers, possess 'an attitude of high moral seriousness about literature', which they share with their creator.[22] While many reviewers and critics claim that Byatt's novels are too caught up in the world of literature and intellectual seriousness,

Naughton's conclusion seems to imply the opposite. He claims that the novel's outcome implicitly criticizes literature, demonstrating that 'ultimately [it] is a mighty bloodless substitute for life'.[23]

In spite of some reservations, the reviews we have encountered so far from the British press have been favourable and encouraging of Byatt's novel. In contrast, one of the few reviews in the American press, R. L. Widmann's review for *The Washington Post* is entirely negative. The title of this review, 'Shades of Brit Lit' [sic], reveals Widmann's main criticism of Byatt's novel, its indebtedness to previous British authors. Widmann claims that the emotions are drawn from D. H. Lawrence (1885–1930), the landscapes from Thomas Hardy (1840–1928), and the characters are 'pale imitations' of Iris Murdoch's or D. H. Lawrence's characters.[24] Indeed, he charges that Byatt fails to develop her characters in 'rational, lively ways'.[25] For Widmann, the shadows cast by these literary predecessors 'paralyze' Byatt's writing.[26] Widmann not only criticizes Byatt's allusions to previous British authors but also attacks her own style. He contends that the narrative voice 'leaps about alarmingly' and that she fails to 'control her language properly'.[27] Widmann concludes with the damning assessment that while Byatt 'tries to make this novel contain everything, in the end it illuminates nothing'.[28] As we shall see, criticisms of Byatt's encyclopaedic tendencies recur in reviews of many of her later novels, and especially in regard to the subsequent novels in the quartet.

That *The Virgin in the Garden* bought A. S. Byatt to the attention of a wider critical and public audience is demonstrated by the appearance of an interview with her in Janet Todd's edited collection *Women Writers Talking* (1983). The interview, conducted by Juliet A. Dusinberre, comes after Penguin had reissued *Virgin* in 1981 and while Byatt was working on the second novel of the projected quartet, later published as *Still Life* (1985). Consequently, both the interviewer and Byatt herself focus on the achievement of the first novel in the quartet. Although she claims that *Virgin* is not an autobiographical novel, Dusinberre introduces the interview with some preliminary remarks about the author's life and the connections between Byatt and one of her protagonists, Frederica. Dusinberre's interview addresses two of the issues that we saw arising in the reviews of the novel: its relationship to realism and its status as a historical novel. Unsurprisingly in an edition devoted to women writers, it also deals with the question of the position of the woman writer.

In her introduction to the interview, Dusinberre places *Virgin* within the tradition of realist fiction that dominated the nineteenth-century novel. However, she recognizes that Byatt's novel cannot be entirely encapsulated within this realist tradition since it 'draws on modernist images and on contemporary interest in the novel as a mirror of itself'.[29] As we shall see in later chapters, Byatt's position in relation to realism, Modernism and postmodernism is a recurring concern of critical responses to her fiction. With regard to *Virgin*, Byatt implicitly draws out the connection with the realist tradition in her account of the genesis of the novel. She states that she began thinking about it when a student in an adult education class asked why novels like George Eliot's *Middlemarch* (1871–72) were no longer written. Byatt then goes on to identify the features of Eliot's classic realist novel that seem to have disappeared from contemporary fiction: 'the large number of characters, wide cultural relevance, complex language'.[30] This connection with George Eliot links the discussion to two other aspects of the interview, *The Virgin in the Garden*'s interest in history and women's issues. Throughout the interview Byatt expresses reservations about being labelled as a feminist writer, which she sees as a challenge to her individuality, 'the source of my identity as an artist'.[31] She argues that '[it] does women a disservice to elevate them as women rather than as writers because it prevents their being judged on merit'.[32] Thus, while she is happy to be identified with George Eliot, she is keen to assert that neither Eliot nor herself should be seen as solely a 'women's writer'. Talking more specifically about *Virgin*, Byatt explains the connections between femininity and creativity in that novel. She notes that in writing *Virgin* 'I wanted to substitute a female mythology for a male one. The male mythology is the Dying God and Resurrection. The female one is birth and Renaissance.'[33] This interest in a female mythology of birth partly prompts the novel's engagement with the Renaissance era and the figures of the two Queen Elizabeths.

Dusinberre's introduction to the novel comments on its 'suggestive double time scheme' in its juxtaposition of the Renaissance era with the 1950s, often referred to at the time as 'the New Elizabethan era'.[34] Dusinberre proposes to Byatt that the novel attempts to capture 'real life' and suggests that 'things become real by moving into the past, and also that literature creates a reality more durable than lived experience'.[35] Byatt concurs with this assessment of her approach to the past: 'Language tries to capture and make permanent a moment in time which won't be captured. ... The present only becomes a real point in time when time has moved on and made it past.'[36] As we shall see in Chapter 5, literature's role in establishing a relationship between the present and the past recurs as a concern in *Possession: A Romance*. For the moment, however, I want to turn to critical accounts of *The Virgin in the Garden* that focus on its status as a historical novel and its depiction of the British past of the 1950s.

THE PRESENTATION OF THE PAST

The titles of Irwin's and Dinnage's reviews hint at *The Virgin in the Garden*'s, and indeed the whole quartet's, engagement with history.

Irwin, however, never really deals with the novel's historical location and Dinnage only mentions it briefly, indicating that not only do 'the 1950s feel as if they happened about 300 years ago' but that the novel 'really does reach back 300 years' in its allusions to the Elizabethan age.[37] The time-frame of *Virgin* is further complicated by the incorporation of a prologue, the events of which take place after those in the succeeding pages of the novel. Thus, three time-frames are operating in *The Virgin in the Garden*: the main action of the novel occurs in the early 1950s, centring around the Coronation of Queen Elizabeth II (born 1926, reigned from 1952); the first Elizabethan age is implicitly juxtaposed with this 'Second Elizabethan age' and is explicitly evoked through Alexander's play *Astraea*; finally, the prologue narrates events which occur in 1968, and so are outside the time-frame of both this novel and the rest of the quartet.

D. J. Taylor's chapter on Byatt's *The Virgin in the Garden* in *After the War: The Novel and England Since 1945* (1994) considers it alongside *Still Life* and argues that these novels present a social study of late twentieth-century English life and are fundamentally 'a study of "ordinary" family life'.[38] For Taylor, Byatt is ultimately a 'social novelist' and as such is connected to the Victorian social novel.[39] Yet, he recognizes that Byatt's novels do not sit entirely comfortably within the tradition of Victorian social fiction as it is no longer possible to present a collective consciousness in the manner of a George Eliot novel. While Byatt's novel addresses similar questions to those asked in the Victorian social novel it incorporates a frame which 'admits of a degree of uncertainty' that Taylor claims was 'unknown' to George Eliot or Elizabeth Gaskell (1810–65).[40] Although Taylor does seem to be acknowledging the more postmodern strands within Byatt's works, he implicitly distances these texts' treatment of the past from the postmodern stance of scepticism. As we shall see in the discussion of *Still Life* in Chapter 3 and *Possession* in Chapter 5, many critics believe that Byatt is engaging with *both* postmodern attitudes towards the past and more traditional, in certain cases Victorian, ones. For Taylor, there is a sense that Byatt's engagement with the past demonstrates an ethical responsibility towards accurately representing the past. He states that: 'There is a concreteness about Byatt's view of history, a sense that human beings operate in fixed and assimilable periods of time – even if that assimilability may be called into question by knowledge subsequently acquired.'[41] Despite this sense of responsibility towards the past, Taylor concludes that neither *Virgin* nor *Still Life* are realistic novels; rather, '[l]ike the decade they purport to describe, these are transitional novels, open-ended and unresolved'.[42] Moreover, he suggests that *Virgin* is at least partly a nostalgic novel which, 'seems at times to be taking place in a sort of prelapsarian gap'.[43]

LANGUAGE AND REALITY

The question of this novel's position in relation to realism also recurs in Kathleen Coyne Kelly's discussion of *Virgin*'s treatment of language. As with her discussion of Byatt's first two novels, there is still evidence of the autobiographical impulse in Kelly's discussion of *Virgin* and *Still Life*. Kelly notes that the setting of the novel corresponds to Byatt's own time at Cambridge and that the heroine, Frederica, 'follow[s] the same trajectory' as her author.[44] Although Kelly hints at a feminist perspective in these two novels, she focuses on their engagement with art. While this is most explicit in the title of the second novel in the quartet, Kelly claims that the title of the first novel, *The Virgin in the Garden* 'seems borrowed from an allegorical tableau'.[45] Allegory is an important concept for *Virgin* since it is explicitly concerned with the possibilities and limitations of metaphoric language. Indeed, Kelly claims that *Virgin* is 'an exuberant celebration of metaphor'.[46] This self-conscious focus on the nature of language is often taken to be a postmodern feature of Byatt's work, but Kelly here suggests that *Virgin* needs to be understood as a realist novel that is informed by a postmodern awareness of the 'slipperiness of language'.[47] As we shall see, the dual impulses towards tradition and experimentation, realism and self-reflexivity, frequently recur in Byatt's fiction. For Kelly, this novel manages to sustain the balance between the two as a result of its complex time-frame. She claims that the 'temporal disjunction' between the 1950s setting of the novel and the Renaissance era it constantly evokes allows Byatt to combine the 'dominant tropes' of both periods, that is Renaissance metaphor and twentieth-century realism.[48]

Alexa Alfer's essay 'Realism and Its Discontents' (2001) examines the relationship between realism and experimentation in the first two novels of Byatt's quartet, *The Virgin in the Garden* and *Still Life*. She argues that literary criticism perpetuates the notion of a dichotomy between realism and experimentation, despite the productions of writers such as Doris Lessing (born 1919), Angus Wilson (1913–91), Julian Barnes (born 1946) and Graham Swift (born 1949) whose fictions, she claims, question 'the … categorical opposition between "old realism" and "new experiment"'.[49] Alfer aligns Byatt with these writers. While Byatt explores this relationship in her criticism, most explicitly in the essay 'People in Paper Houses', which will be discussed in Chapter 4, it is in her fiction that 'the curious symbiosis of tradition and transformation, realism and experiment, storytelling and abstract thought unfolds its real potential'.[50] Alfer focuses on *Virgin* and *Still Life* since she believes that Byatt's 'literary allegiances' in the quartet belong to realism.[51] More interesting, however, is Alfer's positioning of the quartet in relation to the genre of historical fiction. Taylor judged the first two novels of the quartet as socio-historical novels, distancing their depiction of the past from the postmodern scepticism subtly imparted through the narrator. In contrast, Alfer claims that the quartet serves as a 'counterpoint' to the more traditional historical fictions Byatt writes later in her career.[52] She claims that these novels 'explore the fractured historical sense of the postwar period alongside...the possibility (or, as the case may be, impossibility) of its representation'.[53] As we shall see in Chapters 4, 5 and 6, however, the Victorian novels Byatt later writes are equally distanced from 'traditional' historical fictions in their incorporation of a postmodern awareness of the impossibility of representing the past.

Alfer argues that Byatt's novels both continue and challenge the realist tradition and that their experiments prompt a reassessment of the nature of realism itself. Byatt's novels question the view of realism as 'epistemologically naïve', suggesting instead that it is 'a potentially profoundly self-conscious mode of storytelling'.[54] Although dealing specifically with *Virgin* and *Still Life*, this assessment provides a useful way to evaluate Byatt's oeuvre. Critics often find it difficult to locate Byatt's fiction since it occupies an uneasy position between the traditions of realism and postmodernism. Alfer's comment, however, implies that the reason Byatt's fiction is so difficult to situate is because it reveals the untenable nature of such rigid boundaries between realism and postmodernism, tradition and experimentation. Alfer claims Byatt's novels reveal realism as concerned not only with 'the "faithful representation of reality"' but also with 'the problems and pitfalls of our desire for such representations and the always essentially textual strategies we employ in pursuit of them'.[55] As we shall see in the following chapter, this concern recurs in *Still Life*'s preoccupation with the relationship between verbal and visual representation.

Elisabeth Anne Leonard's article, '"The Burden of Intolerable Strangeness": Using C. S. Lewis [1898–1963] To See Beyond Realism in the Fiction of A. S. Byatt' (1998), similarly explores the position of *The Virgin in the Garden* in relation to realism. Leonard begins by quoting from an interview with Nicolas Tredell, in which Byatt stated that, in spite of appearances, neither *Virgin* nor *Still Life* were 'classical realist novels'.[56] Although she claims that Byatt's departure from realism is more apparent in her short stories, particularly *Sugar and Other Stories* (1987) and *The Djinn in the Nightingale's Eye* (1994), and her later works, such as 'The Conjugial Angel', Leonard's essay explores how *Virgin* 'contains elements outside the realm of realism'.[57] In particular, Leonard focuses on the figure of Marcus, claiming that it is through his visions, and also those of his teacher Lucas Simmonds, that Byatt incorporates non-realist elements in her novel. Leonard recognizes that most of Marcus's and Lucas's visions can be accounted for by the mental illnesses these characters suffer from and, as such, 'remain within the

scope of the realist novel'.[58] She claims, however, that there are two
events that are not explained away in this manner and thus represent
the intrusion of non-realist elements into the otherwise realist frame of
the novel.

The first of these instances occurs at Owger's Howe: Marcus and
Lucas both black out and when they come around they realize that
the bottle of milk they had put out is empty. As Leonard puts it, Byatt
'presents only the emptiness of the beaker and leaves it to the reader
to decide what happened'.[59] This event, then, remains unaccounted
for and so represents, for Leonard, 'a place where one can see the
novel spilling over into the realm of the fantastic' since the possibility
of a supernatural or metaphysical explanation for the events is not
foreclosed.[60] The second event is the instance of telepathy between
Marcus and Lucas that occurs during Stephanie's wedding. Leonard
claims that in this instance 'the novel moves firmly outside the realm
of established realism' since there is 'no authorial ambiguity' over the
veracity of the telepathic communication.[61] This incident also serves to
mark the distinction between Lucas and Marcus as it is after this event
that Lucas loses his grip on reality and descends into madness. Thus,
while the novel reveals that 'Lucas's crackpot theories of the universe
are crackpot' there is a sense that 'what Marcus sees is real'.[62] This
distinction between the visions of Lucas and Marcus hinges on their
attitudes towards science; Lucas 'deteriorat[es] beyond the range of science' whereas Marcus is committed to the notion of 'a rational and
orderly and scientific universe'.[63] Leonard claims that Byatt is similarly
committed to conventional science and that it forms 'a vibrant part of
[her] fiction'.[64]

Despite Marcus's grounding in science, Leonard argues that his visions
should be seen as 'fantastic or supernatural and read with an eye towards
possibility and reseeing the world that fantasy offers'.[65] By incorporating
Marcus's visions and 'granting him the possibility that they exist', Byatt
is transgressing the boundaries of the realist novel and allowing for the
possibility of 'an alternate reality, or [at least] an alternate way of perceiving a reality that does exist outside the usual range of perceptions'.[66]
Leonard's insightful exploration of the incorporation of non-realist
elements within *Virgin* is slightly undermined by the autobiographical
reading she presents at the end. For Leonard, the connections between
Marcus's visions and those of Henry Severell in Byatt's first novel, *Shadow
of a Sun*, suggest 'the possibility [that] these experiences are in some way
Byatt's own'.[67] Leonard concludes that this autobiographical link renders
Marcus's visions 'both fantastic and real'.[68]

Juliet Dusinberre's essay, 'Forms of Reality in A. S. Byatt's *The Virgin
in the Garden*' (1982) argues that Byatt's novel incorporates both realism
and experimentation simultaneously. The majority of Dusinberre's

essay explores an issue that, as we shall see in the subsequent chapters, becomes a central feature in critical responses to Byatt's oeuvre: the role of the artist and the possibilities of representation in language. Dusinberre demonstrates that Byatt's attitude towards the artist has changed from *Shadow of a Sun* to *Virgin*. In the first novel, Henry's position as an important artist remained uncontested, despite the fact that his writing was unimportant for the action of the novel. In contrast, *Virgin* leaves the question of the 'absolute artistic merit' of Alexander's work open while at the same time incorporating him as a 'serious presence' in the novel.[69]

Dusinberre claims that in *Virgin*, all of the characters are given a version of Byatt's 'own quest as a writer for a sense of the real and for forms to embody reality'.[70] Most of the characters are revealed to be 'more competent to deal with art than life'.[71] Dusinberre argues that the novel depicts a 'battle ... between real people and images' and that throughout, '[t]he reader is harried between opposing perceptions of the power of the imagination and its impotence'.[72] Ultimately, she claims that the novel 'exposes the characters' final failure to find forms in which to accommodate and define their experiences'.[73] The conflict between reality and imagery, between the real thing and the words used to describe it, is not confined to the characters but is an overriding concern of the narrative in *Virgin*. The book ends with a self-conscious comment on the process of novel writing: 'That was not an end, but since it went on for a considerable time, is as good a place to stop as any.'[74] For Dusinberre, such a comment reveals that which the 'naturalistic characters' in the novel reject, 'that the real exists through the mediation of the unreal verbal form'; that reality can only be accessed through the problematic medium of language.[75] Such a conclusion is what leads many critics to align Byatt's fiction with postmodernism.

The most interesting of these versions of the artist's quest belongs to Marcus, one of the few characters whose concern with reality is not caught up in verbal forms. Dusinberre links Marcus to the figure of Henry Severell from *Shadow of a Sun* since both characters experience geometric visions. Through Marcus, Byatt is able to reveal that reality is 'without shape or order until the mind has placed it in time and so given it form'.[76]

The figure of Marcus has interested many critics and reviewers. As we saw, Irwin found him to be one of the most interesting characters in the novel and Leonard used Marcus to trace the novel's engagement with, and ultimate transgression of, realism. Kelly goes a step further, identifying Marcus as the key figure in *Virgin*. She claims that it is through Marcus that Byatt explores 'the thin line so celebrated by the Romantics between madness and creative imagination'.[77]

THE VISIONARY CHILD

Judith Plotz's essay 'A Modern "Seer Blest": The Visionary Child in *The Virgin in the Garden*' (2001) connects Byatt's novel with the tradition of Romantic literature. According to Plotz, in the Romantic era, the artist and the child both came to be seen as the 'normative human type', a 'Seer blest' in the words of William Wordsworth (1770–1850).[78] The child was considered to be a visionary and as such was thought to share qualities of perception similar to that of the artist: 'idealism, vision, holism, animism, and self-sufficient isolation – which are the source of spiritual authority'.[79] Plotz links Marcus to the figure of the child visionary, since he is 'a solitary visionary whose world becomes increasingly full of over-arching meaning'.[80] However, Marcus is distinguished from the Romantic tradition and is 'ironically diminished by his realistic twentieth-century setting'.[81] Thus, Plotz suggests, Byatt is not merely presenting the Romantic notion of the visionary child but rather questioning the position of such a figure in the modern era.

Plotz analyses and explains the two different types of visions that Marcus experiences. The first type is referred to as 'spreading', which Plotz explains as an out-of-body experience in which Marcus has the sensation of 'diffusing his consciousness over a vast space'.[82] The second type of vision Marcus experiences is defined as 'photism', a type of light hallucination. Plotz claims that while these visions provoke 'a sensation of complex completeness' they ultimately provide 'no particular meaning'.[83] When experiencing these visions, Marcus becomes 'the point of intersection' for 'the finite and the infinite, the mortal and the immortal'.[84] Plotz claims that while the patterns these intersections produce are 'gratifying' in fiction the novel's depiction of Marcus's terror and isolation reveal that 'it is no model for a human life'.[85] In this assessment, Plotz implicitly distances Marcus from the figure of the visionary child encountered in the Romantic tradition who possessed spiritual authority. This distance is signalled by the novel's narrative structure. In Romantic literature, that authority usually comes in part through 'explicit authorial endorsement' whereas in Byatt's novel Marcus's visions are presented from his own subjective point of view, 'a point of view of extreme isolation'.[86] As a consequence of this lack of authority, the presentation of Marcus in the novel places him as 'a victim rather than an adept of vision'.[87] Plotz argues that Lucas's interpretations and explanations of Marcus's visions provide a temporary sense of authority, which is subsequently eroded as a consequence of their sexual encounter and Lucas's descent into madness. Combined with the lack of authorial endorsement for Marcus's visions, then, Plotz claims that *Virgin* ultimately fails to validate or explain the significance of Marcus's experiences. Interestingly, Plotz places *Virgin* alongside Byatt's first novel, *Shadow of a Sun*, since Henry Severell is shown to share Marcus's experiences of photisms. Plotz argues that while Marcus's visions are characterized by 'narrative reticence', Henry's are endorsed as legitimate; it is Henry's 'literary genius [that] certifies these experiences as revelations rather than delusions'.[88]

Ultimately, Plotz claims that Byatt's novel offers a 'much more guarded' view of the visionary child than that encountered in Romantic literature.[89] Rather than being blessed by his visions, Marcus 'embodies the terrors and loneliness of childhood that are inseparable from the condition of not knowing oneself'.[90] This comment recalls Irwin's assessment of the novel as a Bildungsroman concerned with the emotional development of the three Potter siblings. Many critics of *The Virgin in the Garden*, and indeed the quartet as a whole, focus on the figures of Stephanie and Frederica, relating them to Byatt's concern with the position of women in the 1950s and reading the novel in autobiographical terms. Although some critics recognize the importance of Marcus in the novel, few provide a detailed engagement with his character. While Elisabeth Anne Leonard's article focuses on the figure of Marcus, she is more concerned with the formal qualities of Byatt's novel and its position in relation to realism. Plotz's essay, by contrast, presents an interesting and insightful reading of the character of Marcus. In doing so, she draws out the connections between Byatt's novel and the Romantic tradition, an important context for Byatt's work since she has often indicated her admiration for Samuel Taylor Coleridge and indeed wrote a critical study entitled *Wordsworth and Coleridge in Their Time*. The connection of Byatt with Romantic authors highlights an important element of her fiction that is often elided by the debate about her position in relation to realism and postmodernism; a debate which becomes more prominent in Byatt's later fictions, as we shall see in the following chapters.

CHAPTER THREE

Verbal and Visual Art: *Still Life* (1985)

Published in 1985, *Still Life* continued the quartet that Byatt had begun with *The Virgin in the Garden* in 1978. As the second instalment in the quartet, most reviewers discussed *Still Life* in relation to the first novel in the sequence and the projected future volumes. Indeed, some reviewers sought to make claims about the quartet's project as a whole based on the approach of the first two novels.

REVIEWS

In his review for the *London Review of Books*, Patrick Parrinder explicitly positions the novel in relation to its predecessor, claiming that it is 'deeper and darker-toned'.[1] Despite its overt concern with art, Parrinder claims that *Still Life* is as concerned with language as *The Virgin in the Garden* was; painting is 'an alien art' to Byatt and as such 'does not determine her sense of narrative form'.[2] Rather, the discussions on painting ultimately lead back to issues of language and the problems of verbal representation. Parrinder furthers this argument by aligning Byatt's novel not with the Post-Impressionist school of artists to which the Dutch painter Vincent van Gogh (1853–90) was assigned by the art critic Roger Fry (1866–1934), but rather to the realist tradition of George Eliot, and in particular of *The Mill on the Floss* (1860). Parrinder's suggestion that the Cambridge parts of the novel have 'a feeling of thesis-illustration' recalls the criticisms of intellectualism encountered in reviews of the earlier novels.[3] Despite this, however, Parrinder suggests that Byatt's characterization of the minor characters is more successful. As with many reviewers, he praises the descriptions of Stephanie's childbirth, claiming that it positions Byatt alongside Arnold Bennett (1867–1931) and Marcel Proust (1871–1922) and their approach of 'celebrating ordinary things and everyday life'.[4] Parrinder concludes that Byatt inspires 'a strong conviction that [she is] showing us living things and morally significant characters'.[5] Parrinder's review identifies many of the touchstones that other reviewers of Still Life focus on: the importance of the Cambridge context, the novel's relationship to nineteenth-century realism, the presentation of childbirth and the 'ideas versus characters' debate that we have already encountered in reviews of Byatt's previous novels.

In his review for The Spectator, Lewis Jones notes that the Cambridge context, and in particular Leavis's values, are 'part of the fabric' of the novel.[6] Jones views Still Life as an intellectual novel interested in 'the tricky and exhilarating business of thinking about art'.[7] The intellectual aspects of the novel, however, are balanced by the presentation of characters who are not involved in intellectual pursuits. In particular, Jones singles out Mrs Orton and Gideon Farrar as providing this 'light relief' and links them to George Eliot's Mr Bulstrode from Middlemarch.[8] The other counterpoint to the intellectual aspects of the novel comes in the descriptions of the physical experiences of pregnancy and childbirth which, Jones claims, are 'among the best ever written'.[9] Jones contends that ultimately these two elements of the novel, the intellectual and physical worlds, are shown to be one. He concludes with a prediction about the quartet as a whole, which he asserts will 'be an ornament to the Great Tradition'.[10] This comment explicitly connects the novel to Leavis, whose major study of the English novel was called The Great Tradition (1948), and to the writers Leavis applauded in that book, such as George Eliot.

In his review of new fiction for New Statesman Roger Lewis dedicates almost a third of the space to a discussion of Still Life, and is unreserved in his praise. He, like Jones, aligns Byatt with the tradition of Victorian literature, claiming that she embraces it 'with a knowing love'.[11] Lewis sees Still Life as ultimately a novel about art, but he distances it from the solipsism associated with many postmodern self-reflexive texts. Indeed, he contrasts Still Life to the fictions of Jorge Luis Borges (1899–1986), claiming that Byatt demonstrates how 'a novel can think about itself without resorting to nervous Borgesian paper-puzzles, tricks, tics'.[12]

The review for The Times Literary Supplement, by novelist and short-story writer Adam Mars-Jones (born 1954), similarly positions Still Life within a nineteenth-century tradition of literature, claiming that it possesses a 'fullness and density' that is lacking in much contemporary fiction.[13] Mars-Jones praises Byatt's characters, claiming that they are 'buil[t] up ... relentlessly'.[14] In contrast to these elements, which are implicitly aligned with the realist tradition, Mars-Jones identifies the presence of a more experimental voice in the novel, the voice of the narrator. He suggests that the 'informality and self-doubt' of this voice is 'jarringly incongruous' with the authoritative tone of the rest of the novel.[15] Mars-Jones's criticism of this approach seems to assume that readers unquestioningly accept the fiction they are reading as reality. Consequently, such self-conscious questioning of the novel by the narrator is likely to leave the reader feeling 'disoriented'.[16] Ultimately, then, Mars-Jones praises the traditional elements of the book while judging the experimental elements as 'not the most successful'.[17] The traditional elements seem to outweigh the experimental features though, as he concludes that *Still Life* is both 'an impressive episode in a mighty undertaking and a seriously good novel in its own right'.[18]

The review for *The Times*, by the poet James Fenton (born 1949), concentrates on the stylistic elements of *Still Life* and, in particular, Byatt's claim that she had intended to write the novel without metaphor. Fenton criticizes this self-reflexive comment from the narrator, claiming that it is 'irrelevant to the resultant novel'.[19] He recognizes that this is part of a wider concern in the novel with the possibility of perceiving innocently, but claims that 'the point becomes untrue with overstating'.[20] Implicitly, then, Fenton is criticizing the novel's intellectualizing. Like many other reviewers, Fenton singles out the passages on childbirth for praise, claiming that there Byatt 'tell[s] her story directly and vividly'.[21] Oddly, Fenton comments that Byatt depicts pain and misery well; it is when she is dealing with her pleasures, primarily intellectual pleasures, that she 'becomes so perverse'.[22] The negative tone of Fenton's review extends to his comments on the historical aspects of the novel. He claims that Byatt 'thinks in labels' and resorts to clichés to evoke the historical periods she is concerned with.[23] As we shall see, discussion of Byatt's treatment of the past recurs in more extended analyses of the novel.

Peter Kemp's review for *The Sunday Times* equally disparages the self-conscious elements of the novel. He laments the fact that the narrative is often interrupted for 'some less than riveting bulletin from the writing-desk'.[24] Indeed, he notes a 'lecture-like atmosphere' to the novel.[25] Kemp believes that the intellectualism of the novel is a hindrance, particularly to the characters, who end up 'resembling *papier-mâché* constructs moulded from pulped-up reading lists'.[26]

In contrast, Paul West's review for *The New York Times* claims that Byatt is above all a 'psychological novelist' in whose novels plot is subordinated to character.[27] West identifies Byatt's range in her incorporation of both hearty Yorkshire speech and Cambridge literary chit-chat. While he recognizes the need for this outside world to counterpoint Byatt's 'long searches into human opacity', he feels that she uses too much 'expendable dialogue' where she might have conjured up Cambridge 'synoptically, through allusion'.[28] In contrast to the criticisms of her previous novels, West's review implies that in *Still Life* it is the characters who intrude upon and hamper the intellectual aspects of the novel.

West's review implicitly draws out *Still Life*'s feminist concerns, claiming that the passages on pregnancy and giving birth are among the 'most effective and memorable parts' of the novel.[29] Moreover, West links Byatt to a tradition of female writing, claiming that she is continuing the project of Virginia Woolf, a project which West claims only Eva Figes (born 1932) has 'dared to follow'.[30] This tradition is characterized by an interest in the psychological experiences of women and the technique of interior monologue, which presents the character's inner thoughts and impressions to the reader. As we shall see in the discussion of Stephanie's death in the novel, Byatt seems to continue this tradition in rendering the experience from Stephanie's point of view.

Michael Westlake's discussion of *Still Life* for *PN Review* in 1989 positions the novel as ultimately concerned with the possibilities and limitations of language as a form of communication. For Westlake, Byatt's novel is engaging with the problematic questions of the nature of language raised by post-structuralist theories. While aware that post-structuralism challenges the notion of a direct relationship between language and the world, Byatt retains a commitment to the possibility of expressing truth through language. Thus, *Still Life* deliberately oscillates between a belief in the transparency of language, an approach often aligned with the realist tradition, and a commitment to post-structuralist ideas. Ultimately, however, Westlake argues that for Byatt there is a sense that language can represent and express the world of things; she presents 'a version of reality which the reader is not encouraged to question'.[31] Thus, while aware of post-structuralism, Westlake implies that Byatt is ultimately on the side of realism. This commitment to realism is similarly apparent in Westlake's conclusions about the novel's treatment of visual modes of representation. Westlake connects this concern with the novel's treatment of language, claiming that vision becomes 'the chosen metaphor for the articulation of truth'.[32] He concludes that the novel suggests that 'experience precedes representation of it, and that language necessarily falsifies, or at least restricts, the abundance of reality'.[33] The notion that reality exists prior to language would seem to align Byatt with realist views on language, yet the comment that language distorts reality seems to assert the post-structuralist view that it is impossible to access a reality prior to language. In this comment, then, Westlake encapsulates the tension between realism and post-structuralism in Byatt's work. Ultimately, although Byatt is aware of and incorporates post-structuralist ideas into her novel, this does not prevent her from striving towards a sense of truth.

Although he identifies verbal and visual modes of representation as the central focus of the novel, Westlake's article also makes some other interesting comments on *Still Life*. He connects the woman in the prologue to *Still Life* with the woman who accompanies Lady Antonia Fraser (born 1932) in the prologue to *The Virgin in the Garden*, seeing them both as an 'authorial simulacrum'.[34] This phrase enables Westlake to hint at some of the connections between the two novels and their author's life without resorting to autobiographical criticism of the sort which, as we have seen, Byatt dislikes. Moreover, it implies a contemporary, or postmodern, interest in the processes of fiction, which, as we shall see in the next chapter, becomes more pronounced in her works from *Possession* onwards.

The other important point Westlake notes relates to the historical location of the novel. As we saw in the previous chapter, the complexities of historical location were also noted in relation to *The Virgin in the Garden*. For many reviewers, the projected quartet represented an ambitious project of historical fiction, which attempts to make the present history. As D. J. Taylor remarked of the first two novels in the quartet, 'they show every sign of developing into a weighty *roman-fleuve* of English Life in the second half of the twentieth century'.[35] For Westlake, however, *Still Life*'s historical location seems more problematic since he claims that it prevents the novel from addressing the problems and concerns of its own time. However, many critics claim that the novel does incorporate the perspective of its own time. Indeed, Westlake himself implicitly suggests this in the connections he makes between the novel and the post-structuralist theories that had become fashionable in the literary academy of the 1980s.

PAINTING IN *STILL LIFE*

Still Life explicitly asserts its interest in art, and specifically van Gogh; its title immediately indicates a genre of painting and one of the main characters, Alexander Wedderburn, is writing a play about van Gogh, *The Yellow Chair*. As Parrinder's review suggested, this concern with art prompts Byatt to muse self-consciously upon the modes of representation within which she is working, particularly language. Some critical attention, however, has been given to Byatt's engagement with visual art and its implications for the novel's wider concerns.

Although Michael Worton's essay 'Of Prisms and Prose: Reading Paintings in A. S. Byatt's Work' (2001) addresses Byatt's overall engagement with visual forms of representation, it focuses on *Still Life*. Worton begins his essay by pointing out that previous Byatt criticism is hindered by its focus on the 'textual and intertextual' aspects rather than the 'more broadly cultural and intergeneric'.[36] Worton attempts to redress this imbalance by focusing on one aspect of what he calls the 'non-verbal extra-text or paratext' within Byatt's work, painting.[37] For Worton, the world created in Byatt's texts is a 'highly referential one in which language ... also refers the reader outwards *from* the text to a world that is decidedly non-verbal'.[38] In this assessment, Worton positions Byatt's work within the debate that Westlake traced concerning post-structuralism, suggesting that her novels reveal the possibility that language can refer to something outside of itself. Byatt's engagement with painting reveals an intimate connection between reading and writing; for Worton, her texts are 'performative responses to paintings' which challenge the reader into the realization that every act of reading is 'the trace of an encounter' and therefore prompts 'writing of and for the self'.[39]

Despite this, Worton concludes that by incorporating paintings, although not literally, into her texts, Byatt highlights the tension between verbal and visual modes of representation. He claims that Byatt distinguishes paintings from texts, recognizing that paintings can never be captured in words; 'she experiences them "sensationally", allowing ... [them] to move her emotionally'.[40] For Worton, this sensory experience of painting is the defining characteristic of Byatt's engagement with visual art. From this general discussion of Byatt's approach, Worton turns to a more focused analysis of specific texts, identifying three artists as key to an understanding of how painting operates in Byatt's texts: van Gogh, the French artist Henri Matisse (1869–1954) and the Spanish painter Diego Vélazquez (1599–1660) are linked to *Still Life*, *The Matisse Stories* and 'Christ in the House of Martha and Mary' in *Elementals*, respectively. Matisse's position in *The Matisse Stories* will be considered in more detail in Chapter 9.

As we have already seen, the connection between *Still Life* and van Gogh is made explicitly by Byatt, and is explored by Worton in his essay. Worton claims that van Gogh influences *Still Life* not only at the level of plot but also at the level of style; van Gogh's approach to colour and use of 'colour adjectives' is seen to impact both Alexander's and Byatt's writing style.[41]

Worton claims that all Byatt's fiction share an overriding concern with balance; this concern characterizes the tension between verbal and visual modes of representation in *Still Life*. In van Gogh, Byatt finds an ability to hold things together, a model of the balance that she is continually striving for. Worton claims that in examining the tension between verbal and visual representation Byatt does not seek to prioritize either form, but rather recognizes that the very tension can lead to 'a dynamic balance'.[42] Worton argues that for Byatt the relationship between verbal and visual representation is a 'dialectical relationship' and thus 'the central issue is not one of hierarchical supremacy, but the fundamental question of the nature and adequacy of representation'.[43]

Worton concludes that by incorporating paintings into her fictions, Byatt is not attempting to 'fashion a verbal analogue of the painting' but instead, to render 'the painting present as something sensationally perceived'.[44] Oddly, though, Byatt never actually incorporates paintings into *Still Life*, but describes them verbally. Thus, as Parrinder suggested in his review for the *London Review of Books*, it is still the verbal mode of representation that dominates in *Still Life*.

Sue Sorensen's essay 'Something of the Eternal: A. S. Byatt and Vincent van Gogh' (2004) similarly recognizes the quest for balance within *Still Life*, but reaches a radically different conclusion from Worton. Sorensen focuses on the characters', rather than Byatt's, quest for balance within the novel, their desire to achieve 'dual authority in images and words'.[45] She concludes, pessimistically, that they 'are limited by modern and postmodern beliefs that thwart their forward movement'.[46] Sorensen sees *Still Life* as marking a turning point in Byatt's oeuvre; while the early fiction was marked by a confidence in the power of the visual, after *Still Life* her texts 'increasingly demonstrate a sharp awareness of the limitations of all kinds of language and the unattainability of truth'.[47] In *Still Life*, however, there remains a sense of the possibilities of communication through verbal representation. Sorensen claims that van Gogh's work represents 'a time of innocent knowledge no longer attainable in the era of postmodern scepticism'.[48]

Sorensen equally suggests, as Worton did, that van Gogh's influence is evident in Byatt's style, but she comments that Byatt makes unusual use of him, choosing to emphasize his realist rather than expressionist impulses: 'In *Still Life*, Byatt takes van Gogh at his word – that he wanted to get at the truth of objects, of light, of colour.'[49] Sorensen's assessment of *Still Life*'s style, however, is ultimately negative. She claims that it is 'at times, an uneasy blend of pastiche, myth, fabulism, modernist aestheticism and artistic commentary' and that the finished novel 'demonstrates just how incompatible realism and thesis-driven writing can be'.[50] For Sorensen, this incompatibility is centred on the treatment of character; realism is 'necessarily anchored in character' yet '[r]ealist characters do not adhere to a thesis'.[51] Once again, then, we have the charge that the intellectualism of the novel obscures the characterization.

Sorensen's pessimistic evaluation of the novel is most evident in her discussion of Stephanie. Alongside van Gogh, Sorensen claims that Stephanie is the character who is most successful in terms of Byatt's 'ideal conception of communication'.[52] For Sorensen, Stephanie's quest for balance is intimately related to her position as an intelligent young woman and mother in the 1950s as she seeks to balance 'her intellectual and domestic identities'.[53] This hints at another strand of criticism of the novel, feminist criticism which, as we shall see, centres on the figure of Stephanie and particularly on the circumstances of her death. In this essay, Sorensen examines Stephanie's death in terms of its connection to the quest for balance she has been discussing. Sorensen concludes that Stephanie's death is not 'just a death' but rather 'a judgement on a character with the temerity to conjoin sight and word, to entertain high hopes both for thought and personal life'.[54] Sorensen sees a parallel between Stephanie's fate and Byatt's engagement with van Gogh, which 'investigat[es] the possibility that visual and verbal language can amalgamate in some revelatory manner, and com[es] to a similarly pessimistic conclusion'.[55] Sorensen implies that, ultimately, Byatt's novel accepts the post-structuralist notion that the gulf between language and reality cannot be bridged.

AN ACCIDENTAL DEATH?

Stephanie's death at the end of the novel has dominated critical responses to *Still Life* and, as we shall see in the later chapters, influences perceptions of the quartet as a whole. Responses to Stephanie's death tend to focus on the circumstances of her death; that she is electrocuted by a refrigerator and that her final thought is of her children. This reading draws on the critical belief that Byatt creates an opposition in the first two novels of her quartet between Frederica and Stephanie, allowing her to examine the conflicting roles of women in the 1950s. Taylor, who sees *The Virgin in the Garden* and *Still Life* as deriving from the tradition of the Victorian social novel, argues that through the contrasting positions of Frederica and Stephanie 'the life of the mind and the familial hearth remain in sharp contention'.[56] In this context, and taking into account the fact that two volumes of the quartet remained unwritten at the time of his writing, he concludes that Stephanie's death 'seems a steely exhibition of authorial resolve'.[57] Taylor's comment here implicitly draws on a connection between the author and Frederica, assuming that since Byatt has chosen the path of a novelist in her own life she must prefer that path for her female characters.

Stephanie's death has provoked much debate among readers, reviewers and critics because of its banal and apparently unnecessary quality. In his chapter on *Still Life*, ' "Real Accident": Plotting and Pattern', Richard Todd resents Stephanie's death since it is 'not *necessary* to the plot'.[58] The 'appalling truth' of the novel is that it fails to make sense of Stephanie's death or to offer any consolation to the reader or the characters that are left behind: 'Even though … patterns can be discerned, their purpose is not to console so much as to reflect desolately on an inscrutable universe.'[59] Although Todd recognizes the sense of unease Stephanie's death prompts in the reader he sees it as evidence of Byatt's 'moral honesty, which is of the highest order'.[60] Todd's comment implicitly indicates Byatt's commitment to a realist mode of writing since deaths often lack meaning or purpose in real life. This view is extended in more sustained analyses of Stephanie's death and is also applied to Byatt's treatment of childbirth in the novel.

Sue Sorensen's essay 'Death in the Fiction of A. S. Byatt' (2002) presents a comprehensive overview of the treatment of death in Byatt's fiction, identifying four types of death: natural, symbolic, suicidal and accidental. Although Sorensen spends considerable time tracing the range of deaths within Byatt's fiction, her essay focuses on the accidental death of Stephanie in *Still Life*, which she claims is among Byatt's 'greatest written achievements'.[61] Sorensen's wide-ranging essay locates Byatt's oeuvre within a broad tradition of literary deaths, arguing that the treatment of death in literature underwent a shift with the onset of Modernism. Sorensen locates the emergence of this shift within *The Brothers Karamazov* (1880) by Fyodor Dostoevski (1821–81), arguing that in this and subsequent novels '[d]eath no longer automatically earns respect and fear; increasingly it ceases to be a matter of consequence'.[62] Sorensen traces the cause of this shift to language theory, claiming that in the light of theories such as structuralism and post-structuralism, 'the arbitrary nature of language exposes death as a void' and so '[e]ven death has lost its authority'.[63] It is interesting that Sorensen identifies language theory as the cause of this shift in the treatment of death since Byatt's works are often seen as engaging with the possibilities and limitations of language. Indeed, as we have already seen, this is a key feature of criticism on *Still Life* itself.

Sorensen argues that Byatt's presentation of death is an explicit response to the effect of language theories on the treatment of death, claiming that Byatt 'carefully takes up the challenge of representing meaningful death'.[64] For Sorensen, the key point of departure between Byatt's treatment of death in *Still Life* and other literary depictions of death is her adoption of 'the point of view of the dying consciousness'.[65] She claims that Byatt's purpose in *Still Life* is two-fold: to present death plainly and to focus on a type of death that has been under-represented in fiction, accidental death. Predictably, Sorensen makes use of autobiographical details, claiming that Stephanie's death in *Still Life* draws on the death of Byatt's son in 1972, a connection which she also relates to the figure of Mrs Thone in *The Virgin in the Garden*, and Byatt's domestic electrocution in the early 1960s. Yet, as with much biographical criticism, Sorensen fails to do more with this connection between life and fiction than merely point out the correspondences. Her essay is much more interesting, however, when she moves away from Byatt's life to focus on the fictional treatment of death in its own terms.

Sorensen explores the complex responses that Stephanie's death provokes, claiming that this complexity is prefigured in the novel's title. While she suggests that the French translation of the title as 'nature morte' hints at the death the novel contains, she claims that its position within a larger project, combined with the English phrase's suggestion of the continuity of life, does nothing to prepare the reader for Stephanie's death. Sorensen's reading of Stephanie's death draws on feminist responses to Byatt's work. Feminist discussions of *The Game*, *The Virgin in the Garden* and *Still Life* see in Byatt's depiction of two sisters an engagement with the opposition between woman as wife and mother and woman as careerist; an opposition between a biological and an intellectual identity. Although not explicitly presenting a feminist response to the novel, Sorensen connects Stephanie's death to the novel's opposition between body and mind. Sorensen claims that Stephanie is 'the victim of her community's inability to arrive at an equilibrium of body, mind, and spirit'.[66] In this context, Sorensen makes much of the fact that the scenes immediately preceding Stephanie's death see her attempting, if unwillingly, to provide comfort and support to various figures from within the community. For Sorensen, then, the sparrow is 'the distillate of this semiunwilling compassion'.[67] In Stephanie's final word, altruism, Sorensen sees 'an affirmation that her personal life (as opposed to her public function) has meaning that death, despite its imperative power, cannot efface'.[68] Despite this claim, Sorensen remains troubled by Stephanie's death, mostly because she feels it functions as a religious sacrifice which conflicts with the agnostic or atheistic world view she identifies as dominant in both Stephanie's life and Byatt's novel. Ultimately, despite arguing that Byatt is working against the trend that has stripped death of its meaning in literature, Sorensen seems unable to make sense out of Stephanie's death, questioning 'why [is there] the need for a character to bear the sins of others?'.[69]

THE LABOUR OF CHILDBIRTH

An interesting counterpoint to the critical attention given to Stephanie's death in the novel is Tess Cosslett's article 'Childbirth from the Woman's Point of View in British Women's Fiction' (1989). The title of Cosslett's article reveals a connection between her argument about Byatt's treatment of childbirth and Sorensen's argument about the depiction of death. For both critics, the distinguishing feature of Byatt's approach is her decision to narrate the experiences of both childbirth and death from the point of view of the character involved. Indeed, Sorensen's discussion of Stephanie's death incorporates a brief consideration of her childbirth experiences, claiming that Byatt is attempting to present both experiences 'plainly'.[70] Cosslett equally considers the connections between death and childbirth in *Still Life*, stating that the births 'mark stages in a pattern of decline and defeat' which culminates in Stephanie's death towards the end of the novel.[71] Indeed, she claims that '[t]he violent imagery [of Stephanie's second birth] prefigures her death'.[72] Cosslett's article presents a more explicitly feminist analysis than Sorensen's treatment of Stephanie's death.

Cosslett's article examines the treatment of childbirth in Byatt's *Still Life* alongside a much earlier novel, *The Squire* (1938) by Enid Bagnold (1889–1981). Both these novels are seen to depart from convention in making the births central to their plot and in depicting childbirth from the woman's point of view. Although Cosslett argues that these novelists are working against literary convention, she recognizes the impact of cultural discourses on their treatment of childbirth. She claims that Bagnold's and Byatt's representations of childbirth are 'remarkable achievements' which creatively engage with 'contemporary and inherited "voices", language, images, in order to give childbirth from the woman's point of view its own literary shape'.[73] Cosslett locates these novels within the context of varying discourses about children and childbirth; in the case of *Still Life* these discourses include natural childbirth, the postwar promotion of motherhood as the ultimate ideal for women, feminist discourses of the 1980s, and, less obviously, Romantic poetry. As we have seen, the time-frame of *Still Life* is quite complex and, as Cosslett's article shows, implicitly impacts the depiction of childbirth in the novel. For Cosslett, Byatt's story reflects 1980s attitudes towards childbirth more than the 1950s attitudes of the novel's location. She argues that the 1970s/80s backlash against hospitalization influences the perspective of the narrator, who implicitly compares the attitudes of the time of the novel's action with those current at the time of its production. Indeed, Cosslett suggests that Stephanie's consciousness might also be informed by the author's position in the 1980s. By drawing attention to the varying discourses that inform Byatt's novel, and contrasting them to the context of Bagnold's novel, Cosslett reveals the cultural construction of such discourses. The most interesting discourse with which these novels engage surrounds the notion of 'natural childbirth' which, as Cosslett points out, was pioneered by a male writer. Cosslett argues that '[b]oth women claim natural childbirth as a woman's unaided power and marginalize or render invisible its male cultural origins'.[74] In *Still Life*, Stephanie's 'natural' responses to childbirth are thwarted by the nurses' imposition of an unnatural and repressive birthing regime. Indeed, Cosslett sees Stephanie's whole experience of pregnancy and labour as negative: 'Stephanie feels the experience as a painful splitting between her real self and the fetus that has taken over her body.'[75] This notion of a split in Stephanie is, as we shall see, central to Cosslett's analysis of the novel.

The other discourse to which Cosslett devotes considerable attention is Romantic poetry and its view of childhood as an innocent state. As we saw in the previous chapter, this has also been identified as an important context for the depiction of Marcus in *The Virgin in the Garden*. Cosslett analyses Stephanie's life-pattern in terms of its parallels to the Romantic poem 'Ode: Intimations of Immortality from Recollections of Early Childhood' (1807) by Wordsworth. This parallel is explicitly signalled to the reader as Stephanie reads Wordsworth's poem while waiting in line at the antenatal clinic. Wordsworth's poem laments the gradual darkening that occurs as a result of ageing; the movement from '[t]he innocent brightness of a new-born Day' to '[t]he clouds that gather round the setting sun'.[76] Cosslett argues that Byatt transforms the Wordsworthian model to account for a distinctly female experience: 'it is not the coming of adulthood...that dims Stephanie's light, but specifically marriage and motherhood'.[77] This connection is made more explicit as Stephanie's first experience of childbirth is described in specifically Wordsworthian terms. Despite the negative experience of pregnancy and childbirth, Stephanie experiences an unexpected ecstasy when she first meets her child, William. This experience is explicitly cast in Wordsworthian terms by both Stephanie and Byatt and prompts the name of Stephanie's first child. For Cosslett, by focusing on the physicality of the birthing experience, Byatt is implicitly revising the Wordsworthian myth, which sidelines woman's physical role in the process of giving birth.

For Cosslett, the treatment of childbirth in these two novels is explicitly related to feminist concerns about the subjectivity and identity of women. Cosslett argues that in both Bagnold's and Byatt's novels the experience of childbirth is presented as transitional, 'a potentially empowering transformation that takes place in some special area outside normal society'.[78] For Cosslett, this again draws on the 'Romantic model in which the innocent, semi-divine, and asocial child has to fit into the ordinary social world of "common day"'.[79] Cosslett connects the transitional experience of birth in *Still Life* to the conflict between women's roles as mother or career woman. Like many other critics, Cosslett analyses the opposition between Frederica and Stephanie in terms of the conflict women experience between the demands of the body and those of the mind. As we have seen, Cosslett interprets the births in *Still Life* as part of a larger pattern of decline in Stephanie's life that leads to her death, which is juxtaposed with 'the upward trajectory of Frederica's [life] to academic and sexual success'.[80] For Cosslett, Stephanie's fate is the consequence of her life-choices, her rejection of academia and a career in favour of marriage and motherhood. This connection between birth and death is made even more explicit by Cosslett when she comments that 'the births seem to make her more vulnerable to physical accident. ... physicality, and hence mortality, is the property only of the mother; the other main characters transcend it by virtue of being men or taking on male roles'.[81] Cosslett seems to be implying, then, that Byatt punishes Stephanie for adopting a more 'feminine' role, for choosing the role of mother and wife over the role of the intellectual.

BYATT ON *STILL LIFE*

Byatt's essay 'Still Life/Nature morte' examines her approach to writing the second novel in her quartet, an approach intended to 'forgo metaphor' but which she claims ultimately failed.[82] Byatt's essay deals with many of the issues that have been identified in the various critical responses to the novel. For instance, she explores the novel's concern with language and the possibilities of expressing truth which, as we have seen, was identified as a key feature in Michael Westlake's article. Byatt talks of being both drawn to and repelled by, 'both afraid of, and fascinated by' contemporary language theories such as post-structuralism.[83] She concludes that *Still Life* operates within the assumption 'that accuracy of description is possible and valuable. That words denote things.'[84] In talking of the novel's approach, Byatt draws an explicit contrast with her previous novel, *The Virgin in the Garden*. She explains the movement from the first to the second novel in her quartet as a shift from 'an undissociated paradise to our modern dissociated world'.[85] The terms in which Byatt conceptualizes this shift are drawn from the theory of the dissociation of sensibility proposed by the Modernist poet and critic T. S. Eliot. According to Eliot, a 'dissociation of sensibility' occurred during the seventeenth century. Prior to this, there was a natural and unbreakable connection between language, thought and the world. Thus, it would seem that in *Virgin* Byatt was trying to return to this idealized state of the natural connection between language and the world, whereas *Still Life* accepts that it is part of the modern world in which the naturalness of that connection has been called into question. As Byatt, and indeed many of her critics, have claimed, however, there is a persistent commitment to strive for accuracy and truth in language. Indeed, in her essay 'Ancestors', Byatt refers to Eliot's theory as a myth, dismissing it as 'nonsense'.[86] In an essay on her collection, *Sugar and Other Stories*, Byatt asserts that 'I do believe that language has denotative as well as connotative powers.'[87] This comment helps us to understand Byatt's approach in *Still Life*; that novel is attempting to explore langauge's ability to represent the thing itself rather than just to conjure it up through association. Byatt is opposed to theories that claim language can only ever refer to itself – rather, she is attempting to demonstrate language's power to represent the world, even if she recognizes the failure of that project in her novel *Still Life*. The prime example she gives to explain this is van Gogh's Yellow Chair which is a persistent presence in the novel, not least in providing the focal point for Alexander Wedderburn's play. Byatt describes how she originally chose the chair for its denotative qualities, but later discovered it was 'a complex metaphor, psychological, cultural, religious, aesthetic'.[88] Ultimately, as with the image of the Yellow Chair, *Still Life* combines both a denotative and connotative approach to language and as such needs to be seen as both continuing and yet diverging from the stylistic strategies of its prequel, *The Virgin in the Garden*.

Chapters 7 and 8 of this guide will show how the third and fourth volumes of the quartet transgressed even further the stylistic strategies established in the first two novels. Before that, however, came Byatt's neo-Victorian fictions which, as we shall see in the following three chapters, occupy an uneasy position in relation to contemporary theories. As with *Still Life* and post-structuralism, Byatt's neo-Victorian texts seem aware of postmodernism while refusing to subscribe entirely to it.

CHAPTER FOUR

Postmodernism vs. Realism: *Possession: A Romance* (1990)

1990 was Byatt's year: the publication of *Possession: A Romance* brought her both critical and popular success and she was awarded a CBE in recognition of her contribution to British literature. Indeed, Richard Todd goes so far as to call it her '*annus mirabilis*', wonderful year.[1] Given the reception of *Possession* and its impact on Byatt's subsequent career, such a claim seems entirely legitimate. Byatt, however, appears to resent the prominence given to *Possession* and the suggestion that it brought her success. In an interview with Mervyn Rothstein, Byatt counters this claim, defending her earlier works as 'perfectly good novels that were written about quite a lot.'[2] Despite such assertions, however, *Possession* still occupies a central place in Byatt's oeuvre, which is mirrored by its position in this Guide.

Possession was greeted with favourable reviews from the outset, which continued with its Booker Prize success and subsequent transition to the American market. Although reviewers often identified similar qualities to those found in Byatt's earlier work, where they had been criticized previously, they were praised in *Possession*. Whilst the novel was considered to be literary and intellectual it was felt that this was balanced by a popular appeal; it managed to combine postmodern concerns with a revival of Victorian fiction. Thus, the debate over Byatt's position in relation to postmodernism and realism became particularly prominent in reviews of *Possession*. As Byatt's most popular and successful novel, *Possession* received a great deal of attention in the press. In the reviews section that follows, I discuss a range of key reviews which characterize the various responses to the novel. In particular, I indicate how these reviews position *Possession* in relation to postmodernism and realism.

REVIEWS

Peter Kemp's review for *The Sunday Times* claims that *Possession*'s opening scene, set in a library, might worry readers familiar with Byatt's previous novels *The Virgin in the Garden* and *Still Life*. In those two novels, 'literary allusions [are] strewn around...with daunting voluminousness'; by contrast, *Possession* manages to maintain these intellectual qualities without getting 'bogged down' by them.[3] Kemp praises Byatt's 'brilliant sequence' of imitations of nineteenth-century poetry, claiming that 'with uncanny flair, she re-vivifies [the] past'.[4] The contemporary elements of the novel, however, are judged less successful, especially when they emulate the 'tones and techniques' of Iris Murdoch.[5] Although Kemp prefers the Victorian over the modern elements of *Possession*, he concludes that the novel itself is less interested in creating an opposition between the two eras than in drawing out the 'continuities and connections' between the present and the past.[6]

In his review for *The Times Literary Supplement*, Richard Jenkyns' preference for the Victorian elements of the novel is most evident in his response to the characters. For Jenkyns, Byatt's portrayal of the nineteenth-century characters is much more successful than that of the twentieth-century characters, who are 'cardboard'; consequently he argues that 'Roland remains shadowy, and Maud never comes alive'.[7] He reaches a similar conclusion in his assessment of Byatt's multiple ventriloquisms. Of the nineteenth-century texts Byatt incorporates, Jenkyns concludes that despite a few lapses in tone they are generally 'a brilliant achievement of sheer technique'.[8] In contrast, he is entirely disparaging of her ventriloquism of texts by the twentieth-century figures, particularly the extracts from Cropper's biography of Ash.

This privileging of the Victorian over the postmodern elements of *Possession* extends beyond Byatt's characterization. Jenkyns criticizes the most overtly postmodern passages as reminiscent of 'the university novel at its most arch and banal'.[9] For Jenkyns, the book's quality lies in its solidity, a feature he aligns with the Victorian literary tradition. Whilst Jenkyns recognizes that at times the novel's symbolism reduces it to merely 'a mechanical pattern', he concludes that it does not mar the book.[10] Overall, Jenkyns aligns *Possession* with a recuperative strand in contemporary fiction, claiming that it 'restore[s] the Victorians to honour, with an especial admiration for their emotional lives'.[11]

Danny Karlin's review for *London Review of Books* similarly views *Possession* as combining the intellectualism of Byatt's previous novels with a new-found freedom. This freedom prompts a change in tone which is evident in the precursors Byatt invokes. Karlin suggests that George Eliot, whose moralism had dominated the previous novels, has been replaced by Charles Dickens (1812–70) as 'chief Victorian precursor'.[12] Specifically, he identifies *Bleak House* (1852–3) as an important intertext in its combination of 'family romance, Gothic quest, detective thriller'.[13] Despite identifying such Victorian precursors, Karlin prioritizes the modern elements. He claims that the romance between the contemporary pair, Roland and Maud, is 'done with more assurance' than the relationship between Ash and LaMotte.[14] Unlike many reviewers, Karlin seems unconcerned with the question of the accuracy of Byatt's imitations of Victorian poetry. Indeed, he claims that the novel's position as a romance renders the question of accuracy 'irrelevant'.[15] What is important, though, is the use to which these poems are put, and here Byatt comes in for harsh criticism from Karlin. Since her Victorian poets are fictional, she is able to make them serve her own purposes; consequently, Byatt is 'too knowing and too coercive' in her use of the poetry. In particular, he criticizes Byatt's presentation of LaMotte who is 'required to be too many kinds of writer'.[16] Implicitly, then, Karlin raises the frequent charge that Byatt's characters are made to serve her intellectual purposes.

Christopher Lehmann-Haupt's review focuses more on *Possession*'s affinities with postmodern literature than its connections to Victorian fiction. He aligns Byatt's novel with one of the most well-known texts of postmodern literature, *The French Lieutenant's Woman* (1969) by John Fowles (1926–2006) and also with *The Quincunx: The Inheritance of John Huffam* (1989) by Charles Palliser (born 1947). By identifying these two novels as 'precursors' of *Possession*, Lehmann-Haupt positions Byatt's novel within a British tradition of 'neo-Victorian fiction', a contemporary genre which, as we shall see in the next chapter, is distinguished from postmodern literature by its commitment to the historical specificity of the past.[17] Yet, Lehmann-Haupt seems unaware of the particularities of this genre, focusing instead on the features of Byatt's novel that are considered 'hallmarks' of postmodernist fiction: its concern with language and 'the pleasure of reading'.[18] Lehmann-Haupt's bias towards postmodernist fiction is apparent in his assessment of the nineteenth-century texts Byatt incorporates into her novel; for him, Byatt's 'brilliant mimicry' of Victorian poetry is marred by the fact that it captures 'its tedium as well as its complexly patterned obsessiveness'.[19] He sees *Possession* as marking a 'release from realistic fiction' which he implies had characterized Byatt's previous novels.[20]

Liz Heron's review for *The Times Educational Supplement* examines *Possession*'s treatment of contemporary theory. She claims that Byatt is working within the genre of the campus novel but that the various strands of academia are 'treated with amusement but not mockery'.[21] Consequently, the novel reveals 'the partial nature of theory rather than disposing of it'.[22] Heron reaches a similar conclusion about the novel's attitude towards postmodernism. She claims that *Possession* is 'a postmodern text that rejects the emptiness diagnosed by so much postmodern argument.'[23] As we shall see, this claim is elaborated in Bo Lundén's and Jackie Buxton's analyses of the novel.

Jay Parini's review of *Possession* identifies both its Victorian and postmodern elements. This is most apparent in the various analogues Parini identifies, invoking such diverse authors as P. G. Wodehouse (1881–1975), David Lodge and Charles Dickens. Parini is one of the few reviewers who seems willing to accept *Possession*'s deliberate combination of realist and postmodern features. He recognizes *Possession*'s connections to postmodern literature, commenting that the novel increasingly comes to resemble a text by Jorge Luis Borges, a writer known for his highly self-conscious style. Yet Parini simultaneously draws out the connections to Victorian literature in his description of the final revelation as 'a supremely Dickensian one ... that plays wittily with the convention of coincidence.'[24] Parini's closing assessment of Byatt's novel recognizes that its appeal is in part a result of this combination of Victorian realism and postmodernism: ' "Possession" is a tour de force that opens every narrative device of English fiction to inspection without, for a moment, ceasing to delight.'[25] Thus, Byatt successfully combines the metafictional approach associated with postmodern fiction with the pleasures of reading Victorian literature.

One review that clearly diverged from the trend of universal praise was Donna Rifkind's article for *The New Criterion*. Despite being published after the announcement of the Booker Prize, Rifkind swims against the tide of critical opinion in her negative review of *Possession*. She criticizes one of the elements praised by most reviewers, saying that Byatt is 'deplorably inept' at imitating Victorian poetry.[26] For Rifkind, the greatest fault is that these imitations are presented 'unsmilingly, without so much as a hint of irony', suggesting that Byatt considers them as on a par with the poems produced by her Victorian models.[27] Despite these criticisms, Rifkind argues that it is the twentieth-century characters in the novel who come off worst, particularly Maud and Roland. Rifkind asserts that this pair are denied a romantic union so that Byatt can demonstrate the superiority of the nineteenth century over the twentieth century. Ironically, then, 'a pair of properly repressed Victorians managed to be a lot sexier than today's sexually well-informed scholars'.[28] Whilst many reviewers have shared Rifkind's assessment of the passionless nature of the twentieth-century romance, her claims are slightly undermined by her failure to take into account the fact that Roland and Maud do embark on a relationship at the end of the novel.

Although it does not explicitly engage with the question of *Possession*'s position as a postmodernist or Victorian novel, Rifkind's review implicitly comes down on the side of postmodernism. For her,

Possession is distinguished from Byatt's earlier novels by its rejection of 'traditional plotting' in favour of 'literary game-playing'.[29] In addition, she considers the novel's central concern as being the state of romantic love and sexuality in the postmodern age. Rifkind concludes her article with a bold claim about the future success of the novel, suggesting that once the Booker hype subsides *Possession* will come to be seen as 'an outdated literary curio'.[30] Obviously, as the very existence of this Guide and the numerous critical responses that it encapsulates reveals, Rifkind's predictions proved false.

POSSESSION AS A VICTORIAN NOVEL

The tendency to construct an opposition between *Possession*'s postmodernist and Victorian elements has continued to be a feature of much criticism on the novel. Jackie Buxton examines the postmodernist credentials of the novel in her article ' "What's love got to do with it?": Postmodernism and *Possession*' (1996). According to Buxton, '[r]eviewers are unanimous in their praise, and virtually unanimous in their implicit or explicit tagging of the novel as postmodernist', yet, although '[h]ighly forthcoming in their approval, they are less forthright in outlining the reasons for this postmodern classification'.[31] In its inversion of the detective genre, Buxton sees affinities with postmodernist strategies: '[t]hus, to rework a term of [Linda] Hutcheon's, the novel is a historiographic (detective) metafiction, one in which "possession" acts as both *arche* [origin] and *telos* [end], question and solution'.[32] Linda Hutcheon defines 'historiographic metafictions' as 'novels that are intensely self-reflexive but that also both re-introduce historical context into metafiction and problematize the entire question of historical knowledge'.[33] For Hutcheon, 'historiographic metafiction' is the postmodern genre *par excellence* because it encapsulates the very contradictions at work in postmodernism itself. Whilst she acknowledges the self-conscious elements of the novel, Buxton argues that there is a distinction between self-consciousness and the self-reflexive nature of postmodernist fiction, concluding that '[f]or all of its postmodern gestures, *Possession* is first and foremost a "straight" narrative, a realistic fiction'.[34] She argues that a distinction needs to be made between the attitudes of the characters in the novel and the approach of the novel itself: '[w]hile Maud and Roland exhibit a scholarly postmodernist sensibility, the text itself exhibits a strong suspicion of that epistemic condition, even a condemnation of it.'[35] Thus, despite her essay's title, Buxton concludes that '*Possession* is in many ways a Victorian novel, for it replicates the realism of its forbears in capturing the nineteenth-century ethos.'[36] This nineteenth-century approach is most apparent in Byatt's characterization. Buxton claims that for all its postmodern posturing, *Possession* never questions the reality of the characters it presents. She continues: '[o]ne world is obviously given ideological priority in this text, and it is the Victorian one, this literary Golden Age from which the present one is constructed as a falling away.'[37] Oddly, Buxton dismisses one of the most obvious instances of Victorian realism in *Possession* as a postmodern device. Chapter 15 represents a departure from the reliance on textual remains that has characterized the depiction of the nineteenth-century characters up to this point. Instead, the reader is taken back to the nineteenth-century and given direct access to an encounter between Ash and LaMotte for which there are no textual remains. Buxton aligns this narrative strategy of adopting a 'hypothetical observer' with the infamous metafictional frame-breaking of John Fowles's *The French Lieutenant's Woman*:

■ Implicitly, the reader (and writer) is that observer, projected into the novel as a fellow traveller. Although certainly not as emphatically authorial as Fowles' intrusion, the situation, description, and tone of this episode echoes Fowles' embodied entrance into his own fiction.[38] ☐

In aligning this strategy with Fowles's novel Buxton elides the connections to the forms of Victorian realism, connections that in fact are present in Fowles's novel as well. For example, George Eliot's *The Mill on the Floss* opens with the corporeal presence of the narrator leaning on a stone bridge surveying the scene at Dorlcote Mill.

Despite arguing throughout her essay that *Possession* is distinguished from postmodern fiction by its commitment to the Victorian literary tradition, Buxton concludes that '[u]ltimately, I suspect that *Possession* will be denied access to the canon of postmodernist texts [because it] offers modernist ideology in postmodernist guise.'[39] At the start of her essay, Buxton had explained that whilst Modernist and postmodernist literature could be seen to employ similar techniques they differed in terms of their 'informing sensibilities'.[40]

■ While modernists recognized a decentred, fragmented world, their quest for adequate ways to represent it went hand in hand with a desire to transcend it. In contrast, postmodernists, although no less artful, revel in the loss of formal order, accepting the incoherent, random nature of experience.[41] ☐

Buxton's invocation of *Possession*'s affinities with Modernism is interesting since most critics entirely overlook this element in their eagerness to enter the realism versus postmodernism debate. Whilst Byatt is occasionally associated with Modernist authors such as D. H. Lawrence and

Marcel Proust critical accounts of her fiction generally fail to consider her position in relation to Modernism.

Although Bo Lundén's study *(Re)educating the Reader: Fictional Critiques of Poststructuralism in Banville's* Dr Copernicus*, Coetzee's* Foe*, and Byatt's* Possession (1999) does not explicitly focus on the question of postmodernism, it implicitly addresses similar concerns to those found in Buxton's article. The focus on contemporary theory in the texts Lundén discusses leads to the assumption that theory is endorsed in them and they are consequently classed as postmodernist texts. Buxton highlights the need to distinguish between the attitudes of the characters in *Possession* and the overall approach of the novel itself. Similarly, Lundén differentiates between the novel's explicit depiction of critical theory and its overall attitude towards it claiming that in *Possession*, Byatt's 'critique of contemporary theory can be seen as both *implicit* and *explicit*'.[42] He acknowledges that '[t]hese texts can be read as theoretical discourses in fictional disguise' but argues that 'they also insist on exposing purely theoretical discourse as limited'.[43] Lundén's central argument is that all three novels critique poststructuralism, and contemporary critical theory more generally, by invoking a 'residue' that is not accounted for in the theories: 'This residue – the emotional, the spiritual, the mystical, the affective, and the intuitive – can be seen as creating a tension in the novels insofar as it effectively elides the highly sophisticated play of ideas in twentieth-century theories.'[44] In the case of *Possession*, Lundén explicitly connects this 'residue' to the Victorian elements of the novel: 'The literary scholars' (re)covery of the residue (emotions, desire, instincts) can be seen as an implicit influence from the Victorian plot'.[45] Lundén concludes that 'these novels want to make their readers respond not only cognitively but also affectively', in terms of feeling as well as intellect.[46] Whilst the Victorian characters provoke an affective response the twentieth-century figures remain unknowable to the reader at an emotional level, they fail to come alive for the reader. Thus, Lundén implies that Byatt privileges the Victorian world of emotion over the sterile world of contemporary theory. Byatt's attitude towards the Victorian era is revealed through her adoption of a dual plot. Lundén links this strategy to John Fowles's *The French Lieutenant's Woman* since both novels juxtapose the Victorian past and the present and, moreover, both texts 'fuse realism and postmodern self-reflexivity'.[47] Despite adopting similar narrative strategies, Lundén argues that the target of the parody in Byatt's novel is different from Fowles's; *Possession* is 'intended as a parody and critique of a literary academic world of the latter twentieth century and not, as in Fowles's case, as a parody of the Victorian age.'[48] Indeed, as we shall see shortly, Byatt herself is keen to distinguish her fictional project from that of *The French Lieutenant's Woman*.

POSSESSION AS A POSTMODERN NOVEL

In contrast to Buxton who claims that *Possession* is best understood within the Victorian literary tradition, Chris Walsh prioritizes the postmodern features of the novel, claiming that its defining characteristic is its self-reflexive concern with reading. In his essay 'Postmodernist Readings: *Possession*' (1999), Chris Walsh provides both a reading of *Possession* as a postmodernist novel and an analysis of *Possession*'s self-reflexive, and for him postmodern, interest in reading. For Walsh, this self-conscious interest in reading is the most significant feature of the novel:'[i]t is a novel pre-eminently about reading and the intertextual and indeterminate nature of the process...in a double sense'; not only does the reader encounter various different texts, but some of these are 'themselves readings, or "stories of readings"'.[49]

Walsh's comment highlights the metafictional nature of the novel. When examining its approach to reading it often appears as if *Possession* has a Chinese-box structure. For instance, the reader encounters Roland reading Cropper's biography of Ash, thus there are multiple levels of reading. Walsh sees this interest in reading as 'part of a more general postmodernist movement towards an increasingly "self-reflexive", knowing "critical creativity"'.[50] This interest in reading is further identified as a postmodernist feature in the assertion that 'To read *Possession*...is to read conscious of plurality, self-deconstruction and, ultimately, indeterminacy'.[51] Walsh claims that Byatt's novel 'proves that postmodernist fiction can be pleasurable to read. Part of the pleasure of reading *Possession* derives from the reader's consciousness of its nature and status as "historiographic metafiction"'.[52] Whilst he recognizes that the novel's metafictional focus on reading could prove a stumbling block for some readers, Walsh ultimately sees it as a positive aspect of the novel. That the intertextual aspect of the novel provides one of the pleasures of reading is further evident in the number of reviewers who revel in identifying various intertextual echoes in the novel. Walsh concludes that *Possession* explores the reader's freedom, including 'the freedom of the reader to read and misread, to interpret and to misinterpret'.[53]

■ *Possession*, in presenting the reader with so many different kinds and examples of reading and misreading, draws attention to reading's infinite possibilities. It shows us restrictive, monologic, authoritarian, closed, coercive readings for what they are, and promotes an ideal that is the product of thoughtfulness – liberal, dialogic, democratic, open, pluralistic; in

> short, it exposes *possessiveness*, and encourages *freedom* – the freedom
> to criticize, the freedom to interpret.[54] □

Walsh implicitly positions the restrictive, coercive readings as Victorian in opposition to the liberal and open readings prioritized in postmodern texts. Byatt's critical writings, as we shall see, seem to suggest that the opposite is true, that supposedly open texts actually provide less freedom for the reader.

In her essay 'Romancing Difference, Courting Coherence: A. S. Byatt's *Possession* as Postmodern Moral Fiction' (1996), Elisabeth Bronfen understands the opposition between the postmodern and Victorian elements of Byatt's novel as being endowed with moral import: 'For even as authority is implicitly at work in her effort to place her fiction in the tradition of the moral realism of 19th-century literature, her postmodern scepsis towards any such morally encoded messages in turn reflects disempowerment.'[55] Bronfen argues that Byatt adopts the genre of romance because it is 'one of the modes of textuality that maps ethics onto postmodernism'.[56] She claims that romance is related to postmodern ideas because it demonstrates 'a knowledge of its own fictionality'.[57] Once again, then, the self-conscious, and supposedly 'postmodern', elements of the novel are prioritized. Bronfen argues that Maud and Roland 'embody Byatt's demand for a cross between moral realism and experimental fiction precisely by virtue of the fact that they trace the gesture of oscillation between a sceptical postmodern self-consciousness and the unconditional surrender to love required by the romance genre'.[58] Thus, Bronfen seems to imply that it is the romance genre which enables Byatt successfully to combine realism and postmodernism. For some critics, however, *Possession* does not merely combine postmodernism with realism but rather presents a critique of postmodernism.

BEYOND POSTMODERNISM?

Susanne Becker's essay, 'Postmodernism's Happy Ending: *Possession!*' (2001), argues that Byatt's novel signals a movement beyond postmodernism, or at least 'the threshold between postmodern thought and new forms of more realist representation'.[59] This boundary between postmodernism and realism is just one of the many boundaries that Byatt's novel encompasses. Indeed, Becker argues that *Possession* engages with a subgenre of the novel that 'like no other has thrived on the connectedness of extremes: the gothic'.[60] Becker sees 'excess' as the defining characteristic of gothic fiction; an excess which contributes both to its challenge to realist narrative and its popular appeal.[61] She states that the excess in gothic is 'a transgression of the real, the natural and the rational' and that the 'excessive emotional experiences of desire, terror and pleasure become liberatory reading experiences'.[62] Becker's association of *Possession* with the gothic tradition comes in part from its epigraph from the American novelist Nathaniel Hawthorne (1804–64). She states that Hawthorne often applied the category of romance to gothic and that here 'Byatt follows suit'.[63] Moreover, Byatt's novel adopts the gothic strategy of excess in the presentation of an 'abundance of literary characters and narrative forms'.[64] Yet in Byatt's novel this principle of excess is not passively adopted but is actively turned upon the genre of the gothic itself, so that it too is presented through excess in the 'intertextual' mingling of various gothic forms with other narrative modes.[65] Becker acknowledges that this 'narrative play with the expectations of realism and gothicism' can be seen as a 'parodic – and postmodern – move'.[66]

Ultimately, however, Becker claims that the parody in *Possession* is replaced by 'an illuminating perspective' on modern society which suggests the presence of needs and desires that postmodernism cannot account for.[67] The 'excess' of postmodernism, then, is 'the pronounced need for answers' or the 'desire to know' that Becker claims underpins the contemporary plot of *Possession*.[68] This desire to know is the key component of the experience of reading *Possession* and Becker argues that there is a real sense at the end that 'we actually possess something'.[69] Moreover, this desire for knowledge is in part a nostalgic desire representing a 'fatigue with postmodernism's infinite deferrals'.[70] Becker claims that this desire for knowledge represents the transition from the 1980s acceptance of such postmodern ideas as epistemological uncertainty to the 1990s when such ideas were being questioned, especially by post-colonial and feminist critics. In the 1990s, academic culture became increasingly interested in the emotions that are sidelined by the intellectual movement of postmodernism. To return to *Possession*, then, Becker claims that Byatt exploits both of these intellectual climates as her twentieth-century plot incorporates 'an important paradox: knowledge defers the emotional happy ending, while the desire for knowledge that motivates the plot nevertheless works to liberate those emotions'.[71] Thus, the happy ending is deferred for the characters since they have no knowledge of the events in the Postscript, yet the quest for knowledge has enabled Maud and Roland to break free of their theoretical constraints and experience emotions first-hand through their love affair. Becker's argument about the emotional excess of *Possession* recalls Lundén's argument about the 'residue' that is not accounted for in the critical theories Byatt evokes. Whilst Lundén sees this as evidence of Byatt's challenge to poststructuralism, and by extension, postmodernism, Becker takes this a step further in arguing that the emotional excess of *Possession* signals the end of postmodernism and the re-ermergence of realism, albeit in a slightly modified guise. Turning specifically to the Postscript, Becker claims that it is a 'scene of gothic sublime' and as such is 'suspended between nostalgia and desire'.[72] She links the Postscript to the tradition of feminine gothic, claiming that, like the happy endings of those fictions, 'it both undercuts classical realist closure and enforces the pleasurable reading-effect of possessing...a secret'.[73] Despite questioning the possibilities of closure, the Postscript ultimately allows the reader access to the novel's secret and thus provides a neat ending reminiscent of realist fiction.

POSTSCRIPT: A ROMANTIC ENDING?

As we have seen, critical opinion is divided over the issue of whether *Possession* is a realist or postmodernist novel. This division of opinion is equally apparent in discussions of the novel's ending. Whilst some critics see it as one of the postmodern features of the novel others see it as marking a return to the type of endings found in Victorian realist fiction. Hulbert attempts to read the novel's ending as both Victorian and postmodern:

■ the poets' lives have a ragged modern ending, their paths leading off in different directions and their messages to each other lost in transmission. The young professors, meanwhile, are on their way to an old-fashioned happy ending, two chill souls warming each other at last.[74] □

Interestingly, the endings seem to be inverted; whilst the Victorian characters have a modern, open, ending, the modern characters achieve a happy ending reminiscent of Victorian fiction. Hulbert's assessment of the ending, however, fails to take into account the Postscript, which proves a particularly contentious issue in critical discussions of the text.

In her essay 'The Redemptive Past in the Neo-Victorian Novel' (1997), Dana Shiller claims that the Postscript to *Possession* 'calls attention to what is left out of histories' and thus relates it to the novel's views on historiography which will be explored in more detail in the following chapter.[75] For now, though, I am interested in Shiller's assessment of the strategy for closure adopted by Byatt. Shiller writes:

■ A typically neat Victorian ending (Randolph dies, clutching the letter to his breast) is evaded through a quintessentially postmodern lacuna: Randolph never reads the letter, but Maud, Roland and their cohorts do, and it augments (and changes irrevocably) their versions of the life stories of Randolph and Christabel.[76] □

Whilst Shiller implicitly positions the Postscript as a 'postmodern' feature of the novel she fails to engage explicitly with the complexities it raises; indeed, the postmodern lacuna she identifies actually occurs in the chapter that precedes the Postscript.

Chris Walsh's analysis of *Possession* explicitly engages with the question of the novel's closure, relating it to his consideration of the novel's treatment of reading. Walsh argues that most of the readers in the novel are driven by a need for narrative closure. In discussing the novel's ending, however, he distinguishes between the ending presented to the readers and the one that the majority of the novel's characters are left with:

■ The novel's readers are the privileged spectators of all these events, and for us the narrative may be said to reach a satisfactory conclusion both cognitively (the main loose ends are tied up neatly ...) and emotionally. The ending is by no means a conventionally 'closed' one, however, as far as the knowledge and destinies of the protagonists (especially the 1980s figures) are concerned: many questions are left unanswered, many possibilities are left open. In this respect, the ending of *Possession* is decidedly indeterminate.[77] □

Walsh's conclusion that the ending of the novel is 'decidedly indeterminate' corresponds to his assessment of the novel as a postmodern text in which the reader is 'conscious of plurality, self-deconstruction and, ultimately, indeterminacy'.[78] However, whilst the ending for the characters seems to confirm the novel's postmodern position, Walsh implicitly aligns the satisfactory conclusion provided by the Postscript with Victorian fiction.

Jackie Buxton similarly aligns the Postscript with Victorian fiction in her claim that it contributes to the novel's overall critical stance towards postmodernism:

■ The postscript is clearly a playful sideswipe at postmodern historicism, for it concerns things that 'are not spoken or written of, though it would be very wrong to say that subsequent events go on indifferently, all the same, as though such things had never been' .... What Byatt presents here is not a textual construction, but a living human being, a materiality as opposed to a discursive trace.[79] □

Thus, Buxton argues that '[w]hile the conclusions reached by the grouped academics at the end of *Possession* (retrospectively) underline the impossibility of any totalizing knowledge, the reader's experience is exactly the opposite.'[80] Again, then, the twentieth-century characters experience an indeterminate, postmodern open ending whilst the readers are granted a neat, closed, and by implication Victorian, ending.

Frederick Holmes's assessment of the novel's conclusion as a 'festive denouement in which characters are rewarded and love triumphs' connects not only the Postscript but also the preceding conclusion with the typically neat endings of Victorian fiction.[81] Holmes's comments recall the famous criticism of Victorian endings made by Henry James (1843–1916). For James, the endings of Victorian novels were too neat and artificial in their 'distribution at the last of prizes, pensions, husbands, wives, babies, millions, appended paragraphs, and cheerful remarks'.[82] Interestingly, in a later work, Holmes suggests that since the Postscript is so 'parodically overdetermined' it actually denies the reader 'the full measure of satisfaction that the ending of a romance narrative could otherwise give'.[83] Thus, there is a sense that the reader's enjoyment is limited by the authorial control demonstrated in the inclusion of the Postscript.

BYATT ON REALISM

In her critical works, Byatt similarly examines the opposition between postmodernism and realism and explores its implications for issues of readerly freedom and authorial control. Whilst Victorian realist novels are thought to demonstrate authorial control through their adoption of an omniscient narrator, Modernist and, later, postmodernist texts are usually thought to allow readerly freedom in their experimental form. Byatt challenges this view, however, arguing that realist narratives actually provide more space for the reader than overtly playful and experimental novels. 'If I have defended realism, or what I call "self-conscious realism," it is not because I believe that it has any privileged relationship to truth ... but because it leaves space for thinking minds as well as feeling bodies.'[84] Byatt goes on to address theoretical concepts of the opposition between 'closed' and 'open' texts, adopting terminology from semiotic studies of literature such as *The Role of the Reader* (1981), by Umberto Eco (born 1932). Whilst clearly tackling theoretical issues, Byatt's discussion is textually grounded as she explores the concepts of 'closed' or 'open' texts with reference to specific authors. As an example of supposedly closed texts Byatt chooses the novels of George Eliot, arguably the high point of Victorian realist narrative, which are characterized by the presence of an omniscient third-person narrator. In contrast, she proposes the experimental works of Samuel Beckett (1906–89) and Alain Robbe-Grillet (born 1922) and *Tristram Shandy* (1760–7), the proto-postmodernist novel by Laurence Sterne (1713–68) as examples of 'open' texts. From these examples, then, it is clear that Byatt is examining the opposition between realist and experimental, or Victorian and (post)modernist, fiction. Byatt reverses the assumption that the experimental texts are more open, arguing instead that George Eliot's novels are the most open and leave most space for readerly freedom:

> ■ And yet if we think about it, which is really the more *coercive*, the more exclusive of mental activity in the reader, Eliot's measured exposition and solidly sensible embodiment, or Sterne's legerdemain playfulness? It is Sterne who manipulates, who teases the reader and demands total admiration and assent. Eliot lays out her evidence and conclusions, speaks sometimes as 'I,' sometimes to 'you' and sometimes as 'we.' But despite her passionate morality, her reasonable proceedings leave room for dissent and qualification – indeed, she demonstrates and argues the case for independent thought in reader as in character and writer. ... but in Sterne's world, and in Beckett's and Robbe-Grillet's, the reader's freedom is framed quite differently by the novelist's strategies. You – or I – may 'play freely' or 'create' – but with the freedom of the ludo player, or the magic slate-pencils of my childhood.[85] □

In her essay 'People in Paper Houses: Attitudes to "Realism" and "Experiment" in English Post-war Fiction' (1979), Byatt explores these issues of readerly freedom and authorial control in relation to the question of endings. She focuses on Fowles's *The French Lieutenant's Woman*, which is notorious for its inclusion of alternate endings, a feature that is often cited as proof of the novel's postmodern credentials. While many critics consider Fowles's adoption of multiple endings as an instance of readerly freedom, Byatt argues that they actually close off freedom and instead assert authorial control:

> ■ Fowles claims he did not control his characters, but his projected endings do not suggest a plurality of possible stories. They are a programmatic denial of the reality of any....these alternative endings are neither future nor conditional, but fixed, Victorian, narrative past. They, therefore, cancel each other out, and cancel their participants, rendering Fowles as arbitrary a puppet-maker as he declared his desire not to be. For the writer, whilst the plural endings are possibilities in the head, they intensify the reality of the future world. For the reader, now, they reduce it to paperiness again.[86] □

Obviously, Byatt's decision to discuss this novel is significant since it has often been identified as an important intertext for *Possession*. Indeed, in an essay in *On Histories and Stories*, Byatt explicitly positions her novel in relation to Fowles's text, although she distances her project from such 'modern diminishing parodies'.[87]

Byatt's essay, 'People in Paper Houses', also presents a more general account of the relationship between realism and experiment in fiction. She conceives of literary history as a series of movements between acceptance and rejection of previous modes. Thus the 1950s saw the 'reaction against experiment' associated with Virginia Woolf and James Joyce (1882–1941) in favour of a return to prior literary modes. By the 'avant-garde' of the 1960s and 1970s, however, there was a rejection of this rejection. This period was dominated by the 'desperately hectoring voice' of B. S. Johnson (1933–73), 'berating writers who do not realise that "literary forms do become exhausted, clapped out [...]," and that "the nineteenth-century novel" was finished by the outbreak of the First World War: "No matter how good the writers are who now attempt it, it cannot be made to work for our time, and the writing of it is anachronistic, invalid, irrelevant and perverse"'.[88]

Byatt's decision to write *Possession* can be seen as countering Johnson's claims that the nineteenth-century realist novel was an exhausted literary form. Yet, it is significant that she does not merely return to the Victorian novel but rather combines it with postmodern techniques. Ultimately, then Byatt's novel rejects the view that realism and experimentalism are oppositional forces in contemporary fiction and provides an example of how these impulses can be successfully combined. Considering Byatt's reluctance to being labelled a female novelist, it is interesting that her examples of experimental authors, from whom she distances her work, are all male authors. In contrast, the exemplars of the realist mode, with which she more comfortably aligns her own fiction, are women writers, George Eliot and Iris Murdoch.

WOMAN AS ARTIST

As the previous chapters have demonstrated, Byatt's fiction is aware of and presents a challenge to masculine conceptions of artistic imagination. Indeed, in an interview with Nicolas Tredell, Byatt stated that all her novels could be seen as presenting the issues surrounding women artists. As usual, however, she is resistant to any attempts to classify her work as feminist. Despite this, there have been some significant feminist analyses of the role of the artist in *Possession*, in particular focusing on Christabel LaMotte.

As we saw in Chapter 1, Christien Franken's study, *A. S. Byatt: Art, Authorship, Creativity*, proposes that criticism of Byatt's fiction must engage with the issues of gender and feminism. Thus, Franken explicitly examines the position of women artists in three Byatt texts, *Shadow of a Sun*, *The Game* and *Possession*, linking the central female artist figures to the myths of the Lady of Shalott, Cassandra and Melusine respectively. In the chapter on *Possession*, 'Melusine, or the Writer as Serpent Woman', Franken explains the centrality of Byatt's best-selling novel to her study: '*Possession* is a crucial book, because it imagines models of female artistic subjectivity and thoughts about art and authorship which are even more fascinating than Byatt's revisions of the Lady of Shalott and the mythical Cassandra.'[89] Franken accepts the assessment of Byatt found in reviews as 'a nostalgic recorder of a time long past who dislikes the twentieth century and its modern literary theories'.[90] Indeed, she argues that Byatt 'disengages herself from Christabel LaMotte and the feminist nature of LaMotte's work'.[91] She acknowledges that Byatt overtly criticizes feminist literary theories, most evidently in the satirical portrait of Leonora Stern. But, Franken claims, '[w]hat disappears completely behind the image of the nostalgic writer … who identifies herself with Ash and disengages herself from LaMotte and modern literary theories, especially of the feminist kind, is that *Possession* also contains a counter-figuration of artistic female subjectivity'.[92] This counter-figuration is present in the frequent allusions to Melusine, the serpent woman:

■ The Melusine mythology in the nineteenth-century plot of *Possession* is used to investigate the subject of a woman artist's autonomy. It revises the usual idea of the nineteenth century, confining women to their homes, imprisoning them. LaMotte prefers it this way, because it enables her to live the only life she wants to have: the life of the mind, of language, of art. She is able to secure this by living out her ideal with another artist, Blanche Glover.[93] □

Franken considers the focus on motherhood as the most significant, and unique, aspect of Byatt's use of the Melusine myth: 'The nineteenth-century story about Ash and LaMotte resists an image of Melusine as an evil woman and a monster by emphasizing the fact that Melusine is both a mother and a daughter'.[94] Franken concludes that '*Possession* writes beyond LaMotte's and Melusine's ending by creating Maud'.[95] Thus, Byatt constructs a female genealogy that prioritizes both mother-daughter relationships and art in the link from LaMotte to Maia to Maud. As we shall see, the relationship between mothers and daughters and women's (often problematic) engagement with art is a recurring theme in Byatt's fiction, especially the stories in *Sugar* and *The Matisse Stories*.

Deborah Denenholz Morse's essay 'Crossing Boundaries: The Female Artist and the Sacred Word in A. S. Byatt's *Possession*' (2000) similarly claims that the novel establishes a female genealogy, connected through art. This genealogy is most apparent in the connections between Maud and her ancestor, LaMotte, who both 'struggle to maintain their identities as artists'.[96] For Denenholz Morse, Maud's and LaMotte's artistic endeavours signal the novel's feminist critique of the Romantic conception of the poet. As we saw in Chapter 1, *Shadow of a Sun* has similarly been seen as presenting a feminist critique of the Romantic notion of the artist as a solitary genius. Denenholz Morse points out the literary allusions encoded in Maud's name, particularly the reference to Tennyson's poem 'Maud' (1855) and Maud Gonne (1866–1953) who was the poetic muse for W. B. Yeats (1865–1939). Byatt's Maud, however, is not confined to the role of muse but is a writer in her own right. The role of LaMotte's daughter, Maia, is more problematic, however, as is revealed through her association with Proserpina. Denenholz Morse claims that 'the separation of mother and daughter leads to a kind of death of female creativity in May [Maia], who rejects the art Christabel creates in unrequited desire and sorrow.'[97] Denenholz Morse concludes that this reveals the extent to which a maternal genealogy is necessary for women artists to create. Indeed, she sees Blanche's suicide after LaMotte's departure as evidence of the need for 'female identification and community for women's art to flourish'.[98] Denenholz Morse regards the novel's ending as optimistic about the possibilities of reconciling these conflicting impulses; Maud's burgeoning relationship with Roland suggests that she will be able to live with a poet without compromising her own identity as a writer. Yet the novel also suggests that the opposite is true, that LaMotte can only be free to create her art by rejecting the role of mother. In this sense, *Possession* returns to the issue of the conflict between the biological and intellectual roles of women that was explored in *The Virgin in the Garden* and *Still Life* and recurs in the later novels in the quartet.

CHAPTER FIVE

The Presence of the Past:
Possession: A Romance (1990)

As we saw in the previous chapter, critical responses to *Possession* are preoccupied with locating Byatt's novel within the traditions of realist and postmodernist fiction. This concern resurfaces in accounts of Byatt's engagement with the past. The question of *Possession*'s position as a historical novel implicitly connects it to *The Virgin in the Garden* and *Still Life* but Byatt's postmodern concerns in this novel distinguish it from her previous historical project. As we observed in Chapter 2, Taylor considers Byatt as a 'social novelist' and thus aligns her quartet with the historical fictions of the Victorian era.[1] In contrast, most critics position *Possession* within the postmodern category of 'historiographic metafiction' which we encountered in the previous chapter. In Hutcheon's definition, 'historiographic metafiction' combines a realist commitment to presenting the past accurately with a postmodern scepticism about the possibility of such a project.

POSSESSION AS A HISTORICAL NOVEL

In her essay 'No End of History: Evidence from the Contemporary English Novel' (1995), Del Ivan Janik lists Peter Ackroyd (born 1949), Julian Barnes, Kazuo Ishiguro (born 1954) and Graham Swift as the most prominent among a generation of writers who were born after World War II and began writing professionally in the 1980s. The novels these writers produce are specifically concerned with history, but they are also marked by 'a foregrounding of the historical consciousness'.[2] Born just prior to World War II, Byatt technically belongs to the preceding generation, yet Janik aligns her historical approach with that of the postwar generation. Indeed, she claims that *Possession* demonstrates this approach 'most directly and clearly, if not most provocatively'.[3]

Janik's discussion of history in these novels responds to claims that postmodernism lacks historicity, that 'there stands before us or about us only a perpetual present'.[4] She challenges this view of the contemporary situation, arguing that these authors 'insist upon and demonstrate the validity, necessity, and difficulty of acknowledging, confronting, and dealing with the past, both private and public'.[5] While this commitment to the past separates these novels from postmodernism more generally, they equally do not sit easily in the category of the historical novel since they incorporate an overt self-consciousness about the nature of history. According to Janik, these novels transform the traditional historical novel by 'add[ing] the modernist emphasis on epistemology – modes of knowing – and often also the postmodernist fascination with ontology – modes of being'.[6] This concern with the modes of knowing the past is most evident in the emergence of a new breed of protagonists in these novels who are, 'for the most part[,] explorers of history (in the broadest sense) by profession or avocation'.[7] Thus, these novels combine a commitment to the past found in the traditional historical novel with a postmodern self-consciousness about the possibilities of narrating the past.

Turning specifically to *Possession*, Janik claims that Byatt's novel vividly demonstrates these concerns as it 'centers on a very conscious and purposeful quest for knowledge of the past'.[8] Another feature which links *Possession* to the other novels Janik examines is its dual plot. Janik sees in this technique, an 'affirmation of the importance of history to the understanding of contemporary existence'.[9] Despite this adoption of a dual plot, however, these novelists avoid the 'perpetual present' that postmodernism supposedly creates through their commitment to the past itself.[10] Janik claims that *Possession* presents two alternative models for engaging with the past, both within the novel and in the title itself. Byatt distinguishes between 'proper (that is, positive, life-enhancing) and improper (objectifying, life-denying)' approaches towards the past.[11] A proper approach towards the past is one that understands it on its own terms, rather than merely co-opting it into the present. Implicitly, Janik suggests that such a positive engagement with the past resembles Byatt's own approach and isolates Chapter 15 of *Possession* as a good example of this. In that chapter, Ash and LaMotte 'become sufficiently "real" to present on the same fictional plane as the contemporary characters'; thus, Byatt presents them to the reader in their own terms, rather than through the lens of the twentieth-century characters engaged in reading their textual remains.[12] Despite the self-conscious knowingness that Janik identifies in *Possession* she remains hesitant about assigning it to the category of postmodern literature. In part, this is due to her broader argument that the contemporary British novelists she has been discussing are undertaking a project that counters claims about postmodernism's lack of interest in history. In part, however, that hesitation derives from *Possession* itself since Janik claims that it has 'all the earmarks of a Victorian "good read"'.[13] Thus, Janik seems to imply that *Possession*'s popularity is a result of its Victorian elements, which may explain the preference for the Victorian plot encountered in several of the reviews discussed in the previous chapter.

As its title indicates, Frederick M. Holmes's study *The Historical Imagination: Postmodernism and the Treatment of the Past in Contemporary British Fiction* (1997) is also concerned with the nature of the contemporary historical novel. In a similar vein to Janik, Holmes argues that contemporary historical fictions differ from the traditional historical novel in their tendency to 'comment self-consciously upon the historical matter which they dramatize'.[14] Thus, they are not only concerned with the past 'as setting', but also with 'the methods by which we know the past and the uses to which we put knowledge'.[15] This self-conscious engagement with the modes of knowing the past indicates the novels' postmodern impulse, yet it is combined with a realistic use of the past as 'setting'. In this regard, Holmes's account recalls Hutcheon's definition of 'historiographic metafictions'. For Holmes, though, this incorporation of realism is a peculiar feature of British postmodern historical fiction. He suggests that while British postmodernism is 'subversive of the realist tradition' it is 'more closely attached to that tradition' than postmodern fiction from elsewhere.[16] Holmes explores this hypothesis by examining key texts by several British authors, including A. S. Byatt.

One of the defining features of *Possession*'s presentation of the past is its reliance on historical documents; the nineteenth century is mediated to the twentieth-century characters, and by extension the readers, through textual remains. This incorporation of textual remains distinguishes *Possession* from traditional historical fictions, which 'sustain throughout the pretence of supplying direct access to the past in all its fullness and particularity'.[17] By revealing the extent to which our knowledge of the past is textually constructed, *Possession* is seen to partake of a postmodern 'blurring of the distinction between history and literature'.[18] Despite this postmodern scepticism, however, Holmes notes that *Possession* maintains a commitment to the past it depicts. He argues that 'in full awareness of the forces at work against such an endeavour', Byatt seeks to 'establish continuity with and make sense of the past'.[19] Although the results are often 'tenuous and ephemeral', Holmes asserts that this purpose remains.[20] The incorporation of textual remains might initially suggest a postmodern awareness of 'the constructedness of any account in language of the way things are'.[21] Ultimately, though, Holmes argues that it is through these textual remains that the novel 'prevents schism from occurring' making it possible for the present to forge a connection with the past.[22]

One of the broader questions Holmes addresses is the issue of nostalgia. He suggests that these British novelists take one of two 'contradictory attitudes' towards the past, which ultimately depends on 'whether the processes of historical change are experienced as damaging or nourishing'.[23] Holmes suggests that Byatt belongs to the first group as she 'exploit[s] the nostalgia pervasive in British high brow culture for the Victorian past', a past that is thought to be characterized by 'confidence, stability, and unclouded sense of purpose'.[24] This notion of nostalgia for the lost certainties of the Victorian era implicitly goes against the assertion by Jean François Lyotard (1924–98) that postmodernism is not only characterized by a loss of belief in meta-narratives but also by a lack of nostalgia for that lost incredulity. For Holmes, these novels reveal that while '[f]aith in the grand design of history may have lapsed, ... the desire for what has been lost remains'.[25] Despite this nostalgic impulse, however, Holmes claims that the novelists he examines are 'too sophisticated and sceptical to subscribe wholeheartedly to a "golden age" myth'.[26] Consequently, they 'also subvert the notion that the past really was superior to the present'.[27] It is surprising to encounter this view of Byatt's novel since, as we saw in the previous chapter, most reviewers felt that it betrayed a preference for the Victorian era over our own time. Holmes claims that *Possession* demonstrates that 'our envied Victorian forbears ... suffered from the same epistemological and existential difficulties which affect us'.[28] This does not preclude a nostalgic approach, however. In a recent interview with Jonathan Noakes, Byatt explains the attraction of the Victorian era for her:

■ One of the things that I feel about the Victorians in both [*Possession* and *Angels and Insects*] is that they had very rigorous rules about what they should and should not do – which meant that if they broke them, it was a real act of violence.[29] □

While Byatt suggests that the Victorian era was equally a time of transgression and challenges, she retains a nostalgia for it in contrast to the modern era: 'We have so few rules that there is almost nothing that we should not do – which almost means that there is nothing that is really interesting to do.'[30]

NEO-VICTORIAN FICTION

Byatt's approach towards the past should be understood not only in relation to the opposition between realism and postmodernism but also in terms of the contemporary genre of neo-Victorian fiction. Although Byatt is not responsible for initiating this genre (most commentators posit the appearance of John Fowles's *The French Lieutenant's*

Woman in 1969 as its starting point) *Possession* is generally thought to be responsible for its popularization. Indeed, Byatt has become one of the most important practitioners of this genre, returning to it for two subsequent fictions, *Angels and Insects* and *The Biographer's Tale*, which will be discussed in the next chapter.

Dana Shiller provides a sustained account of neo-Victorian fiction in her essay 'The Redemptive Past in the Neo-Victorian Novel' (1997). She sees the genre as combining the dual impulses of postmodernism and realism that were identified by several critics as a key feature of *Possession*. Thus, neo-Victorian fiction is both 'characteristic of postmodernism and imbued with a historicity reminiscent of the nineteenth-century novel'.[31] It is this sense of historicity that distances the genre from standard accounts of postmodern fiction. Indeed, Shiller addresses this with reference to one of the most influential theorists of postmodernism, Fredric Jameson (born 1934). Shiller summarizes Jameson's criticism that postmodern depictions of the past 'strip away its specific political content to focus on its aesthetics'.[32] Consequently, he believes that 'the past as historical referent is dissolved in self-reflexive textuality' in postmodern texts.[33] While neo-Victorian fictions retain this self-reflexive consciousness, about both the nature of fiction and the nature of historical representations, Shiller argues that they incorporate a sense of historicity that is committed to 'recuperating the substance of bygone eras, and not merely their styles'.[34] The other criticism Jameson levels at postmodern historical fictions is the 'false continuity' they establish between the past and the present by focusing on the similarities and projecting the present onto the past.[35] Again, Shiller distances neo-Victorian fiction from this charge on the grounds that it 'respect[s] the radical difference' of the Victorian era.[36] This is exemplified in the ensuing discussion of *Possession* in which, Shiller suggests, Byatt's preference for the Victorian era reveals her 'ability to differentiate between the two historical periods' of the novel.[37] Specifically, this preference is for the love plot of Ash and LaMotte in contrast with the 'relatively sterile "romance"' of the twentieth-century protagonists.[38] As we saw in the previous chapter, this preference appears to have been communicated to reviewers, who usually felt more drawn to the Victorian story than the modern plot of the novel. For Shiller, this demonstrates Byatt's commitment to the historical referent since she is sensitive to 'the ways her characters' Victorian mores enriched their love affair'.[39] In asserting neo-Victorian fiction's commitment to the historical specificity of the past, Shiller distances the genre from Jameson's account of postmodernism and implicitly aligns it with a more realist approach towards history.

Shiller does note the presence of a characteristically 'postmodern' self-consciousness about the possibilities and limitations of historical knowledge in neo-Victorian fiction. Indeed, she asserts that neo-Victorian texts are 'motivated by an essentially revisionist impulse' towards the past.[40] Yet for Shiller, such a revisionist approach is not purely postmodern; in fact, she associates it with George Eliot's notion that history is dependent on 'unhistorical acts'.[41] Consequently, even in their seemingly 'postmodern' questioning of historical narratives, neo-Victorian fictions retain an awareness of Victorian attitudes towards history. Shiller implicitly connects *Possession* to Eliot's notion of history when she describes the Postscript as 'call[ing] attention to what is left out of histories'.[42] She concludes that neo-Victorian fictions reveal an 'unflagging desire' to engage with the past, in spite of a supposedly postmodern 'doubt' about the possibilities of recovering the past.[43] Shiller connects the neo-Victorian attitude towards the past to George Eliot's notion that 'the past [is] entirely redemptive'.[44] The notion of the past, and its literature, as redemptive implies a moral impulse behind neo-Victorian fiction that again distances it from playful postmodernism, connecting it instead with the moral realism of Victorian writers.

TEXTUAL REMAINS

Accounts of *Possession*'s status as a historical fiction have peripherally dealt with the issue of the incorporated texts in the novel. The incorporation of multiple texts is often seen to be a characteristic feature of postmodern fiction, but for some critics it is part of Byatt's realist commitment to the historical specificity of the past.

Suzanne Keen's *Romances of the Archive in Contemporary British Fiction* (2001) presents a sustained account of the fictional engagement with the archival past. While she acknowledges that this is a feature of many postmodern texts, part of a general postmodern scepticism about the accessibility of the past, Keen's focus is broader. Thus, many of the texts she considers are 'conservative, nostalgic, defensive' in their presentation of the past and are often 'insufficiently sceptical about finding the truth'.[45] Indeed, Keen suggests that, in some texts, this concern with the 'material traces' of the past is a backlash against postmodernism, demonstrating that '[t]he truth ... has not been irrevocably lost'.[46] Keen proposes *Possession* as the exemplar of the type of fiction she designates as 'romances of the archive'. Such texts do not merely reflect an antiquarian interest in the past but rather are concerned with the relationship between the present and the past. Keen uses Byatt's novel to delineate the defining characteristics of the genre: a focus on a literal, and frequently literary, archive; a central character who is engaged in archival research; a quest structure that brings the novel close to a detective story; and the incorporation of texts from the archive.

Keen questions the categorization of *Possession* as a postmodern novel, since it centres around 'successful truth-seeking' which ultimately has transformative effects on the lives of Roland and Maud.[47] She claims that assertions of *Possession*'s postmodern status are usually grounded in consideration of its narrative strategies. In fact, she suggests that '[e]ven the overtly knowing narrator of nineteenth-century real-ism can appear a postmodern trick' since it provides the reader with information denied to the characters and so highlights the impossibil-ity of ever attaining a full account of the past.[48] Yet Keen argues that Byatt uses such postmodern-seeming techniques 'playfully, in order to affirm more traditional representational aims'.[49] Thus the Postscript, which some critics have viewed as a postmodern aspect of the novel, actually 'reinforces the reader's certainty about "what really happened", in contradistinction to the usual aims of postmodern undecidability'.[50]

Keen identifies the postimperial condition of Britain as an important context for the development of the romance of the archive, noting that these novels frequently depict a past in which 'the British (often English) national story is central and influential'.[51] This context is certainly apparent in her reading of *Possession*:

■ Not only redemptive, but escapist, defensive, nostlagic and revisionist…, *Possession* uses the past for the pleasure of evoking a vanished world and time, for articulating the significance of the humanities (particularly English literature and historical research), for the dress-up fun of imitating the Victorians, and for celebrating undervalued British national treasures.[52] □

This bias towards the British is apparent in the characterization of the novel. As several reviewers and commentators have noted, the American figures generally represent negative approaches towards the past whereas the British characters, and in particular Roland and Maud, eventually discover a positive and life-enhancing way to engage with the past. Moreover, Keen argues that the positive outcomes at the end of the novel, Roland's job offers and the acquisition of the Ash–LaMotte letters, enact a 'conservative fantasy [which] flouts American money'.[53] It is in this discussion of the novel's national context that Keen makes an interesting observation; she states that '*Possession* triumphantly defeats the forces of contemporary forgetfulness, while at the same time inducing selective amnesia about the past'.[54] That is, while *Possession* asserts the importance of the material traces of the past and thus demands knowledge of the past, its insistence on the need to keep British heritage in Britain elides the fact that many British cultural institutions contain the heritage of other countries.

John J. Su's article 'Fantasies of (Re)collection: Collecting and Imagination in A. S. Byatt's *Possession: A Romance*' (2004) similarly links Byatt's concern with the archive of the past with a wider cultural interest in heritage. Su's views on the heritage industry are framed by the arguments of Robert Hewison (born 1943). As the title implies, Hewison's book *The Heritage Industry: Britain in a Climate of Decline* (1987) views the heritage industry negatively. Su summarizes Hewison's view that the heritage industry 'neither preserves the past nor provides guidance for a nation struggling to envision its future. Rather, it stifles the possibility for creative change'.[55] Su interrogates these statements by exploring the position of heritage in Byatt's *Possession*. Specifically, he is interested in the social function of heritage in that novel and whether 'material traces' can prompt 'an accurate or truthful depiction of the past'.[56] He asserts that Byatt's novel does not indulge in Hewison's pessimistic attitude towards the fascination with heritage; rather, *Possession* demonstrates how an active engagement with the past can 'help individuals to imagine alternative identities'.[57]

For Byatt 'a preoccupation with material traces is not always motivated by escapism'; instead, in *Possession*, collecting provides a means to regain a meaningful relationship to the past.[58] Su claims that the process of collecting initiates 'a kind of role-play' which encourages the collectors to 'use their imagination to position themselves within the worlds that the collected objects evoke'.[59] The use of the imagination, however, is limited by Byatt's commitment to 'a historically accurate representation of the past'.[60] In fact, the ability to imagine alternate identities is achieved as a result of 'an intimate identification with the past, an identification made possible only by acquiring significant historical knowledge'.[61] Unlike Hewison, who suggests that heritage objects create a 'screen' between the present and the past, Byatt indicates how they can provide a way to engage with its historical specificity.[62] Examining the correspondence of Ash and LaMotte, Roland and Maud become aware of the distance between their own beliefs and those of the Victorian poets. Only when they are able to think outside their own theoretical frameworks can they begin to imagine, and eventually confirm, the relationship between Ash and LaMotte. Thus, Byatt seems to be suggesting that 'greater attention to material traces might provide the basis for accurately reconstructing the poets' beliefs and attitudes'.[63] Moreover, it is only after they have discovered the relationship between Maud and Roland that they are able to recognize, and eventually rectify, the absence of romance in their own lives. So, this positive transformation of the twentieth-century characters' social identities can only occur as a result of a direct engagement with the past, an engagement that begins with a close examination of its material traces.

While Byatt reveals the possibilities of forging a connection with the past through an engagement with its textual remains, Su suggests that the novel itself presents a 'gross simplification' of the Victorian past.[64] He claims that *Possession*, because of its position as a romance, 'aestheticizes the past in order to make it more accessible'.[65] This is not necessarily a failing, however; Su claims that Byatt's novel reveals a 'preference for what might be called a usable past over an absolutely accurate one'.[66] The idea of a usable past is linked to the possibility of transforming social identities which, Su claims, is for Byatt a more important goal than fidelity to an accurate but isolated past. As we have seen, though, this usable past must always begin from a close identification with the physical reality of the past.

In a recent interview with Jonathan Noakes, Byatt implicitly addressed the role of textual remains in discussing the position of poetry in *Possession*:

■ I was actually trying, as university teacher and as writer, to say that poetry is more real than criticism. Poetry does more things at any given moment than any critical account of it. It is not a historical object. It isn't a theory, it is a *thing*.[67] □

Interestingly, then, Byatt seems to suggest that the texts of the past can have an existence that transcends their role as an historical object. Byatt claims that the valuation of poetry over criticism is the fundamental point of the novel, not, as some have mistakenly concluded, a prioritization of the past over the present. Yet, the novel seems to present a clear division between the nineteenth-century poets and the twentieth-century critics. Consequently, it is possible to see in her valuation of poetry over criticism an implicit valuation of the past over the present.

THE POLITICS OF THE PAST

Louise Yelin's article 'Cultural Cartography: A. S. Byatt's *Possession* and the Politics of Victorian Studies' (1992) suggests that the novel's attitude towards Victorian literature is symptomatic of its wider views on the Victorian era. Yelin sees the technique of ventriloquism that dominates Byatt's novel as 'an art at once Victorian and postmodern'; thus, Byatt's literary technique encompasses both the past and the present.[68] Yet Yelin claims that, ultimately, the Victorian texts (even if they are written by Byatt herself) are privileged over the contemporary texts in the novel. She asserts that for Byatt 'Victorian literature is an inscription of value...that makes it more enduring, more worthy than its ventriloquizing, belated, postmodern epigones'.[69] The textual mediation of the Victorian era similarly implies a privileging of it on Byatt's part. Yelin claims that the incorporated texts establish a distance between the nineteenth and twentieth centuries, revealing the Victorian past as 'an essence unavailable to the grasping moderns and postmoderns – us – who only want to possess it'.[70] Indeed, Yelin not only claims that Byatt privileges Victorian literature but also prioritizes the Victorian tradition as the primary context for Byatt's novel. For Yelin, *Possession* is 'stuffed' with 'the kinds of metonymic details that constitute what, in an earlier, less self-conscious critical era, one would have called *the* Victorian novel'.[71]

Despite asserting that Byatt's novel favours the Victorian past over the modern present, Yelin still recognizes a critical element in Byatt's approach towards the past. *Possession* intends to reinstate the Victorian notion of culture as the best of what has been thought and said, as propounded by Matthew Arnold (1822–88) in *Culture and Anarchy* (1869). Yet Yelin sees in Byatt's novel an implicit critique of the exclusion of the feminine in Arnold's view of culture. This critique occurs in the figure of the 'unconventionally feminine' Christabel who questions the 'association of same-sex female eroticism with demonic possession of a passive victim' found in Samuel Taylor Coleridge's poem 'Christabel' (1816).[72] In this account, then, Byatt's gender politics seem more radical and contemporary than the Victorian world she is depicting. Interestingly, however, Yelin hints at a more conservative attitude towards gender in the twentieth-century plot, resolved as it is through the wealth of Euan, who is significantly both male and part of the Yuppie class brought about by the policies of the Conservative government led by Margaret Thatcher (born 1925; Prime Minister 1979–90).

Richard Todd's essay 'The Retrieval of Unheard Voices in British Postmodernist Fiction' (1994) views *Possession*'s engagement with the past as an engagement with literary tradition. Again, he focuses on Byatt's technique of ventriloquism, claiming that it presents 'specifically intertextual rewritings of English literary as well as cultural history'.[73] Like Yelin, Todd views Byatt's novel as implicitly questioning the gender bias of the past by 'reinscrib[ing] ... those voices, often but not exclusively those of women, that have been excluded by patriarchal ... tradition'.[74] Todd concurs with many reviewers in his suggestion that the nineteenth century is prioritized over the twentieth century since Ash and LaMotte, and to a lesser extent the other nineteenth-century characters, 'appear more vivid and colourful than their twentieth-century counterparts'.[75] Indeed, he suggests that the twentieth-century characters are subordinate to their predecessors, and that they exist merely to permit 'the retrieval of the nineteenth-century originals'.[76] Todd pays particular attention to the position of Blanche Glover in the novel, claiming that though her voice is only 'retrieved' when it is seen to have significance to the Ash–LaMotte plot, she does in a sense have a twentieth-century counterpart in the figure of Val. Todd points out the 'striking ... literal echo' of a phrase from Blanche's suicide note, 'I'm a superfluous creature', by Val.[77] In this instance, the 'interplay of heard and unheard voices' reveals a difference in the gender attitudes of the novel's two time-frames.[78] For Blanche, this realization 'proves fatal' yet it 'proves enabling to Val'.[79] Like Yelin, then, Todd implies that Byatt does not merely indulge in escapist nostalgia for an idealized past but rather is aware of and critical of certain negative aspects of the Victorian past, especially with regards to gender politics. Unlike Yelin, however, Todd sees the twentieth-century plot as more progressive than the Victorian story in terms of its gender politics.

POSSESSION – THE MOVIE

Byatt's preoccupation with texts in *Possession* might make it seem an unlikely candidate for a Hollywood film adaptation yet its popular appeal and success ensured the film rights were snapped up and a film version directed by Neil LaBute (born 1963) appeared in 2000. Sue Sorensen's article 'Taking Possession: Neil LaBute Adapts a Postmodern Romance' (2004) considers the film adaptation in relation to Byatt's original novel and, generally, finds it wanting. Sorensen begins her article with a brief discussion of the book which she claims is 'huge and varied' and deals with a range of areas in 'alarming and allusive detail'.[80] She sees Byatt's novel as 'maximalist' in its combination of various genres and styles, which include 'parody, poetry, fairy tales, and a postmodern detective story'.[81] Ironically, despite dropping the subtitle, it is the romance elements of the novel that LaBute's film has 'resolutely emphasized'.[82] Not only does LaBute narrow down the novel's concerns to emphasize its romantic plot, but he also contracts the book's exploration of the 'shades of the meaning of "romance"' by focusing on the 'conventional form' of romance.[83]

Although Sorensen accepts that the demands of the film medium meant LaBute and his screenwriters had to 'trim the novel', she fears that 'they have taken away too much'.[84] Most interesting is Sorensen's assertion that, despite being 'some sort of feminist', LaBute 'turns a blind eye to the [novel's] feminist themes'.[85] In particular, she criticizes the decision to include many of the minor male characters who are 'less amusing and less individual' than the minor female characters that are, for the most part, omitted in the film.[86] Consequently, Sorensen claims, 'an adaptation of a feminist novel is undercut by the director's fear of the strong women who made the novel delightful'.[87] Moreover, despite the film's focus on the romance plots of the novel, Sorensen claims that LaBute 'rarely faces up to sexual power'.[88] In contrast, she claims that in the novel Byatt 'communicates a fullness of possibility and danger in sexual passion'.[89] The film lacks the erotic charge of the novel, in part because the long, drawn-out courtship of both the Victorian and twentieth-century couples is too contracted. Specifically, she contrasts the treatment of Maud and Roland's emerging relationship in the novel and the film. In the film, Maud's hair is unloosed at the end immediately prior to her and Roland's lovemaking. Byatt, however, has Maud unloose her hair midway through the novel yet still delays the lovemaking until the end of the novel, resulting in a 'slower and more satisfying erotic engagement'.[90]

One of the key problems Sorensen identifies with LaBute's film is his avoidance of the category of postmodernism. Sorensen claims that Byatt's novel 'offers a smorgasbord of postmodern tricks' while at the same time questioning 'if this is what we truly desire from fiction'.[91] The point about Roland and Maud, in the novel, is that they are thoroughly postmodern subjects, constrained by their theoretical positions which are expressed in 'deliciously silly, stuttering conversations'.[92] In LaBute's film, this awareness of their postmodern positioning is replaced by the phrase 'Yes, aren't we just modern?'[93] Sorensen criticizes this replacement claiming that '[m]odernism is practically the only topic that Byatt does not tackle' in the novel.[94] For Sorensen, Modernism is characterized by the fact that 'for all its experiments, [it] took art and life seriously', whereas postmodernism is seen as 'dabbl[ing] in parody and even nihilism, suggesting that art and morality have little meaning'.[95] In claiming that Byatt's novel does not deal with Modernism, then, Sorensen seems to be implying that *Possession* does not take art and life seriously. As we saw in Chapter 4, *Possession* has more affinities to Modernism than Sorensen allows. Indeed, while Jackie Buxton conceived of the opposition between postmodernism and Modernism in similar terms, she reached an entirely different conclusion. For Buxton, Byatt does take art and life seriously and it is this moral commitment that ultimately aligns *Possession* with Modernist rather than postmodernist literature.

Sorensen recognizes that the decision not to tackle postmodernism may have been a necessary concession to the audience but laments that in avoiding this issue LaBute fails to grasp the point of the novel. For Byatt, the point, or as she sees it 'joke', of the novel is that 'the dead are actually much more alive and vital than the living'.[96] In her recent interview with Jonathan Noakes, Byatt similarly implies that the film adaptation has missed the point of the novel:

> ■ When they made the film, I think they assumed – because they were Hollywood Americans – that the story is a story about the young modern lovers whereas actually almost all readers know that the story is an occluded story about the Victorian lovers, and the other two are there for finding it out.[97] □

Byatt's comment implicitly prioritizes the book over the film and suggests that readers are more intelligent than filmgoers. A similar view is implied in Sorensen's final pronouncements on the film. She asserts that LaBute has 'compromised too much and trusted the audience too little'.[98] Thus, while the novel presents a 'detective story to which only the readers, not the characters, have full access', LaBute removes this detective process from the viewer's experience by resolving the mysteries 'instantaneously'.[99] Consequently, the viewer's only role is to 'admire the admittedly attractive folds of Christabel LaMotte's voluminous gowns and hooded cloaks'.[100] The film, then, seems to have succumbed to the mere surface representation of the past that the novel was mostly felt to have avoided. Ultimately, then, the film, like the twentieth-century characters in the novel, is seen to be a thin and papery version of the 'original' on which it is based.

Byatt insists, however, that she is not trying to revive Victorian literature in her novels: 'I believe that both *Possession* and *Angels and Insects* are modern novels, written by a modern novelist, who is not trying to recreate the atmosphere of a Victorian novel, but only to hear the rhythms of one.'[101] Byatt was to return to the 'rhythms' of Victorian fiction twice more with *Angels and Insects* and *The Biographer's Tale* and, as we shall see in the next chapter, many of the concerns we have encountered in responses to *Possession* resurfaced in relation to those texts.

CHAPTER SIX

Neo-Victorian Fiction:
Angels and Insects (1992) and
The Biographer's Tale (2000)

After the success of *Possession*, it is unsurprising that Byatt kept her winning formula in her next fictional work, *Angels and Insects*. After taking a short break to write *Babel Tower* she returned to the Victorian era with the publication of *The Biographer's Tale* in 2000. Along with *Possession*, these novels comprise a significant contribution to the genre of neo-Victorian fiction. Indeed, as we shall see in the reviews sections that follow, most reviewers judged these novels in relation to *Possession*.

ANGELS AND INSECTS (1992)

Reviews

Coming so soon after the publication of *Possession* it was predictable that the initial reviewers of *Angels and Insects* would place it alongside that novel. What is perhaps more unexpected is that it was often viewed more favourably than its Booker Prize-winning predecessor. Marilyn Butler's review for *The Times Literary Supplement* claims that with *Possession* Byatt found the 'postmodern historical manner' that seems to suit her so well.[1] This approach appears to sit uneasily between the modes of faction and fiction, leading Butler to propose a new form for which she suggests the term 'ficticism'.[2] Like reviewers and critics of her earlier works, however, Butler seems reluctant to locate Byatt wholly within postmodernism, claiming instead that she is 'a Victorianist Iris Murdoch'.[3] Butler recognizes that Byatt's Victorianism is inflected by the twentieth century, presenting a critique of Victorian ideals of family values. Interestingly, Butler locates this critique in 'The Conjugial

Angel' but the climactic revelation of 'Morpho Eugenia' means that it is equally present in that story. Overall, Butler judges *Angels and Insects* to be '[m]ore fully assured and satisfying' than its predecessor, *Possession*.[4] Indeed, she goes so far as to claim that the novellas represent Byatt's 'best work to date'.[5] Considering previous criticisms of her intellectual style, it is interesting that Butler's claim rests on the assertion that in the novellas Byatt has embraced 'full-hearted literariness'.[6]

The title of Kathryn Hughes's review for *The New Statesman*, 'Repossession', indicates that she is firmly locating *Angels and Insects* as a direct successor to *Possession*. While the novel maintained the 'safety net' of a twentieth-century frame for its Victorian story, the novellas of *Angels and Insects* are judged to be 'both resolutely mid-Victorian in tone and content'.[7] Despite this, Hughes recognizes that the erotic elements of the two novellas diverge from the Victorian tone of the stories. Although this is not seen as a failing in itself, Hughes does indicate some shortcomings in the novellas. She claims that Byatt's concern with the relationship between history and fiction is a 'familiar point' and expresses the fear that Byatt's 'longing for authenticity' threatens to dominate the text entirely.[8]

Mary Hawthorne's review for *The New Yorker* similarly opens with a discussion of *Possession* in which she identifies a 'deep sense of mourning' that belongs as much to Byatt as to her creation, Roland.[9] She claims that Byatt is still 'wearing widow's weeds' in *Angels and Insects*, in which she becomes a 'kind of medium – our conduit to a lost world'.[10] Yet, there is a suggestion that Byatt's engagement with the Victorian past is not entirely healthy in the connection Hawthorne establishes between Byatt's approach and the 'compulsive hoarding' of Alabaster in 'Morpho Eugenia'.[11] However, Hawthorne recognizes that there is at least an attempt at imposing order; she suggests that Byatt's task in the novellas is to 'make sense of the Victorians' intellectual and spiritual legacy'.[12] While Hawthorne appears to appreciate Byatt's re-creation of the Victorian past, an old criticism of her style recurs in the comment that the characters are 'pressed into the service of Byatt's ideas'.[13]

The status of Byatt's recreation of the Victorian world is as much a question in reviews of *Angels and Insects* as it was in reviews of *Possession*. *The Times* review, by biographer and novelist Victoria Glendinning (born 1937), asserts from the outset that the novellas are neither 'pastiche [nor] parody' but rather 'the nearest that a late-20th-century author can get to actually writing' a nineteenth-century text.[14] Adopting Byatt's own terminology, Glendinning claims that she is 'possessed' by the Victorian era, particularly 'the physical texture of the past'.[15] In this regard, she sees a connection between the spiritualist activities of Mrs Papagay and Byatt's own project in writing of the Victorians;

both are in a sense mediums who resurrect the dead. As we shall see, the connections between writing and spiritualism have been traced in critical responses to 'The Conjugial Angel'. Interestingly, Glendinning mistakenly attributes the most vivid spiritual manifestation in the story to Emily Jesse, when in fact it is Sophy Sheekhy who sees Arthur Hallam. Like Hughes, however, Glendinning notes that the novellas diverge from nineteenth-century fiction in their depiction of eroticism. Despite these 'satisfactory sexual shocks', Glendinning finds the novellas too didactic.[16]

Walter Kendrick's review in *Yale Review* places *Angels and Insects* alongside not only *Possession* but also other precursors of the neo-Victorian genre. He suggests that while the novellas are set entirely in the nineteenth century, the narrators inevitably betray a 'modern perspective' at points.[17] Yet he commends Byatt for avoiding the pitfalls of 'hindsighted patronizing' that he claims 'mars' the first neo-Victorian novel, John Fowles's *The French Lieutenant's Woman*.[18] Kendrick implies that, unlike Fowles, Byatt approaches the Victorian era with 'sympathy and affection' since it represents an 'escape' from the modern world.[19] He explores the narrative techniques of the novellas in relation to Victorian fictional preferences; in using Arturo Papagay to forge a connection between 'Morpho Eugenia' and 'The Conjugial Angel', Byatt is honouring the Victorian preference for happy endings. Similarly, he claims that while the climax of 'Morpho Eugenia' could never have been incorporated into a Victorian novel it is again a homage to their taste for 'shocking discoveries'.[20]

John Barrell provides an extensive if equivocal review of *Angels and Insects* in the *London Review of Books*. He opens with the declaration that he was unsure what to make of the novellas; not because he had doubts about their quality, but rather because he was unclear of the purpose of re-creating the Victorian era in fiction. He suggests that Byatt's success in recreating Victorian fiction is part of the problem, since it merely serves to demonstrate 'the irredeemable pastness of the past'.[21] Indeed, he claims that recreation of the Victorian style is too contrived and as such the novellas felt 'more remote' than Victorian fiction.[22] Moreover, he laments the deliberate anachronisms which he felt laboured the point of the distance between the Victorian era and our own times. Similarly, he notes that while both novellas are 'urgently didactic', their moral fails to have the impact Byatt seems to desire because it seems to belong more to the Victorian world of the characters than the modern world of the reader.[23] Ultimately, he concludes that '[t]hese Victorian novellas of ideas are resolutely novellas of Victorian ideas'.[24] Turning to style, Barrell's comments recall many earlier opinions on Byatt's fiction in their criticisms of its intellectual qualities. While he marvels at the 'impressive intelligence' that has 'inextricably interwoven' the various narrative threads, he experienced a loss of readerly control as a result of the 'claustrophobia' the style provoked.[25] Barrell prefers 'Morpho Eugenia' to 'The Conjugial Angel', suggesting that in the later novella the convoluted style which was meant to demonstrate the text's 'Victorianness' finally overpowered the narrative.[26]

Michael Levenson's review for *The New Republic* seeks to locate Byatt's fiction within a tradition that predates postmodernism. While he accepts that there are postmodern elements in her work, he also claims that there is 'an earnest attempt' to return to the Victorian project.[27] Consequently, he proposes that she be understood as a 'postmodern Victorian'.[28] This phrase recognizes that Byatt's return to the Victorian era is not an attempt to deny the modern world, but rather to indicate that 'the road into the twenty-first century winds exactly through the middle of the nineteenth'.[29] For Levenson, this approach is what connects her most clearly to Iris Murdoch. Turning his attention to *Angels and Insects*, Levenson claims that the novellas demonstrate 'the reach and the promise' of Byatt's neo-Victorian project.[30] He connects Byatt's approach to that of George Eliot, claiming that Byatt wants to follow in Eliot's footsteps as 'the natural historian of a post-Christian spiritual life'.[31] Ultimately, Levenson sees Byatt as a realist, who is committed to depicting the Victorian era with 'respect and ... love'.[32]

Criticism

Sally Shuttleworth's article 'Natural History: The Retro-Victorian Novel' (1998) seeks to account for the appearance in 1992 of two texts which 'dramatise the Darwinian moment in Victorian history': A. S. Byatt's 'Morpho Eugenia' and Graham Swift's *Ever After*.[33] Before discussing Shuttleworth's analysis of 'Morpho Eugenia' I would like to briefly examine her designation of the subgenre 'retro-Victorian fiction', which is related to the genre of neo-Victorian fiction discussed in the previous chapter. Shuttleworth argues that retro-Victorian texts combine 'an informed post-modern self-consciousness in their interrogation of the relationship between fiction and history' with 'an absolute, non-ironic, fascination with the details of the period, and with our relations to it'.[34] This definition corresponds to the combination of postmodern and realist impulses that many critics identify in Byatt's fiction more generally. The term Shuttleworth adopts for this subgenre is connected to Fredric Jameson's comments on postmodernism. She explicitly refers to Jameson's account of 'the appetite for "retro"' in contemporary society, 'where styles of the past swiftly replace one another, without any sense of the cultural and social baggage they had previously carried'.[35] Shuttleworth claims that 'retro-Victorian' fiction does not partake in this process since it displays 'a deep commitment to recreating the detailed texture of an age'.[36]

Although Shuttleworth is making some general claims about the subgenre of retro-Victorian fiction, her essay focuses on a subset of this in its analysis of texts that display a preoccupation with Darwinian ideas. Shuttleworth sees 'Morpho Eugenia' as part of a wider explosion of cultural interest in Charles Darwin (1809–82). Along with Graham Swift's *Ever After*, Shuttleworth identifies Fowles's *The French Lieutenant's Woman* as an important 'progenitor of the Victorian natural history novel'.[37] Indeed, Byatt's own *Possession* is seen as part of this genre, establishing the 'exploration of the Victorian preoccupation with natural history' that Byatt develops in 'Morpho Eugenia'.[38] Shuttleworth claims that Victorian natural history was characterized by a 'celebration of the world of the minute' but that it was this attention to the minute forms of nature that prompted Darwin's revelations in *On the Origin of Species* (1859).[39] Consequently, Shuttleworth suggests that in Victorian natural history '[t]he study of the order of nature transmuted into a lament for its disorder'.[40] Both 'Morpho Eugenia' and Swift's *Ever After* are located at this precise point in history and so present that moment of crisis in their texts. For Shuttleworth, the Darwinian crisis is nostalgically invoked by these authors since it provoked 'a decisive crisis of faith, a sense that the world was shaking under them, an ecstatic agony of indecision', which seems impossible in the postmodern era where there are 'no fixed boundaries of belief'.[41] Shuttleworth suggests that 'Morpho Eugenia' not only presents a natural history in Adamson's study of the ant colonies but is itself 'a natural history of the lives and beliefs of the protagonists who are alike subjected to the scrutiny of the magnifying lens'.[42] Although Shuttleworth points out the structural similarities between Byatt's novella and the forms of Victorian natural history, she does not extend this connection any further. Yet, it is not too much of a step to notice that the shift Shuttleworth identified in Victorian natural history is replicated in the narrative structure of 'Morpho Eugenia' itself; the seemingly ordered world of Bredely Hall is shown to be in a state of both natural and moral disorder in the climactic revelation of Eugenia's incestuous relationship with Edgar. Shuttleworth argues that 'retro-Victorian' fiction is responding to the 'mythical realm of Victorian Values' being promoted by politicians of the time, most notably the British Prime Minister Margaret Thatcher.[43] In particular, she claims that in the frequent depiction of incest and family secrets, 'retro-Victorian' texts challenge the 'idealised visions of Victorian family values' being celebrated by Thatcher at that time.[44] Thus, Shuttleworth implies that Byatt's novella, and by extension the entire genre of retro-Victorian fiction, complicates our view of the Victorians. As we saw in Chapter 4, Byatt distances her fiction from the 'diminishing' approach towards the Victorians that she finds in Fowles's *The French Lieutenant's Woman*.[45]

Shuttleworth claims that 'Morpho Eugenia' is, like *Possession*, a romance and as such she reads the ending optimistically. She claims that '[s]urvival, not destruction, is the message' of the novella and that it therefore serves to reinforce the Victorian ideology of 'the energy of the individual'.[46] As we saw in Kendrick's review, however, Arturo Papagay establishes a subtle connection between 'Morpho Eugenia' and 'The Conjugial Angel' and so it is naïve to consider the ending of the first novella without reference to the second one. Indeed, for the majority of the second novella the reader is led to believe that Arturo has drowned aboard his ship, the same ship on which the protagonists of 'Morpho Eugenia' were travelling. While Arturo returns at the end of 'The Conjugial Angel', the fact that there is no such narrative resurrection for Matilda and William undermines Shuttleworth's optimistic reading.

Hilary M. Schor's article 'Sorting, Morphing, and Mourning: A. S. Byatt Ghostwrites Victorian Fiction' (2000) proposes that contemporary novelists return to the Victorian era in an attempt to rediscover the 'confidence of psychological realism'.[47] Although this seems to suggest that writers are drawn by a nostalgic desire to return to the lost stabilities of the Victorian world, Schor comments that '[t]he Victorians ... matter not for their answers, but for their bewilderment'.[48] The inclusive impulse that many commentators have noted in Byatt's previous texts is, for Schor, part of her commitment to Victorian fictional forms. She claims that the idea that a novel acts as a 'kind of organizational structure', whose purpose is to incorporate everything, is 'an instinct much more akin to the Victorian than the postmodern novelist'.[49] Thus, Schor connects the intellectual elements of Byatt's fictions to the postmodernism versus realism debate that recurs in critical accounts of her work and explicitly aligns Byatt's neo-Victorian fictions with a realist, rather than postmodernist, project.

Schor moves from this general discussion of Byatt's position in relation to the Victorians to a more specific consideration of *Angels and Insects*, which she sees as Byatt's 'most extended incarnation as a Victorian'.[50] Interestingly, Schor implies that the novellas forego the comforts of the traditional realist novel, in particular plot, in favour of the technique of 'layering', which she connects to the process of 'laminations' employed in *Babel Tower*.[51] Thus, Byatt's engagement with the Victorians is achieved through the incorporation of Victorian texts, both real and imitations. Schor claims that Byatt's imitation of Victorian literary forms is a process of 'ghostwriting', which operates in two ways. First there is the process of ' "borrowings" ("writing like ...")', which refers to the incorporation of other texts within Byatt's fictions.[52] Schor locates this process as similar to the form of pastiche in postmodern fiction. This explanation is limited by the fact that it conflates two distinct textual practices; the process of incorporating Victorian texts ('borrowing') needs to be distinguished from Byatt's process of imitating Victorian texts ('writing like...'). The second way Schor sees ghostwriting as operating in Byatt's fiction is in a metaphorical sense. She suggests that Byatt's novellas are involved in a process of 'speaking with the dead, not so much as writers but as mouldering bodies, decaying forms'.[53] This sense of ghostwriting draws on the concern with spiritualism in 'The Conjugial Angel' which, as we shall see shortly, is a prominent focus in critical accounts of that novella. Schor connects this concern with reviving the dead to Byatt's interest in returning to Victorian literary forms. She claims that since the realist novel 'is a collection of material things' it is inevitably bound up with the processes of death and decay.[54] It is for this reason that realism 'must always stage the return of matter as a deeper ("lumpier") form of material'.[55] In resurrecting Arthur Hallam in 'The Conjugial Angel', then, Byatt is literalizing this 'uncanny nature of realism'.[56] Schor believes that Byatt's novellas incorporate this awareness that realism partakes of 'ghostwriting' and as such positions her 'less as "postmodernist" than as "pre-realist"'.[57] Ultimately, Schor sees Byatt's neo-Victorian texts as 'reanimat[ing]' Victorian realism to present a 'contemporary version of realism'.[58] Similarly, as we saw in the previous chapter, Byatt considers her neo-Victorian fictions as trying to recuperate the rhythms of Victorian fiction.

Susan Poznar's essay 'Tradition and "Experiment" in Byatt's "The Conjugial Angel"' (2004) addresses Byatt's problematic position on the boundary between realism and postmodernism through an examination of her use of the séance. For Poznar, this problem is 'particularly urgent' in the neo-Victorian texts *Possession* and *Angels and Insects* since as historical texts they 'necessitate both a "realistic" representation of the historical period and an acknowledgement that a differing authorial sensibility is molding those materials'.[59] She claims that Byatt's postmodern sensibility prompts the reader 'into focusing less on the autonomous "origins" and "intentions" of particular texts than on how they intervene, modulate one another, and proliferate'.[60]

Poznar turns her attention to the séances in 'The Conjugial Angel' to explain how postmodernism combines with realism in the novella. She argues that the séance 'aligns different versions of the unfallen and fallen', which she connects to thematic concerns from previous Byatt novels such as the opposition between the spirit (or mind) and the body and the question of whether language can adequately depict the real world.[61] This opposition between the unfallen and the fallen is explored through Byatt's use of metaphor, which combines the two elements; it 'fuses body and spirit, abstract ideas with its linguistic vehicle'.[62] In 'The Conjugial Angel', the purpose is less to combine the fallen and unfallen but rather to indicate their 'simultaneous irrenconcilability and interdependency'.[63] The unfallen nature is linked to T. S. Eliot's notion of undissociated sensibility, which, as we saw in Chapter 3, has been noted as an important intellectual context for previous Byatt texts. Poznar claims that Sophy's vision in the first séance is such an 'undissociated' experience; the creature that Sophy sees reveals 'Byatt's fascination with and exploitation of metaphor's flexibility' since its 'many inner eyes examine itself'.[64]

Indeed, for Poznar, the séance itself 'might figure the functioning of metaphor'; it can be seen as a metaphor for metaphor since séances both create images and provide a means through which to interpret those images.[65] It is in her approach towards metaphor that Byatt most obviously combines the opposing impulses towards tradition and experimentation in the novella. Poznar argues that while Byatt continues to employ metaphor in a 'traditional' way, using the séances to 'represent the power of metaphor in general and dramatize its fissured nature and iconic dimension' is 'a very postmodern move'.[66] Consequently, she concludes that 'The Conjugial Angel' exists 'both as a story with a traditional shape and themes and as a tissue of postmodern issues'.[67] These postmodern issues are primarily concerned with interpretation and the question of intention. Poznar claims that in the séances 'Byatt stages a riddling...querying of the subject and its enunciations'.[68] This is most obvious in relation to the medium figure, Sophy Sheekhy, who becomes a vessel through which spirits can speak, and the automatic writings which seem to come from a source other than the hand that literally writes them. This incorporation of multiple voices is continued in the rest of the novella through the incorporation of passages from Tennyson's In Memoriam (1850) and Arthur Hallam's letters. Poznar argues that while this intertextuality might make it seem 'exemplarily postmodern', 'The Conjugial Angel' does not create 'a world solipsistically constructed of nothing but language games'.[69] Thus, Byatt does not entirely adopt a postmodern attitude, but rather remains 'deeply committed to more traditional literary forms'.[70] However, as with the séance's approach towards the unfallen and the fallen, the opposition between postmodernism and realism is not as stark as this may suggest. Indeed, Poznar claims that Byatt, and her medium Sophy, 'celebrate both evocative language, which magically captures reality, and self-reflexive language, which reveals its material origins and its artifice'.[71] Consequently, Byatt refuses to prioritize either the postmodern or the realist approach to language; thus tradition and experiment are inextricably intertwined in her novella. The result of this is a text that is 'a living creature defiant in its indefinability and anomalousness, yet potently expressive'.[72]

Byatt's concern with ghosts and 'ghostwriting' is also explored in Louisa Hadley's article 'Spectres of the Past: A. S. Byatt's Victorian

Ghost Stories' (2003). This account asserts the importance of historical location to Byatt's neo-Victorian project. Hadley argues that Byatt is sensitive to the fluctuations in attitudes towards spiritualism in the nineteenth century and skilfully incorporates them into her texts to present any easy assumption of twentieth-century superiority.

Hadley's article draws out the connections between gender and spiritualism. That there is an implicit feminist approach to spiritualism in these texts is indicated by Byatt's own comments on *Angels and Insects*. She refers to Alex Owen's sociological study of nineteenth-century spiritualism, *The Darkened Room* (1989), which demonstrated how '[b]eing a medium was one way in which a Victorian woman could have a career'.[73] Hadley explores these feminist concerns through the connection between literature and spiritualism. In particular, she analyses Mrs Papagay's automatic writing, which she claims demonstrates how spiritualism confirmed the Victorian ideology of passive 'femininity' while simultaneously providing an alternative to the domestic confinement that ideology usually necessitated. Hadley points out the significance of the fact that it is her husband's voice that Mrs Papagay seems to be channelling through the automatic writing. Thus, although Mrs Papagay gains access to language which her position as a middle-class Victorian woman denies her, it is ultimately a 'limited liberation' as it can only be achieved 'by appropriating the voice of her husband'.[74] Again, then, this reveals the double bind which spiritualism presented for Victorian women; while it provided a measure of freedom for them it did so by confirming the restrictive ideology of female passivity.

Hadley's article examines the connection between spiritualism and literature that Byatt draws out in these texts, arguing that the relationship between the past and the present is 'experienced through a process of reading' and that the séances operate as a metaphor for reading.[75] Interestingly, 'the most vivid spiritual manifestation' in 'The Conjugial Angel' occurs outside the séances.[76] Hadley discusses three instances of ghosts in 'The Conjugial Angel', although she distinguishes between the different 'ontological levels' that they occupy.[77] At the first level there is Arthur Hallam (1811–33), who appears as a mouldering corpse to Sophy Sheekhy. This instance points to the connections between literature and spiritualism since Hallam's appearance is preceded by Sophy's recital of a poem by John Keats (1795–1821). At the second level is Alfred Tennyson who is alive at the time of the narrative, yet takes on a ghostly quality as his presence in the novella is mostly through his poetry. This not only points to the connection between literature and spiritualism but also enhances the historical specificity of the novella since *In Memoriam* 'had become a great mouthpiece for the spiritual anxiety of the Victorian era'.[78] In Chapter 10, however, Tennyson appears as a character but, as Hadley notes, this chapter is framed by Sophy's imagining of Tennyson and so his presence there is 'almost that of a ghost'.[79] Finally, there is the character of Emily Jesse, who 'adds another dimension to [the] ontological layering of ghosts' in the novella.[80] While Emily is clearly alive within the confines of the fiction, to the reader she is dead and thus Byatt's 'invocation of her in this novella takes on a ghostly quality'.[81] Hadley concludes that this proliferation of ghostly figures 'prevents any clear opposition between the dead and the alive, the past and the present' in 'The Conjugial Angel'.[82]

Drawing on this connection between literature and spiritualism, Hadley proposes some conclusions about Byatt's attitude towards the past and literature's role in accessing the past. She claims that both *Possession* and 'The Conjugial Angel' 'display the power of literature to resurrect the ghosts of the past'.[83] Yet, she suggests that these texts also reverse this relationship; that Byatt reveals 'that it is necessary to connect with the figures of the past, especially authors, in order to bring literature to life'.[84] As we shall see, O'Connor reaches a similar conclusion about Byatt's views on the importance of biography to literature in her reading of *The Biographer's Tale*.

THE BIOGRAPHER'S TALE (2000)

Reviews

Ruth Franklin's review for *The New Republic* judges *The Biographer's Tale* negatively, claiming that it 'reads like a tired rehash' of *Possession*.[85] In adopting the same narrative techniques as *Possession* Franklin notes a 'staleness' to *The Biographer's Tale*.[86] Franklin also identifies similar concerns in *The Biographer's Tale* as in *Possession*, particularly an interest in ordering and categorizing the world and an obsession with 'recovering and uncovering the past'.[87] Like the texts it incorporates, Franklin suggests that *The Biographer's Tale* itself is a 'maddening' combination of fact and fiction.[88] Franklin's review also considers Byatt's critical text *On Histories and Stories* and judges it as harshly as she does *The Biographer's Tale*. She sees both texts as characterized by a 'soullessness' that stems from their intellectual qualities.[89] While the charge of intellectualism has been levelled at many of Byatt's earlier fictions, in this instance, it is the subservience of facts to the illustration of a theory that Franklin seems particularly to be criticizing. Ultimately, Franklin's review of *The Biographer's Tale* seems unreserved in its criticism. While she recognizes that the novel's academic satire 'wickedly hits the mark' this, like so much else in the novel, still falls short of the standards set by the 'perfectly tuned satire' found in the pages of *Possession*.[90]

While Franklin considered *The Biographer's Tale* alongside *Possession*, Ruth Scurr's review for the *London Review of Books* discusses it in relation to *Still Life*. While she sees the second novel in the quartet as characterized by realism, she views *The Biographer's Tale* as 'a lush celebration of allusive and imaginative metaphor'.[91] Although this is not in itself a criticism, Scurr goes on to comment that the novel's inter-textual approach leaves no room for the reader. In a way that recalls Barrell's comments on *Angels and Insects*, Scurr laments the fact that the echoes in the novel 'have all been decided in advance'.[92] One of the echoes that Scurr highlights is Virginia Woolf's *Orlando: A Biography* (1928); but she claims that this merely serves to reveal the failings of Byatt's text. Scurr claims that, contrary to Woolf's novel, in Byatt's text the 'imaginative emphasis' is focused on 'the consumption as opposed to the production of prose'.[93] Scurr points out that the problem with creating a novel that relies so heavily on the echoes of precursors is that those precursors can detract from the novel itself, merely indi-cating its shortcomings. This secondariness, however, could be seen as part of the point the novel is making about both biography in gen-eral and the nature of artistic production in the postmodern era. The frequent criticisms of Byatt's intellectual style are implicitly invoked in Scurr's review. While she absolves Byatt of responsibility for the 'clunk-ing prose' and 'geeky intelligence' of the protagonists' thoughts, she does claim that the novel itself reads more like a 'haphazard' research notebook.[94] Despite these reservations, however, Scurr ends on a posi-tive note, praising Byatt's facility in dealing with misery. Although she draws most of her examples from *Still Life*, Scurr does note a striking example in *The Biographer's Tale* which she claims presents a 'sudden flash of utter misery' amid the intellectual games of the novel, the effect of which is 'unsettling'.[95]

Erin O'Connor presents a reader's response to *The Biographer's Tale* in the book forum section of the journal *Victorian Studies*. This positioning is appropriate for a novel that is explicitly concerned with both the Victorian era and intellectual pursuits. Indeed, O'Connor claims that Byatt should be seen as a Victorianist who works through 'intelligent, searching fiction' to bring Victorian studies to the general public.[96] O'Connor, like many reviewers, positions *The Biographer's Tale* alongside *Possession*, claiming that it perhaps makes most sense to understand it as an 'inversion' of its Booker Prize-winning predecessor.[97] Since *Possession* declares in its subtitle that it is a romance, its twentieth-century protag-onist, Roland, eventually experiences the joys and rewards of academic research; in contrast, O'Connor suggests that *The Biographer's Tale* is an 'academic anti-romance' in which Phineas is never permitted to reap the rewards of his intellectual project.[98] O'Connor believes that in the later novel, Byatt is implicitly lamenting the state of contemporary literary studies which in its rejection of biography has become 'divorced from the very thing that gives it meaning', the writer.[99] What this results in is a 'strangely dehumanized humanities'.[100] While she does not goes as far as to claim that *The Biographer's Tale* is arguing for the restitution of biography in literary studies, O'Connor does claim that it forces a re-evaluation of biography's role. Prompted by this, O'Connor takes the opportunity to propose herself that biography could prove an effective resource in Victorian studies. Perhaps appropriately for a novel that brings such intellectual concerns into focus, what began as a book review has developed into an opinion-piece about the state of modern literary studies and biography's possible role in its future.

Criticism

The title of Celia Wallhead's article, 'Metaphors for the Self in A. S. Byatt's *The Biographer's Tale*' (2003), indicates her dual focus on the nature of subjectivity and Byatt's use of language. In terms of genre, Wallhead recognizes the importance of this novel's engagement with biography and links it to wider developments in both biography and fiction:

■ If the imaginative has now entered biography through conjecture, extrapolation and informed speculation, the reverse has also occurred as a tendency within the novel as historical metafiction has incorporated some of the fact of the biography, inviting the reader to join in the play of juxtaposing fact and fiction.[101] □

Although she notes the presence of both historical and fictional characters in the novel, Wallhead does not really address the implications of Byatt's juxtaposition of historical and fictional characters, of biography and fiction.

Wallhead claims that this novel is a Bildungsroman, that is a novel that traces the growth and development of the central character: '[i]nitially desperate for fact, [Phineas] becomes seduced by words'.[102] Specifically, then, it charts the transformation of Phineas into a writer and so might be better termed a Künstlerroman, a novel that traces the development of the artist. Either way, writing is connected to the formation of identity in this novel: 'it is through writing that one searches for identity ... for writing can change, develop or confer identity'.[103] In particular, the novel, as its title announces, is concerned with the search for the self through biography. Wallhead lists the various metaphors adopted for biography in Byatt's novel (the Maleström, mosaics, radiology, Rubik cubes and marbles, to name just a few) suggesting that they all highlight the process of 'assembling' and that they imply either 'aesthetic patterns' or a 'hidden mystic centre'.[104] This notion of a hidden core which will be revealed through the right combination of words, the correct pattern, seems to underpin the biographical project as a whole. Wallhead further argues that these metaphors apply not only to the biographical project but also to the search for identity. The novel's structure is interpreted as a figuration of the multiplicity of identity. In particular, the numerous 'threesomes' in the novel (e.g. Elmer Bole/Scholes Destry-Scholes/Phineas; Phineas/Fulla/Vera; Linnaeus/Galton/Ibsen) are seen as providing 'the major structure-endowing mechanism of the novel'.[105] Wallhead implicitly links this combination of identities to Byatt's own approach to writing, claiming that it indicates 'metaphorically ... that no writer creates in isolation, but always draws on the work of others in a combination of past, present and future'.[106]

As we have seen, then, for all their postmodern awareness, Byatt's neo-Victorian fictions ultimately suggest that she is interested in reviving the forms of Victorian realism. Similarly, critics of the first two novels of the quartet drew out a connection to the Victorian form of the historical and social-problem novel. As we shall see in the next two chapters, however, the rest of the quartet seems to diverge from this realist project and *Babel Tower* and *A Whistling Woman* are more frequently aligned with postmodern impulses.

CHAPTER SEVEN

Language and Memory:
Babel Tower (1996)

By the time her sixth novel appeared in 1996, Byatt's reputation as an important British novelist was well and truly established. As the first novel that Byatt published after the Booker success of *Possession*, *Babel Tower* was often judged in relation to its immediate predecessor and so had to live up to the high standards it set. Yet *Babel Tower* was never intended as a follow-up to *Possession* but rather marked Byatt's return to the quartet she had begun with *The Virgin in the Garden* (1978) and *Still Life* (1985). Although *Babel Tower* belonged to the quartet, it was, as we shall see, felt to indicate a new direction in the quartet.

REVIEWS

Lucy Hughes-Hallet's review for *The Sunday Times* claimed that *Babel Tower* was a 'voluminous, baggy book' which fans of the 'tight-plotted' *Possession* might find disappointing.[1] Yet she concludes that *Babel Tower* is 'tartly funny, emotionally engrossing and headily intelligent'.[2] As we have seen, reviewers often criticized the intellectual aspects of Byatt's previous novels, but for Hughes-Hallet *Babel Tower* successfully combines 'analytical intelligence' with 'fictional imagination'.[3] Hughes-Hallet identifies two aspects of the novel which came to dominate reviews: its focus on story-telling and its position as an historical novel. She claims that *Babel Tower* is 'a cunning pastiche' which is 'not only a tale which the times might have bred ... but also a tale about the times'.[4] This comment reveals the complex historical positioning of the novels that comprise the quartet, which incorporate the dual perspectives of the time they are set and the time they were written.

Tom Adair's review for *The Scotsman* similarly begins by placing *Babel Tower* alongside *Possession* and judges the later novel as a 'greater pastiche'.[5] The rest of the review, however, is not as favourable. Adair claims that *Babel Tower* incorporates too much pastiche, which ends up seeming 'clever and knowing' and thus intrudes on the enjoyment of the novel.[6] Moreover, he criticizes the novel's prioritization of language over characters; 'its babble of words deserts the book's heart' to the extent that readers end up caring very little for the characters.[7] He reserves his most damning criticism for the end of the review, claiming that Byatt seems to have 'forgotten to heed E. M. Forster's command – and the novelist's duty – "Only connect"'.[8] This criticism seems a little unfair since the urge towards disconnection and fragmentation appears to be deliberate, part of the reconstruction of the ethos of the 1960s, as indeed Kate Kellaway's review for *The Observer* concludes. The other problem with Adair's review is his failure to take account of *Babel Tower*'s position as the third novel in a quartet. Consequently, his criticism that Byatt is 'raiding old novels, as if ... troubled by unfinished business' is wholly unjustified.[9]

Again, Miranda Seymour's review for *The Financial Times* places *Babel Tower* alongside *Possession*, judging it to be 'less compelling and approachable' but 'more ambitious' than its predecessor.[10] Like Adair, Seymour concludes that Byatt's interest in presenting intellectual ideas detracts from the novel. She claims that '[t]he ideas are ... too big for the multi-threaded narrative to contain' and that the characters lack 'the essential ability to hold our interest and sympathy'.[11] Despite these criticisms, Seymour does suggest that the reader can derive enjoyment from *Babel Tower*, particularly in its depiction of the 1960s, which succeeds in 'sharpening our memory of its finer moments of madness'.[12] Thus, for Seymour, *Babel Tower*'s position as a historical novel is its most prominent feature.

Several reviewers commented on Byatt's approach towards the past in *Babel Tower*, linking it to the quartet as a whole. D. J. Taylor's review for *The Guardian* implicitly adopts a similar approach to his chapter 'Reading the 1950s: A. S. Byatt's *The Virgin in the Garden* and *Still Life*'. There, Taylor argued that Byatt was fundamentally a 'social novelist' and that the projected quartet presented a detailed depiction of life in Britain after the war.[13] While *Babel Tower* attempts to continue this project into the 1960s, Taylor implies that it is not as successful since '[s]ome of this decade-mongering is a touch obtrusive'.[14] Taylor has other criticisms of the novel; his most vehement one is of Byatt's decision to kill off Stephanie at the end of *Still Life*, leaving 'only the intolerable Frederica' for the rest of the quartet.[15] Despite these criticisms, Taylor's review ultimately comes out in favour of *Babel Tower*, suggesting that while it may perplex fans of *Possession* it is ultimately 'the better book'.[16]

A similar assessment is presented in Philip Hensher's review for *The Spectator*. He claims that the quartet as a whole presents 'a novelist's history' of postwar Britain; Byatt is not interested in public events in these novels but in 'the subterranean, shifting history ... [depicted by] tracing the history of the imagination'.[17] For Hensher, it is this interest in the imagination that characterizes the quartet as it stands so far. Yet he contends that *Babel Tower* is more than just a collection of ideas; rather it neatly combines intellectualizing with a 'grippingly dramatic plot'.[18] Indeed, whereas many reviewers felt that the characterization suffered because of the novel's preoccupation with ideas, Hensher is impressed by the characters. He implies that in Byatt's previous works characterization is achieved through 'build[ing] up detail to massive, imposing effect'; yet in *Babel Tower* he notes 'a new quickness about the portraits' which nonetheless suffer 'no loss in psychological sharpness'.[19] Overall, Hensher judges the novel favourably, praising its 'exceptional gravity and serious charm'.[20]

Penelope Lively's review for *The Times* focuses on the novel's depiction of historical detail; she claims that *Babel Tower* is characterized by 'compendious writing' which, while it may not suit all readers, will have 'social historians of the future [singing] hymns of gratitude'.[21] The accumulation of period details that are 'minutely catalogued' links *Babel Tower* to *Virgin*, which Lively claims presented a detailed description of a 1950s lower middle-class household.[22] Despite this connection, Lively identifies a 'shift in authorial approach' from *Virgin* to *Babel Tower*, the later novel being 'even more expansive, more discursive'.[23] This returns to the question of the novel's engagement with ideas. Unlike many of the reviewers we have encountered so far, however, Lively sees this as a virtue rather than a vice. She recognizes that the novel is less concerned with narrative and plot than 'meditations and arguments and descriptions', but claims that '[t]hese are what language is for'.[24] This notion of a shift between *Still Life* and *Babel Tower* comes to characterize responses to *Babel Tower* and, as we shall see in the next chapter, the quartet as a whole.

Lorna Sage's review for *The Times Literary Supplement* similarly notes a transition in Byatt's style between the three books of the quartet. Sage claims that the quartet has moved away from being 'a kind of chronicle – though always a bit compromised, and ironized' towards 'a game of hide-and-seek with herself'.[25] The notion of a chronicle implicitly links the first two volumes in the quartet with a realist project of faithfully representing the past while the playful elements Sage notes in *Babel Tower* connect it to postmodernism. This connection between *Babel Tower* and postmodernism continues in Sage's comment that Byatt's novel is 'putting story-telling itself on trial'.[26] The notion that the quartet moves from the realist project of the first two novels to a more postmodern approach is furthered in critical responses to *A Whistling Woman* and the quartet as a whole, as we shall see in the next chapter.

Hugo Barnacle's review for *The Independent Weekend* similarly identifies *Babel Tower* as marking a transition within Byatt's projected quartet. He claims that *Virgin* and *Still Life* demonstrated Byatt's skills in writing 'readable stories about domestic, family and sexual goings-on'.[27] Barnacle notes an 'increasing range of tricksy highbrow embellishments' in Byatt's fiction, which he claims reveals her dissatisfaction with the realist mode of writing she employed in the first two novels of the quartet.[28] He claims that while this paid off with *Possession* it is not as successful in *Babel Tower*. Barnacle also addresses the intellectual aspects of *Babel Tower* in relation to the rest of the quartet. Whereas *Virgin* demonstrated a 'tendency to overdo the intellectual window dressing', in the third instalment of the quartet, this preoccupation with intellectualizing is felt to dominate the characterization.[29] Barnacle claims that Byatt introduces too much extraneous material into the novel, brought in by characters that seem designed merely to be the mouthpiece for a particular intellectual viewpoint. As for Frederica, while Barnacle recognizes that the reader is meant to identify with her as 'our plucky heroine' he concludes that she is 'a right pain'.[30] Ultimately, Barnacle claims that *Babel Tower* shows 'a certain expansive confidence' that is 'not absolutely justified' by the novel itself.[31]

Reviewers of *Virgin* and *Still Life* often dwelt on their concern with the relationship between language and reality and the power of fiction to represent the world. This concern is equally apparent in *Babel Tower* and is explicitly commented on in Kate Kellaway's review for *The Observer*. The illustration that accompanies Kellaway's review shows a caricature image of Byatt building a tower of bricks around her. This image hints at the recurrent criticism of the intellectual elements of Byatt's fiction in its connotations of an 'ivory tower'. Interestingly, despite identifying language as the novel's overriding concern, Kellaway claims it is also 'the great fault of the novel'.[32] For Kellaway, as for Barnacle and Adair, the novel's ideas overpower its emotional aspects: 'The ideas of the novel are its lifeblood: emotions are watery in comparison.'[33] As in *Possession*, Byatt inserts various texts within her novel, but here the pastiches are thought to be unsuccessful and 'inauthentic'.[34] This meta-fictional technique is often identified as a feature of postmodern fiction and Kellaway implies that the novel engages with postmodernism in its trial of language. Byatt 'demonstrates that no story is definitive, no structure firm and no judgement finite', yet she refuses to permit a descent into 'unquestioning subjectivity [by] hold[ing] subjectivity hostage'.[35] Thus, *Babel Tower* is seen to exist in an uneasy relationship to postmodernism; while aware of postmodernist scepticism towards language Byatt never surrenders to it wholeheartedly.

Ann Hulbert's review for *The New York Times Book Review* similarly identifies the tension between postmodernism and realism that was implicit in Kellaway's review. Hulbert claims that although Byatt incorporates a 'post-modern self-consciousness', in *Babel Tower* it 'takes the old-fashioned moralizing form'.[36] As with many of the previous reviewers we have considered, Hulbert aligns *Babel Tower* with the broader fictional project to which it belongs. She argues that after *Virgin* and *Still Life*, *Babel Tower* introduced a much-needed breath of fresh air into Byatt's 'emblematic epic'.[37] Consequently, *Babel Tower* is 'a bolder novel' that refuses to lament the limitations of fiction but rather celebrates and explores 'how much [novels] – or this one, at least – can squeeze in'.[38] Hulbert's only criticism of Byatt's novel relates to the novel-within-the-novel, *Babbletower*, claiming that Byatt is heavy-handed in her treatment of it and that her comments on the power of literature seem didactic.

THE POWER OF LANGUAGE

As we have seen, several reviewers felt that *Babel Tower* is essentially a novel about the possibilities and problems of language. This concern with the possibilities of representation often provides the focal point for more sustained critical responses to the novel.

Celia M. Wallhead's study, *The Old, The New, and the Metaphor* (1999) addresses the engagement with language and the role of metaphor in Byatt's work. Although Wallhead's study focuses on Byatt's earlier fiction, it provides an interesting framework within which to consider *Babel Tower* since it primarily engages with questions about language. Wallhead proposes that all of Byatt's writings 'tackle the relationship between language and the real world, and confront the aesthetic and epistemological difficulties of language and "truth"'.[39] She concludes that metaphor and myth are important tools in a Byatt novel since, 'with their potential for opening up the subject to new meanings, [they] are the only solution to such limitations [of language]'.[40] Wallhead's analysis relies on the titles of Byatt's novels to identify their central image. Thus, in the case of *Babel Tower*, she unsurprisingly identifies the story of the biblical Tower of Babel as the 'central image–metaphor' for the novel.[41] This metaphor operates 'by mapping the myth of the Tower...on to the target domain of the use of a recalcitrant language to create art'.[42] In this interpretation Wallhead explicitly connects *Babel Tower* to the rest of Byatt's oeuvre; the 'target domain' of a Byatt novel is 'always Life and Creativity', it is only the 'source domains or vehicles that vary'.[43] This account is quite reductive; it not only simplifies all of Byatt's work to a single 'target domain' of creativity but also fails to engage in detail with the novels themselves.[44] However, Wallhead does extend her analysis of *Babel Tower* slightly further when she deals with the question of its historical setting. For Wallhead, Byatt's fiction is characterized by 'a specific historicity' and *Babel Tower* is no exception.[45] Wallhead argues that the image-metaphor of the Tower of Babel is not just a consequence of Byatt's concern with creativity but also a specific response to the historical location of the novel. Byatt's decision to adopt the image of the Tower of Babel indicates her view that the 1960s were 'characterised by a total lack of consensus in all spheres, ideological, political, social, etc'.[46]

Babel Tower's treatment of language was explored in much more detail in an earlier article by Wallhead, 'The Un-utopian Babelic Fallenness of Langage: A. S. Byatt's *Babel Tower*' (1997). This article considers the novel's depiction of various discourses and the relationship between language and truth. Wallhead claims that *Babel Tower* is concerned with 'the power of language, the capacities of falsification of different discourses, the freedom of the individual and how far this affects group social life'.[47] The concern with language and the position of the individual are inter-related and are both seen by Wallhead as deriving from the novel's historical location. She argues that both *Babel Tower* and the metafictional narrative within it, *Babbletower*, explore the possibilities of Utopia in relation to language. In contrast, the two trials that serve as the 'dramatic culmination' of the novel, Frederica's divorce trial and the obscenity trial of *Babbletower*, reveal that language 'does not represent the truth' and so is 'fallen'.[48] An 'enormous falsifying discrepancy' exists between the legal discourse of these trials and the discourses employed by Frederica and Jude Mason themselves.[49] Wallhead argues that it is Literature itself that is on trial and that, despite appearances, 'Byatt does not allow literature to fail'.[50] Thus, while *Babbletower* is judged to be obscene, the ruling is overturned due to a technicality: 'truth is not what counts, but persuasive eloquence within the correct discourse'.[51] The truth of this opinion is also evident in the rulings concerning Frederica's divorce trial. While her husband's masculine discourse holds sway in the first hearing, the second, child-custody hearing goes in Frederica's favour because of the discourse of 'the unprepossessing female social worker' and her display of 'expert knowledge'.[52] This view would seem to align the novel with postmodern ideas about the intersections between language and power and the impossibility of asserting truth through language. Indeed, Wallhead explores the novel's connection to postmodernism at both a formal and thematic level. However, as we shall see, she perceives a commitment to realism in Byatt's writing that implies a belief in a moral truth behind language.

The multiplicity of discourses in *Babel Tower* is also seen as part of the formal experimentation of the novel. Wallhead claims that *Babel Tower* demonstrates Byatt's characteristic approach of presenting 'a variety of different discourses interpolated within the general frame of self-reflexive realism'.[53] Wallhead connects the incorporation of *Babbletower* in this novel with the metafictional devices of Alexander Wedderburn's plays in the first two novels of the quartet. Despite this connection, however, she suggests that *Babel Tower* marks a formal divergence from the first two novels in the quartet. She draws on Westlake's comments on *Still Life* in *PN Review*, summarizing his view that it paid 'lip-service' to continental language theories while 'remaining in formal terms firmly with the realists'.[54] She suggests that Westlake 'demands of Byatt a more postmodern approach to narrative'; a demand that she believes is fulfilled in *Babel Tower*.[55] Wallhead claims that *Babel Tower* is 'more daring within the limits of realism' and that her formal experimentation with narrative complements the innovative approach to language at the level of content.[56] These comments again raise the problematic question of Byatt's relationship to postmodenrism and realism. Wallhead suggests that Byatt is 'torn between her devotion to realism as a formula which gives a semblance of truth to the discourse, and to her desires to be on the crest of the wave in fiction, accommodating postmodern theories of identity and narrative approach'.[57] This comment implies that Byatt's engagement with postmodernism is part of a desire to be fashionable and that ultimately she remains committed to realism. This view is also apparent in Wallhead's comments on the relationship between language and reality in Byatt's novel. Wallhead claims that the incorporation of various discourses in *Babel Tower* reveal Byatt's belief that 'reality is not static or univocal'.[58] Yet, she also contends that Byatt maintains a conviction that there are 'underlying moral truths which are disregarded at our peril'.[59] This positing of an ultimate position of truth and meaning within the text seems to undermine the postmodern appearance of the novel. For Wallhead, this 'anchor of truth' comes from the narrator.[60] She claims that this is less explicit in *Babel Tower* than in the previous two novels of the quartet, in part because the narrator of the third volume 'attempts to confine herself to what she could know in the 1960s'.[61] Thus, Wallhead implies that there is less of a temporal disjunction in *Babel Tower* than in the previous two novels, although she recognizes that the temporal disjunction for the reader may actually be greater.

Wallhead examines the various narrative levels that operate in *Babel Tower* as a response to the criticisms that the novel is 'overambitious in [its] formal pretensions'.[62] Specifically, she addresses the criticism that the novel lacks both a beginning and a sense of story. Wallhead stresses the impact of the novel's position as the third volume in a projected quartet and points out that *Virgin* and *Still Life* were equally problematic about the nature of beginnings in their incorporation of prologues dated after the events of the novels that followed. Returning to *Babel Tower*, Wallhead identifies four separate openings to the novel (as we shall see shortly, Noble identifies one more), claiming that this indicates 'the fragmentariness of life, of identity, of language'.[63] Despite claiming that for Byatt 'all are possible [openings] since [they are] *simultaneous*', she recognizes that the linear nature of language, and the novel form, means that one will necessarily be privileged over the others.[64] For Wallhead, there are two privileged beginnings, which she connects to the openings of the first two novels in the quartet. She connects the first opening of *Babel Tower*, which deals with the thrush and genetics, with the prologues of *Virgin* and *Still Life*, claiming that together they form a 'metadiscourse of the self-consciousness of art'.[65] This description of the prologues seems to align them with the postmodern, self-conscious elements of Byatt's fiction. The other privileged beginning is the second one, which indicates the start of the 'metanarrative' of Frederica and which provides the narrative thrust for both *Babel Tower* and the quartet as a whole.[66] This opening, then, seems to represent the realist impulses in Byatt's fiction, the concern with narrating a traditional story.

The other element of *Babel Tower* with which Wallhead implicitly deals is its position as a historical novel. She claims that the novel is a 'recreation' of the 1960s which 'looks at the dark as well as the light sides of the decade'.[67] This focus on the negative aspects of the 1960s marks a departure from the first two volumes of the quartet; leaving behind the 1950s, Byatt also seems to be leaving behind what Taylor saw as the overly nostalgic tone of *Virgin*. Wallhead does not really deal with this shift in tone and focus between *Still Life* and *Babel Tower*. Rather, she sees the third novel as determined by the overarching structure of the quartet as a whole. By the time of *Babel Tower*, Byatt is unable to diverge too far from the narrative she had established with *Virgin* and *Still Life* and from the historical approach of those novels. For Wallhead, this third novel reinforces the view formed from the first two in the quartet that 'an impression of an age...is as important, perhaps more so, in these novels than narrative'.[68] In its engagement with the recent historical past, Wallhead judges the quartet as an 'approximation to the subgenre [of] the Condition of England Novel'.[69] She states that 'Byatt's aim is to explore a person's threefold experience as the Victorians did: as human being, as citizen and as artist'.[70] Thus, Wallhead implicitly draws out the connections with Victorian historical fiction that Taylor made explicit in his discussion of *Virgin* and *Still Life*. Yet, she recognizes that the 1960s world depicted by Byatt is 'not the stable setting with clear political and social purposes and clearly centred meanings of the original, Victorian, Condition of England Novel'.[71] Despite this, Wallhead identifies a commitment to historical specificity in Byatt's novel, which she connects to the underlying moral sense she distinguished beneath the multiplicity of discourses. This is all tied in with her formal commitment to realism, despite some postmodern play, since 'Byatt must continue to create characters with a semblance of a fixed identity and a history in a specific social context' if their 'moral choices' are to have any force for the reader.[72] Consequently, Wallhead seems to align *Babel Tower* with the realist project in terms of its commitment to truth and depiction of the past.

THE ART OF MEMORY

Michael Noble's perceptive essay 'A Tower of Tongues' (2001) analyses *Babel Tower*'s concern with the art of memory and neatly connects it to the classical and Renaissance traditions of memory theatre. Through close reading of the multiple possible openings of the novel, Noble explores the various images for memory that Byatt presents and extrapolates a general attitude towards the art of remembering. Unsurprisingly, given the novel's title, one of the most important images is that of architecture or buildings, which serve as both 'metaphors' and 'mediums' for 'the organization and structure of memory'.[73] Noble connects these buildings to the Elizabethan tradition of memory theatre, whereby a speaker constructed a building in his mind to 'store' the various images that will help them remember the speech. Thus, the act of remembering is like taking a journey through a familiar building. Indeed, Noble, drawing on the research of the historian Frances Yates (1889–1981), points out that the Tower of Babel was a common image in Elizabethan memory theatre and accepts Yates's proposition that this was possibly 'an allegory for the confusion that will be overcome by the art of memory'.[74] Noble concludes that *Babel Tower* equally 'gives order to chaos, if not perhaps to overcome confusion, then to counterbalance it, to ... artfully render it so that it may be at least partially understood'.[75] Indeed, he suggests that there is an implicit order in chaos, that '*deconstruction* implies a flourishing and ambitious *construction*, however paired it may be with the already inscribed and much-touted *destruction* foreshadowed by such structure'.[76] In referring to deconstruction, Noble implicitly connects Byatt's novel to Jacques Derrida (1930–2004) whose deconstructionist approach to texts is influenced by post-structuralist theories about the impossibility of language to convey meaning. The importance of this post-structuralist and postmodern context is indicated by Noble's decision to preface his essay with an epigraph from Borges's story 'The Library of Babel' (1941).

Noble identifies at least five different openings to the novels; drawing on the notion of the Elizabethan memory theatre, he claims that each of the openings creates a 'distinct locus'.[77] The first of these openings occurs prior to the narrative and thus 'highlights the page itself as the site of memory'.[78] In this self-conscious opening, the typography of the page reflects the image of the snail that is described therein. As we have seen, this self-conscious reflection on the possibilities of representation in language was identified as a key feature of the previous two novels in the quartet, *Virgin* and *Still Life*. Noble develops this connection between *Babel Tower* and the novels it continues by claiming that the prologues to the first two novels in the quartet similarly function as memory theatres, which foreground the ideas and events of both the individual novels and the entire quartet. He remarks that the prologues of both novels are located further in the future than the novels themselves reach. For example, the prologue to *Still Life* occurs in 1980 but with *Babel Tower* the quartet has only reached 1967. Consequently, he argues that the prologues are concerned with memory and personal histories but that the significance of the mnemonics they employ does not become apparent until the later novels. In contrast to the first two novels, Noble points out that *Babel Tower* does not have a prologue but rather multiple beginnings and that it is through these possible openings that Byatt explicitly engages with and questions the Elizabethan conceptions of memory theatre.

As I have said, Nobel identifies at least five possible openings to the novel, although he devotes most attention to the first two openings. The second opening equally draws out the connections between language and memory as it follows Hugh Pink's walk and the poem he composes. This experience combines the present and the past as Pink replaces the images he sees with ones from his memory, thus creating 'a palimpsest', which preserves the original text while inscribing a new text on top of it.[79] The notion of the palimpsest is central to an understanding of *Babel Tower*. Ultimately, Noble claims that in its multiple beginnings and endings, *Babel Tower* presents various layerings but that 'the layers are not integrated' and so '[t]here is not one pinnacle of conclusion'.[80] Noble argues that this multiplicity is not presented as something to be overcome but rather to be embraced.

Noble asserts that the Hugh Pink opening could be categorized as stream-of-consciousness, a stylistic technique favoured by many Modernist writers. 'Stream of consciousness' was a term coined by William James (1842–1910) to reflect the notion that consciousness was experienced as an uncontrolled flow rather than in any logical and structured pattern. Many Modernist writers sought to integrate this new concept of consciousness into their depiction of characters and so developed a writing style intended to capture realistically the flow of thoughts experienced by their characters. Although this section of Byatt's novel could be seen as similar to the Modernist approach, Noble distances it from the project of such Modernist writers in terms of its focus. Noble claims that Byatt 'revises and critiques' the Modernist use of 'stream-of-consciousness' by presenting it as 'a deliberate act of consciousness, as a *reconstruction* of the past'.[81] For Noble, this relates to Byatt's overall project in *Babel Tower* since her focus is on 'memory and creation rather than consciousness (or rather on consciousness as memory)'.[82] In this regard, Noble connects Byatt's novel to Marcel Proust's *À la recherche du temps perdu* (1913–27), which was an ambitious project concerning the nature of memory.

The third opening explicitly draws out the connection between the Tower of Babel story and the processes of memory; it depicts Daniel Orton in the crypt of St Simeon's Church, which, we are told, used to have a stained glass window of the Pentecostal flames. Noble claims that these 'tongues of flame' represent both the confusion of tongues created by Babel and the pre-Babel, original tongue. The window, however, was destroyed in World War II and, although it has been reconstructed, it retains the traces of its destruction. Noble claims that 'the introduction of chaos' into the window 'does not…destroy its beauty or its memory function. Rather, it illustrates and remembers the relation of language to reality and to itself.'[83] This is, indeed, the project of *Babel Tower* itself; to acknowledge and incorporate various different voices in order to celebrate and embrace the diversity of language. Unlike some of the reviewers we have encountered, then, Noble does not admonish Byatt's novel for failing to connect all the various strands of the novel but rather praises the attempt to incorporate chaos and confusion into art.

Embracing multiplicity and disorder is often seen as a feature of postmodern fiction and, as we have seen, critical accounts of *Babel Tower* have often drawn out the novel's connection to postmodernism. As we shall see in the next chapter, this relationship to postmodernism is similarly drawn out in responses to *A Whistling Woman* and thus confirms the sense of a split in the quartet.

CHAPTER EIGHT

The Conclusion of the Quartet: *A Whistling Woman* (2002)

With the publication of *A Whistling Woman* in 2002, Byatt completed the quartet that she had begun over 20 years earlier with *The Virgin in the Garden*. While then she was a little-known novelist, standing in the shadow of her more famous sister Margaret Drabble, by the time the final volume appeared she had become an established novelist, both in critical and popular circles. Its position at the end of the quartet means that considerations of *A Whistling Woman* often deal as much with its relationship to the preceding texts as with the novel in its own right. This problem is inherent in the novel itself: as the last in a successful quartet, *A Whistling Woman* is constantly aware of its relationship to the previous three novels. Indeed, many of the issues we have encountered in relation to the earlier novels in the quartet recur in responses to *A Whistling Woman*, in particular: its position as historical fiction, its engagement with feminism, the intellectual elements of Byatt's style and the opposition between postmodernism and realism.

REVIEWS

Steve Davies' review for *The Independent* implicitly sets up the opposition between postmodernism and realism that we have encountered in criticism of Byatt's earlier novels. He claims that Frederica is 'fleshed out with pastiche', a characteristic postmodern style, and that Byatt rejects realism as 'archaic'.[1] He explores this opposition through an interesting analogy to food, suggesting that while the reader might desire a 'solid' bag of fish and chips, good homely food, they are served up an 'airy soufflé of highbrow talk'.[2] Davies, then, comes down on the side of postmodernism, and his criticism of Byatt's characterization of Frederica is extended to the more general accusation that Byatt 'sidelines the human heart'.[3] Although framed in slightly different terms, we have again the opposition between the intellectual and the novelistic elements of the book. Davies does recognize moments when *A Whistling Woman* delves into the realm of the human heart, arguing that the treatment of Josh's inner life is 'at once forensic, profound and humane'.[4] Ultimately, however, he suggests that the intellectual aspects are prioritized, to the extent that the reader will never understand all the allusions. This, Davies asserts, is intentional and consequently the quartet cannot escape an air of condescension towards the majority of its readers. Davies claims that the lack of emotional engagement in the final novel hampers its treatment of the 1960s, which is reduced to 'tiresome clichés'.[5] This comment recalls Fenton's criticism that in *Still Life* Byatt's depiction of the past resorts to adopting simplistic 'labels' for the period she is presenting.[6] In particular, Davies remarks that Byatt's avoidance of feminist politics is '[o]dd' given the novel's claim to 'anatomise the Sixties'.[7] Indeed he goes so far as to claim that the whole quartet is 'reactionary' in terms of its gender politics.[8]

Pamela Norris's review for *Literary Review* draws out the feminist concerns of the quartet, seeing *A Whistling Woman* as continuing the exploration of the 'conflict between biological imperatives and forging a career' that Byatt had begun in *Virgin* and *Still Life*.[9] Norris implicitly links this concern to the novel's epigraph, suggesting that the 'relentless energy' of *A Whistling Woman* is Byatt's attempt to avoid the fate of 'whistling in the wind'.[10] This energy is most apparent in the abundance of literary and scientific references in the novel. Yet, despite praising the novel's energy, Norris again raises the frequent criticism of Byatt's prioritization of intellectual concerns, claiming that at times she 'craved a little less matter with more artistry'.[11] In terms of its project as historical fiction, Norris judges *A Whistling Woman* as less successful than *Possession*. Whereas the earlier novel displayed 'formal order' despite the diverse voices, she considers *A Whistling Woman* to be 'at times both too diffused and too personal'.[12] Norris judges the quartet as 'an extraordinary achievement', both as a whole and as separate novels.[13] Oddly, though, she concludes with expectation for a further novel about Frederica, claiming that the reference at the end of *A Whistling Woman* to *The Winter's Tale* (1610/11), by William Shakespeare (1564–1616), highlights the illusion of the happy ending. Byatt indirectly answers this charge in her interview with Jonathan Noakes, where she defends what is often seen as the artificial nature of happy endings, especially those found in Shakespeare's comedies. She claims that such an ending is 'a very, very beautiful object. It isn't just unreal. It's unreal for very good reasons.'[14] These reasons are to do with the human desire for 'temporary artificial endings where people are all right' and Byatt asserts that if you don't impose the 'proper ending' of death on your characters, 'you have a right to a happy ending'.[15]

Robert MacFarlane's review for *The Observer* considers the quartet's position as an historical fiction, claiming that by focusing on Frederica Byatt is attempting to present history 'as seen from ground level'.[16] He implicitly connects the quartet to another of Byatt's historical fictions, *Possession*, when he comments that Byatt employs pastiche to encourage her readers 'to feel the past'.[17] Despite this implicit praise of the quartet, MacFarlane judges *A Whistling Woman* as a failure. Interestingly, MacFarlane assesses Byatt's novel in relation to the tradition of Victorian literature. He claims that although Byatt is 'the most nineteenth-century of contemporary novelists' this last novel 'lacks the essential clarifying power which narrative can bring to history'.[18] Consequently, he finds the novel 'an over-ambitious jumble'.[19] *A Whistling Woman*, however, is not one of Byatt's 'Victorian' novels, but rather is an attempt to capture the ethos of the 1960s, which was itself characterized by disunity and fragmentation. MacFarlane also criticizes the style of *A Whistling Woman*, particularly the 'ludicrous names' and what he terms 'stylistic botches', occasions where Byatt's intellectual vocabulary seems at odds with the situation being described.[20] Indeed, we see again the criticism that Byatt's novel is too intellectual in MacFarlane's claim that the novel contains 'too many ideas' which merely produces 'bewilderment' in the reader.[21] MacFarlane's criticism is not reserved for *A Whistling Woman*, however, but is extended to the entire quartet. He claims that the stylistic 'sins' of *A Whistling Woman* are present in the earlier novels; they are just more obvious in the last novel.[22]

Lorraine Adams's review for *The New Republic* equally positions Byatt in relation to Victorian literature, particularly George Eliot. Adams explicitly refers to Eliot's famous essay 'Silly Novels by Lady Novelists' (1856), in which she categorized the various types of 'silliness' women authors indulged in as 'the frothy, the prosy, the pious, or the pedantic'.[23] Adams claims that despite being desperate to avoid the charges Eliot laid against lady novelists, Byatt falls into precisely this trap. The source of Byatt's silliness is her pedantry. Rather than seeing Byatt as a 'novelist of ideas', as she is often judged, Adams asserts that she is merely 'a melodramatic pedant'.[24] While she recognizes that the novel is bursting with ideas, and indeed provides an extensive list of all the areas of intellectual activity that *A Whistling Woman* treats, Adams suggests that Byatt's learning is superficial, that she 'prefers wiggly surfaces to sure depths'.[25] As we have seen, a common view of the quartet is that it is a historical project, but Adams claims that Byatt's game-playing with the ways of narrating the past, merely 'obscures her collapse into costumed melodrama'.[26] Adams seems to excuse *Virgin* from these criticisms, claiming it was *Still Life* that revealed Byatt's 'inadequacies' as a writer.[27] Adams's comments on the characterization in the quartet revive the frequent criticism of Byatt's fiction. She claims that the novels fail to bring the characters to life; while she sees points in *Virgin* when 'psychological acuity...seems nearby', ultimately the characters are merely 'figurine[s]', soulless and lifeless.[28] Moreover, she, like many other reviewers, does not seem to like Frederica as a central character, finding her 'annoying' and 'exasperating'.[29] Adams seems less concerned with the unlikeable nature of Frederica, however, and more bothered by Byatt's assumption that presenting Frederica in an unsympathetic and non-idealized way renders her 'complicated'.[30]

In contrast, Amanda Craig's review for *The Times* judges Byatt's quartet as demonstrating her skill for 'creating complex characters'.[31] She suggests that Byatt's ability to make Frederica 'live in the imagination' in spite of her unsympathetic qualities is evidence of this skill.[32] Moreover, Craig seems to praise Byatt's style more generally, claiming her presentation of suffering as 'both exact and poetic' and the descriptions of the anti-university as 'vivid, and unexpectedly funny'.[33] Yet in spite of this praise, she contends that the latter passages 'seem to be by another novelist' and consequently fail to cohere with the rest of the novel.[34] Despite recognizing Byatt's skills at both characterization and story-telling, Craig considers *A Whistling Woman* as a novel of ideas, and as such criticizes it along the same lines as many previous reviewers. She claims that the 'danger' with an intellectual novel is that it fails to reveal the writer's imagination.[35] While she acknowledges that we do turn to fiction for intelligence she feels that it should be 'of a more subtle kind' than that provided in Byatt's novel.[36] Ultimately, Craig's review of *A Whistling Woman* judges it negatively. Not only is it too intellectual, but she claims that its depiction of the 1960s 'strains credibility' in the absence of 'professional prejudice' against Frederica.[37] Here again, then, we have the implied criticism of Byatt's failure to engage with feminist issues. For Craig, this is particularly problematic since it represents a departure from historical accuracy.

Daphne Merkin's review for *The New York Times* recognizes the problems *A Whistling Woman* encounters as the final novel in a quartet. She claims that in this novel Byatt is so focused on 'the vast prospect before her' that she loses sight of the reader.[38] Like other reviewers we have come across, Merkin links Byatt to both George Eliot and Iris Murdoch, but she qualifies this identification, claiming that Byatt is 'more lighthearted' than Eliot and 'less formulaic' than Murdoch.[39] Merkin asserts that *A Whistling Woman* 'rivals' its predecessor, *Babel Tower*, in its range of interests and 'the dense interplay of its refracted realities'.[40] The fairytale that opens the novel is seen to resemble most closely the metafictional techniques 'used to tiresome effect' in *Babel Tower*.[41] She does recognize that Byatt's skill as a writer extends beyond her 'daunting intellectual reach', claiming that the depiction of Joshua Lamb reveals her 'empathic powers'.[42] Here, then, we see a qualification of the criticism that Byatt prioritizes ideas over characters. Moreover, Merkin asserts that Byatt maintains an ability to present 'a straightforward realistic scene'.[43] Merkin proposes that the goal of the quartet as a whole is to present a social and cultural history of contemporary England and that Byatt's approach is that of a cultural anthropologist, providing an accumulation of details about her characters. As with Pamela Norris, Merkin seems unconvinced that *A Whistling Woman* really does represent an end to Frederica's adventures. Publication of the quartet in boxed form in 2003 and the fact that, from the outset, Byatt conceived the project as a quartet seems to suggest that there will not be any more novels. Like Merkin, we can only wait and see if that is the case.

Ruth Scurr's review for *The Times Literary Supplement* draws an interesting line of connection through the quartet by tracing the imagery of blood in all four novels, judging *A Whistling Woman* as 'by far the bloodiest'.[44] Scurr points out that the fiction of Muriel Spark (1918–2006) similarly has 'blood gushing' through it but that it is explicitly linked to her religious beliefs.[45] In contrast, for Byatt there is no such framework. Scurr suggests that Byatt's views about religion are 'in close conversation' with D. H. Lawrence.[46] Scurr's review raises again the criticisms of style that we have encountered in reviews of Byatt's previous novels. She claims that while colours and patterns are 'crucial', their effect is 'intellectually exciting' rather than 'sensual'.[47] Similarly, despite the meticulous description, Scurr contends that clothes serve as 'props' in the novel rather than revealing something about 'a character's sensuality'.[48] This comment seems to identify the pedantry that Adams had criticized in Byatt's novel. Despite these criticisms, Scurr views *A Whistling Woman* as an example of Byatt's best writing. She believes that the 'grandeur' of Byatt's work derives from her treatment of grief, 'its violence and its faltering retreat'.[49]

In his review for *The Scotsman*, the novelist Allan Massie (born 1938) is reserved in his praise when he states that *A Whistling Woman* does stand alone, 'if also sometimes puzzlingly and even infuriatingly'.[50] His assessment of the quartet as a whole is similarly ambivalent. While he finds the three earlier books are 'worth re-reading', he feels that the quartet as a whole is lacking in a sense of unity, at the level of both structure and theme.[51] Again, the charge of intellectualism is laid against Byatt. Massie claims that she is the type of novelist who crams her book with as much as possible and, while this is 'often exhilarating', he laments that the ideas are generally 'too divorced from the characters'.[52] However, he tempers this criticism in the case of *A Whistling Woman*, stating that the novel is not 'aridly intellectual' but rather 'an intellectual adventure, full of energy and vitality'.[53] Massie is similarly ambivalent in his concluding assessment of the novel. Were it not for Byatt's fame, he suggests, the novel might have been improved by the touch of a 'sharply critical editor'.[54] Yet he suggests that a similar claim could be made about *Middlemarch* and goes on to assert that Byatt is 'the George Eliot of our time'; praise indeed for a novelist who at times seems to be striving to recuperate the tradition of the Victorian novelists.[55]

Alice K. Turner's review for *The Washington Post* is unreserved in its praise for *A Whistling Woman*, and implicitly for the quartet as a whole, which she claims as 'important' within the context of postwar fiction.[56] She situates the last novel in relation to its immediate predecessor, *Babel Tower*, asserting that while it is 'much more playful' it remains 'just as complex'.[57] She acknowledges the 'mayhem' of the novel but, unlike MacFarlane, does not judge this as a negative quality in the book.[58] Rather, she affirms, the novel demonstrates 'how to use many voices and formal literary techniques to tell a rousing story'.[59] Similarly, while she recognizes the intellectual demands that the novel places on its reader, she claims that it never feels like work because Byatt combines her intellectual interests with both drama and description. Ultimately, she judges the final novel in the quartet more favourably than its predecessors; whereas she sees the three earlier novels as imitations of other writers, she views *A Whistling Woman* as 'triumphantly [Byatt's] own'.[60] Turner's assessment diverges from the general review response to *A Whistling Woman* which, as we have seen, usually viewed it as the least successful novel of the quartet. However, she implicitly indicates a break between *Still Life* and *Babel Tower*, a critical perspective which, as we shall see, comes to dominate accounts of the quartet as a whole.

Ruth Bernard Yeazell's review for the *London Review of Books* is an extensive treatment of both *A Whistling Woman* in its own right and also its place as the concluding novel of the quartet. Yeazell also points to the break in the quartet that occurred at the end of *Still Life*, although she sees it less as a stylistic shift and more as a shift in attention. She claims that from *Babel Tower* onwards, the quartet has come to focus much more on Frederica, making it seem like 'an extended Bildungsroman'.[61] Moving on to consider *A Whistling Woman* in its own right, Yeazell discusses its position as an historical fiction. While she claims that it is not overtly an historical novel, in the way that *Possession* and *Angels and Insects* are, *A Whistling Woman* recalls the approach of George Eliot's *Middlemarch*, which looks back on events 40 years previously. Yeazell claims that in *A Whistling Woman* Byatt uses this 'temporal gap' to 'vindicate a scepticism she presumably felt from the start'.[62] This comment highlights the discrepancy between the time the novel is set and the time it was published. Although this distance was present from the outset of the quartet, it has grown wider in the final instalment;

while the publication of the novels spans 24 years, the time-frame of the novels themselves only covers 17 years, excluding the 1980 prologue to *Still Life*. In Yeazell's review, the charge of intellectualism again resurfaces as she claims that the quartet 'occasionally suffer[s] from an overindulgence of [its] author's cognitive appetites'.[63] In light of this criticism, then, it is unsurprising that Yeazell judges *Still Life*, with its 'spare design', to be the best novel of the quartet.[64] Yeazell concludes that *A Whistling Woman*, and hence the quartet as a whole, ends on a 'surprisingly hopeful note'.[65] While Byatt is 'too modern a novelist' to solve the conflicts of the novel through a happy-ever-after marriage ending, Yeazell argues that, as in *Possession*, she offers a 'deliberately updated version of nineteenth-century romancing'.[66] Yeazell suggests that in its overt 'wish-fulfilment' the ending of the novel resolves all too easily the difficulties of being an intelligent woman in the 1950s and 1960s with which the entire quartet has been concerned.

Alex Clark's review for *The Guardian* opens by assessing *A Whistling Woman* in relation to the quartet it completes. She concludes that while as a novel it can stand alone, as an intellectual project it is best read in conjunction with the rest of the quartet since 'its most profound themes are continuously being developed and refined'.[67] Clark notes a 'palpable shift' between *Still Life* and *Babel Tower*; she claims that the death of Stephanie at the end of *Sill Life* was incorporated into the 'texture' of the quartet, which became in *Babel Tower* 'both frac-tured and self-consciously ludic'.[68] Clark acknowledges the diversity of concerns that had made up the first three books of the quartet but claims that these are extended even further in the last instalment. Clark lists the various areas of interest in *A Whistling Woman* but unlike many previous reviewers she finds them 'eloquently elaborated' and 'fired with genuine curiosity'.[69] She does recognize the limitations of this interest in intellectual life, however, asserting that the novel essentially presents us with Byatt's 'own fantasy of intellectual life'.[70] Yet Clark also identifies the vitality and energy of the novel, seeing it as 'saturated with sensual and physical detail'.[71] She concludes that, despite the fail-ings of the novel and the quartet, the 'massive ambition' of Byatt's pro-ject remains unquestionable.[72] Clark contends that while Byatt's aim in the quartet was to create 'fictional unity', ultimately she is as interested in the processes of disintegration as unification.[73] This conclusion is particularly interesting in light of *Babel Tower*'s concern with chaos and confusion that we encountered in the previous chapter.

In her review for *The Daily Telegraph*, Lisa Allardice suggests the quar-tet's project as an historical fiction has progressed from the 'family saga' of the first two novels into the 'portrait of an age' presented in the latter two novels.[74] This portrait is not particularly favourable though; indeed, Allardice claims that *A Whistling Woman* is critical of liberalism, both of the time it is set and the time it is written. Like MacFarlane, Allardice connects Byatt's project to the Victorian tradition of historical fiction, in particular George Eliot's *The Mill on the Floss*. She interprets Frederica as a 'modern Maggie Tulliver' and claims that the first two novels in the quartet incorporate 'partly autobiographical scenes of provincial life'.[75] Yet she identifies a shift in the approach between *Still Life* and *Babel Tower*; consequently, readers who want 'the quietly documented "felt life"' that had been presented in the first two novels will find *A Whistling Woman* a disappointment.[76] Despite this, she does redeem the novel from the typical criticism of Byatt's intellectualism, claiming that it also possesses a 'wisdom, humanity and humour that gives it life'.[77] In her final assessment, she judges the quartet to be a 'monumental chronicle' of the past but laments the fact that as the project has progressed the reader has become less and less important.[78]

D. J. Taylor's response to Byatt's intellectualizing differs from that of many reviewers we have encountered so far. He claims that her 'skill' as a novelist comes from her depiction of 'how her characters work, from the inside'.[79] Taylor presents a sensitive assessment of the individual novels in the quartet as well as its progression as a sequence. He, like many other reviewers, sees a split halfway through the quartet, indicated by the 'deliberate act of closure' brought about by Stephanie's death at the end of *Still Life*.[80] Taylor's view of the novels equally seems to be split at the same point; while he judges the first two novels positively, the last two are on the whole viewed negatively. Of *Virgin*, Taylor notes that Byatt's recurring concern with the opposition between mind and body, intellectual and domestic life, is apparent in the novel's structure, combining as it does 'a high-class family saga' with 'a kind of symbolist masque'.[81] Similarly, Byatt's style is praised in *Still Life*, which Taylor claims presents some of the best examples of Byatt's 'naturalistic writing'.[82] Moreover, contrary to the charge that Byatt prioritizes ideas over characters or action, Taylor argues that this second novel contains moments of 'sheer narrative excitement'.[83] With *Babel Tower*, however, Taylor notes a shift in style, indicating that the intellectual demands overtake the demands of storytelling as '[e]verything turns horribly metatextual'.[84] When he finally returns to *A Whistling Woman*, Taylor aligns it with *Babel Tower* suggesting that once again the ideas overwhelm the narrative. He claims that the characters are so '[w]eighed down with intellectual baggage' that the novel becomes merely a 'spectacle of...Byatt thinking'.[85]

SCIENCE AND NATURE

As we have seen, several reviewers have noted a shift between the second and third instalments of the quartet, a shift which could be understood to affect not just the style and tone of the novels but also their field of intellectual interests. In the first two novels, *Virgin* and *Still Life*, literature appears to be central with a focus on Frederica's and Stephanie's experiences as well as Alexander Wedderburn's plays. With *Babel Tower*, however, the scope broadens to incorporate more scientific pursuits, which are extended even further in the last novel *A Whistling Woman*. Obviously, this is a generalization since Marcus, whose interests are very definitely not verbally oriented, was a key figure from the outset of the quartet. There is a sense, however, in which the shift in emphasis changes midway through the quartet so that the focus turns from literature to science. Byatt herself confirms this view: 'if *Still Life* was concerned with the life of the body, *Babel Tower* was designed to look at the life of the mind, especially the nature of language'.[86]

Byatt examines the relationship between science and literature in the quartet in an article published in the scientific journal *Nature* (2005). She begins by discussing the impact of the context in which she was writing, specifically the 'two cultures' debate between F. R. Leavis and C. P. Snow (1905–80) that occurred in the late 1950s and early 1960s. F. R. Leavis favoured what Byatt calls a 'semi-religious attitude' towards literature, believing that it was central to a university education.[87] This semi-religious approach can be seen in the moral standards by which he judges literature in his famous work *The Great Tradition*. Interestingly, despite the fact that many critics identify a Leavisite approach in Byatt's work, she asserts that while at Cambridge she felt that literary creativity could only be possible if 'one had no such exclusive semi-religious attitude'.[88] Byatt's approach to the relationship between literature and science seems to be an attempt to bridge the divide that Snow lamented between the two cultures. So, despite a shift in focus, all four novels clearly incorporate a concern with both literature and science. Thus, *Still Life* is concerned both with the intellect, in its focus on the nature of perception, and in 'biological existence', as Byatt herself claims.[89] As in her fictions, the connections Byatt draws out in this essay depend on both scientific fields of enquiry and literature. Thus, she conceives of the mind–body split that the quartet addresses in terms of T. S. Eliot's theory of the 'dissociation of sensibility' that was discussed at length in Chapter 3. Byatt comments that this idea was foundational for the quartet, which she characterizes as 'about the body–mind problems of a young woman interested in her own sex-versus-intellect conflict'.[90]

In describing the way George Eliot incorporates science into *Middlemarch*, Byatt presents an interesting analogue to her own approach in the quartet, and especially in *A Whistling Woman*. Eliot does not simply refer to scientific advances but rather 'weaves them into the structure of the story, the thought and the metaphorical form of the novel'.[91] Indeed, Byatt conceives of metaphor itself in a very scientific manner; metaphor is exciting because of 'the double, connecting/ conflicting stimulation of a single synapse'.[92] As we have seen, critics and reviewers of the quartet have from the outset identified a concern with the nature of language and the relationship between language and reality. Although the increasing focus on scientific pursuits in the last two novels appears to move them away from the earlier novels' explicit engagement with verbal representation, Byatt's key concern is still underpinning these later novels. Byatt explains how the connections she drew between DNA and snails were based on the linguistic fact that the Latin term for snail is *Helix*. Moreover, she claims that the DNA code is a '"hard-wired" language, that was universally human'.[93] Her resistance to 'self-referring closed language-systems', such as structuralism and post-structuralism, further reveals her attempts to bridge the gap between language and reality, the mind and the body.[94] Although she is aware of and incorporates contemporary language theories into her novels, she retains a firm belief in the possibilities that language can communicate things about the world around us. This commitment to capturing the world is one of the reasons that Byatt is so interested in science and scientists. She claims that scientists hold an appeal for her since they 'do not spend their time deconstructing the world, or quibbling theologically about abstract terms of value'.[95] Byatt seems to be trying to replicate the scientist's approach in her quartet where, she claims, 'I tried to construct, with mnemonics, conscious patterns and colours and rhythms that represented this sense of form'.[96] As we saw in Chapter 4, this commitment to capturing the form of reality in fiction links Byatt to a Modernist project; indeed, she is often connected to the Modernist author D. H. Lawrence.

D. H. LAWRENCE

Peter Preston draws out these connections in his essay '"I am in a Novel": Lawrence in Recent British Fiction' (2003). Preston explores the presence of Lawrence in contemporary British fiction not in terms of influence but, as he puts it, '"Lawrence" as...a signifier'.[97] He argues that while in the novels of contemporary male authors, Lawrence is usually accorded no more attention than a passing reference, the work of contemporary female authors presents a 'more sustained engagement' with Lawrence's work and ideas.[98] He remarks that this situation is surprising given the feminist attack on Lawrence within critical thought and attempts to provide an explanation for this circumstance in his article. In order to explore how and why contemporary female authors incorporate Lawrence into their work, Preston examines *Regeneration* (1991) by Pat Barker (born 1943), *Zennor in Darkness* (1993) by Helen

Dunmore (born 1952) and Byatt's quartet, to which he devotes most space.

Preston claims that in Byatt's fiction Lawrence exists as a 'narrative antagonist, alternately admired and rejected'.[99] This view is reinforced by Byatt's own comments in the foreword to the 1991 reprint of her first novel, *The Shadow of the Sun*, where she positions Lawrence as someone she 'cannot escape and cannot love'.[100] Preston identifies Lawrence's presence in most of Byatt's novels, excluding her three neo-Victorian texts, although his analysis focuses on the quartet. Unfortunately, since *A Whistling Woman* had only recently been published when Preston's article appeared, it does not deal with the final volume in the quartet. Preston refers to Byatt's quartet as 'the Frederica Potter quartet', and focuses on Frederica's response to Lawrence, which Preston claims impacts upon her personal relationships and 'plays a crucial role in defining the scope of action open to her as an educated woman'.[101] Preston traces the alterations that occur in Frederica's response to Lawrence as the quartet progresses. In *Virgin*, Lawrence provides the 'focus of conflict' between Frederica and her father; while for Bill, 'Lawrence's work represents sane and liberating values', Frederica seems keen to resist these values.[102] This rejection of Lawrence's values and 'authority' is continued and developed through Frederica's Cambridge experiences in the second novel *Still Life*. Specifically, Preston connects *Still Life* to Lawrence's *Lady Chatterley's Lover* (1928), seeing Frederica's relationship with Nigel Reiver in terms of Lady Chatterley's relationship with Mellors. Preston argues that Frederica's relationship brings her close to Lady Chatterley's experience of 'florid spreading circles of satisfaction', which 'temporarily detaches her from her commitment to verbal articulation'.[103] For Frederica, this detachment from language is unsettling, not liberating as it is for Lady Chatterley. For Preston, Lawrence's fictions are preoccupied with 'the search for otherness in the pursuit of wholeness and the resulting conflict as the characters...struggle to achieve star equilibrium'.[104] As Preston indicates, these issues in Lawrence's fiction 'are of more than academic interest to Frederica' and, I would argue, to Byatt, as she explores their meaning for herself and for Stephanie.[105] In this respect, Preston is implicitly linking Byatt's concern with the mind–body conflict that faced many educated women in the 1950s and 1960s with her engagement with Lawrence's work.

It initially seems odd for Preston to combine Byatt's feminist concerns in the quartet with an author that many feminists criticize or reject. Yet, this returns us to the central issue of Preston's essay: why do contemporary women authors incorporate Lawrence into their fiction? Preston suggests that one of the reasons might be that Lawrence's 'dramas of change and self-discovery' often focus on female figures.[106] The other, more interesting answer that Preston proposes draws on Carol Siegel's argument in *Lawrence Among the Women* (1991). Siegel argues that Lawrence's writing was in part a response to the Victorian women writers that he read; it marked a deliberate attempt to 'reinterpret' those texts.[107] Drawing on Siegel's argument, Preston concludes that Lawrence 'acts as a bridge between Victorian and modern literature, who, by arousing such a strong reaction in many female readers and writers, enables them to connect more securely to the traditions in which they belong'.[108] This model provides a way to conceive of Byatt's relationship to Modernism, a relationship that is often overlooked in the focus on her position in relation to postmodernism and realism. Byatt's engagement with Victorian realism does not mark a nostalgic desire to return to the past, but rather is self-consciously aware of the distance between the Victorian and contemporary world, a distance that incorporates the Modernist period. Byatt would not object to being aligned with a tradition of Victorian fiction; indeed she often positions herself in relation to George Eliot. Yet given her resistance to being designated as a female novelist, she would probably reject the notion of such a female tradition to which women writers 'belong'. Byatt's work draws as much on the tradition of male authors as it does on female authors, even if, as is the case with Lawrence, she ultimately rejects that tradition. Preston concludes that it is Byatt's interest in language, the position of women and the nature of personal relationships that 'brings her inevitably to Lawrence, and just as inevitably to a rejection ... [of] his "myths of desire"' which are so problematic for women authors, readers and characters.[109]

OVERVIEWS OF THE QUARTET

Preston, like many other critics, refers to the quartet as the 'the Frederica Potter Quartet'. This label reveals an overall approach to the quartet; by highlighting the centrality of Frederica, critics who adopt this phrase imply that the series is best understood as a Bildungsroman, which traces Frederica's development. Thus, in her review of *Babel Tower* Ann Hulbert claimed that the first three novels of the quartet presented 'a portrait of the reader as a young woman'.[110] Although *A Whistling Woman* had not been completed at this point, Hulbert questions whether the final volume will complete the cycle by presenting 'a portrait of the artist'.[111] The fact that Frederica publishes her first novel in *A Whistling Woman* suggests that this supposed trajectory has been fulfilled. The phrase 'Frederica Quartet' also prioritizes the novels's concern with the position of the educated woman in the 1950s and 1960s. Indeed, it has encouraged some critics to read the quartet in an autobiographical light, seeing a connection between the heroine and her creator. Other critics, however, take a more expansive view of the quartet, seeing it as a family saga rather than a story about an individual. This view is indicated in the adoption of the title 'The Potter Quartet' to refer to the novels and relates to the assessments of the quartet as an historical project. Thus, Lisa Allardice's review of *A Whistling Woman* claims that the quartet widens out from being 'a family saga', becoming 'a portrait of an age'.[112]

As we have seen, many commentators locate a shift in the quartet between the second and third novels. As Allardice suggested, this shift is partly to do with content. Indeed, the death of Stephanie at the end of *Still Life* is felt by some reviewers to have prompted a narrowing of the quartet, with the remaining two novels increasingly concentrating on the life of Frederica. The quartet also experiences a stylistic shift; the realism of *Virgin* and *Still Life* is replaced by the more overtly postmodern techniques of *Babel Tower* and *A Whistling Woman*. Interestingly, Pilar Hidalgo claims that in Byatt's original conception of the quartet the second and third novels were to be experimental, while the first and fourth instalments were intended to be more traditional in form.[113] In her review for *The Washington Post*, Alice K. Turner highlights this shift from realism to postmodernism by drawing out the connections between each of the novels that comprise the quartet and other writers of Byatt's generation. She claims that *Virgin* is Byatt's 'Iris Murdoch effort' while *Still Life* is in the style of a Drabble novel, 'mostly domestic realism and Cambridge coming-of-age'.[114] As many other reviewers have done, Turner notes a shift in technique with the third novel, *Babel Tower*, which she claims is like a Doris Lessing novel. Finally, she views *A Whistling Woman* as coming out of the shadow of other writers, a 'terrific show-off whizz-bang' of Byatt's own style.[115] By identifying *A Whistling Woman* as the exemplar of Byatt's own style, Turner seems to be suggesting that she be understood more as a postmodernist, than a realist, writer, at least in the later phases of her career.

Byatt's reputation as a novelist rests on *Possession* and the achievement of the quartet. While attitudes towards the quartet have altered with each succeeding volume, with the later novels generally judged to be less successful than the earlier ones, reviewers remain almost unanimous in asserting the importance of Byatt's project. As we shall see in the next chapter, however, Byatt is also a prolific writer of short stories. Indeed, the short-story collections address many of the same thematic issues encountered in her novels, while managing to avoid the criticisms that are often levelled at Byatt's novelistic style.

CHAPTER NINE

Fiction-Making, Fairy-Tales and Feminism: Short Stories

In an interview with Jean-Louis Chevalier shortly after the publication of *The Matisse Stories* Byatt explained that one of the reasons she turned to the short-story form was to 'accommodate the strange'.[1] As we shall see, many of her short-story collections deal with fantastic events, such as the appearance of ghosts or a woman who turns to stone, and many adopt a fairytale structure. Thus, Byatt seems explicitly to distance her short stories from the realism that, for all the postmodern gesturing, remains fundamental to her novelistic style.

Byatt's first collection of short stories appeared in 1987, when she had already published four novels and was beginning to establish a name for herself as an important writer. After this, her output of short-story collections was fairly steady with four volumes appearing between 1993 and 2003. This chapter will examine each of these collections in chronological order. Criticism tends to focus on the three early volumes: *Sugar and Other Stories* (1987), *The Matisse Stories* (1993) and *The Djinn in the Nightingale's Eye* (1994). The discussion of these collections, then, will combine both review responses and critical analyses of the texts. The two later volumes, *Elementals: Stories of Fire and Ice* (1999) and *The Little Black Book of Stories* (2003), however, have received little critical attention to date and so discussion of these will be limited to review responses.

SUGAR AND OTHER STORIES (1987)

Reviews

In a review of new short-story collections for the *New Statesman*, Sabine Durrant marks Byatt's *Sugar and Other Stories* out as 'more personal' than the other collections.[2] Indeed, as we shall see, two of the stories, 'Sugar' and 'The July Ghost', are often read in explicitly autobiographical terms. Although Durrant's review is limited in scope, she does identify an important thematic preoccupation for Byatt when she states that the best stories in the collection are 'fascinating explorations into the process of creation'.[3] This focus on the story-telling aspect of the short stories is continued in critical accounts, not only of *Sugar* but also Byatt's later collections.

The Times Literary Supplement provided a more extensive review of *Sugar* in Anne Duchêne's article 'Ravening Time'. Duchêne, however, devotes much of her article to a discussion of Byatt's previous novels. Interestingly, Duchêne claims that several of the stories in the collection feel like 'reworkings of episodes from the novels'.[4] In contrast, she particularly praises 'Sugar' and 'Precipice-Encurled' as short stories that 'do not aspire to the condition of the novel'.[5] Of the style of 'Sugar', Duchêne comments that it presents 'brilliant, firm detail ... with an unwavering control'.[6] For Duchêne, these two stories encapsulate the recurring thematic concerns of Byatt's fiction: the role of the artist, the nature of story-telling, and a latent interest in women's issues through a consideration of the position of daughters. This implicit feminist concern is thought to be more prominent in the story 'In the Air', which Duchêne judges a 'quite flawless study in female panic'.[7] Unfortunately, Duchêne implicitly criticizes the story for adopting such a 'sadly familiar' theme.[8] The only other story Duchêne singles out for attention is 'The Dried Witch', which she claims is a 'rogue story' since it shows Byatt moving away from her typical fictional settings.[9] While Duchêne seems to praise Byatt's attempts to adopt a new approach, she ultimately feels that the story is hindered by its setting: 'the conscientious exoticism ... curiously diminishes the authorial presence'.[10] In her concluding remarks, Duchêne returns to Byatt's novelistic output and states her preference for the quartet. She expresses the desire that the 'rather uneven' stories collected in *Sugar* have not hindered the anticipated third volume of the quartet.[11] Interestingly, despite her avowed preference for the quartet, Duchêne mistakenly refers to the heroine of the series as Felicia.

Francis Spufford's review for the *London Review of Books* similarly identifies several of the stories as 'out-takes' from the quartet and, like Duchêne's review, devotes considerable space to a discussion of Byatt's novels, particularly the first two volumes of the quartet.[12] A key preoccupation Spufford identifies in the quartet is Byatt's eagerness to present descriptions of characters observing something. He claims that while these 'set-pieces' contribute to the novels' 'worrying stylisation', taken individually, they 'vindicate her largesse of language'.[13] It is this observation that finally leads Spufford on to a discussion of the new collection, *Sugar and Other Stories*, since he claims that these stories interrogate the act of perception. Spufford also implicitly connects *Sugar* to the quartet in his discussion of the contrasts between the past and the present within the short-story collection. For Spufford, while the stories are about loss, in various different guises, 'the tone is never apocalyptic'.[14] In contrast to responses to the novels, which often focus on the intellectual aspects of the texts, Spufford claims that the stories are more concerned with the characters and are 'elegantly and scrupulously attentive to their struggles'.[15] Interestingly, however, Spufford sees this sympathy with the characters' perceptions as a failing in the collection since he believes that 'loss viewed intimately' constrains the stories.[16]

As we have seen, the relationship of Byatt's fiction to postmodernism has often been discussed in responses to her novels. Spufford's article similarly identifies postmodern characteristics in *Sugar*, particularly in the 'hints of metatextuality' in 'Racine and the Tablecloth'.[17] However, he claims that while these aspects have the playful quality of postmodernism, they lack the postmodern questioning of the position of the author; *Sugar* continues the approach of the novels in its 'confidence...in what a writer can show'.[18] It diverges from the novels, however, in its 'strategically diminished confidence' in the ability of characters to know.[19]

Patricia Craig's review for *The Sunday Times* judges *Sugar* an 'outstanding' collection concerned primarily with 'craftsmanship [and] exactitude'.[20] Craftsmanship forges a connection between the present and the past, a connection that is further drawn out through the various generational relationships depicted in the stories. Craig claims that while many of the stories deal with death, this thematic concern does not overly affect the mood of the stories, which are 'predominantly energetic, enquiring and audacious'.[21] As with Spufford, Craig identifies the self-reflexive elements of some of the stories, but again implies that these are not part of a wider postmodern aesthetic. Rather than questioning the notion of narrative authority, she sees these authorial interjections as 'part of the author's distinctive, invigorating approach'.[22] Thus, instead of undermining the sense of an author behind the text, they actually serve to confirm it.

The review for *The Times*, by the novelist, poet and translator Elaine Feinstein (born 1930), similarly identifies an interest in the past as one of the central features of *Sugar*. Indeed, she claims that this concern links it to the novels, in which Byatt established her reputation for 'a sensitive recreation' of the past.[23] Feinstein connects this concern with the past to an implicit interest in the lives of women, commenting that several of the stories are concerned with the relationships between daughters and mothers. Unlike several of the reviewers who seem to prefer Byatt's novels, Feinstein asserts that the short-story form could be said to 'free' Byatt and that her attention to detail in the language she chooses is similar to 'the pleasure a poet takes in language'.[24]

Although it was her first collection of short stories, Byatt's reputation as a novelist ensured that *Sugar* received attention in the American as well as the British press. Lynne Sharon Schwartz's review for *The New York Times* locates the concerns of *Sugar* as essentially British: 'the struggle between passion and manners, need and propriety'.[25] Indeed, she links Byatt's writing to two great British novelists, George Eliot and E. M. Forster (and one American, Henry James), claiming that like them Byatt seeks to create a 'moral universe'.[26] Unlike those realist writers, however, Byatt combines an interest in the ordinary with a fascination with fantasy; hence the title of the review, 'At Home With the Supernatural'. This combination of the domestic, everyday world of the realist writer with the realm of the fantastical is reminiscent of the combination of realism and postmodernism that we have encountered in many discussions of Byatt's novels. Indeed, Schwartz hints at this combination when she describes the tone of the collection as that of 'a powerful late-Victorian intellect trained on 20th-century social and personal dilemmas'.[27]

Unusually, Schwartz singles out 'The Dried Witch' as the 'most forceful illustration' of the collection's key concerns, although 'The July Ghost' and 'Precipice-Encurled' are equally praised as successful stories.[28] Interestingly, unlike Duchêne, Schwartz claims that Byatt finds a freedom and range in her 'far-flung' stories that is not achievable in the stories that are confined to the realities of the present.[29] In contrast, 'Sugar', which is usually considered the best story in the collection, is deemed to be less successful. Schwartz claims that 'Sugar' fails to confront its subject directly and consequently appears passionless. Like reviewers of many of the novels before her, Schwartz points out Byatt's commitment to detail and exactitude. While she sees this as a positive aspect of Byatt's style in 'The Next Room', she finds that in 'Racine and the Tablecloth' it 'drain[s] away emotion'.[30]

Criticism

As I have said, Byatt's first collection of short stories is often read in autobiographical terms, in particular 'The July Ghost' and 'Sugar'. Telling the story of a mother's grief at the death of her son, 'The July Ghost' is often interpreted as a reflection of Byatt's own experiences of the death of her son in 1972. Claude Maisonnat's article, however, moves beyond a purely autobiographical approach to examine how the story represents the process of mourning and its connection to writing. Maisonnat argues that 'The July Ghost' is characterized by an ambiguity concerning the status of the ghost in the story, an ambiguity that is reinforced by the processes of doubling and repetition that abound in the narrative. Ambiguity is also inscribed into the figure of the lodger, the ostensible narrator for much of the story, who refuses to check the truth of events even when presented with the opportunity. Maisonnat argues that 'such narratorial unreliability casts doubt on the narrative itself'.[31] At the structural level there is also ambiguity; Maisonnat claims that the different narrative levels of the story are blurred so that it becomes difficult to establish a single perspective for the events. Moreover, in terms of time-frame, the events of the story take place over three successive Julys but these time-frames merge rendering them 'indistinct'.[32] Maisonnat connects this ambiguity to the quality of 'hesitation' that Tzvetan Todorov (born 1939) prioritizes in his definition of the fantastic text.[33] Todorov states that 'the purely fantastic text establishes absolute hesitation in protagonist and reader'.[34] Maisonnat judges 'The July Ghost' as a ghost story, although he claims that it adheres to Todorov's definition of the fantastic 'literally but with great subtlety'.[35] This subtlety is mostly conveyed through Byatt's decision to displace the encounter with the fantastic from the grieving mother to her lodger.

For Maisonnat, the key point of the story is that the work of mourning acts as a metaphor for the process of writing. The explicit connection between mourning and writing is signalled by Imogen's response to the news of her son's death, musing on the phrase 'is dead' to the point of obsession. The story concerns both Imogen's inability to come to terms with 'the work of mourning' and the effect that has on her writing process.[36] Maisonnat argues that the role of the anonymous narrator in the story is diminished in favour of the 'ghost-writer' who produces the text, who 'could even be the ghost of the narrator's former self'.[37] The technique of Free Indirect Discourse that Byatt adopts continues the ambiguity of the story since the narrator's indirect discourse is mixed with the language and point of view of the character, making it difficult to distinguish between them. In 'The July Ghost', this operates as the narrator's unconscious; it is able to 'bypass the censor and to say obliquely what cannot be admitted openly'.[38] Maisonnat claims that the use of Free Indirect Discourse allows Byatt to achieve 'the transformation of the imaginary ghost (the visual image of the son which Imogen so terribly longs to see) into a symbolic ghost (the verbal representation of the son through the symbolic code of language)'.[39] It is this transition from the imaginary to the symbolic that allows Imogen to complete the mourning process and grants the ghost the 'immortal status' of a fictional character.[40] This analysis implies that Byatt sees art as providing an adequate outlet for mourning, that in some way art has a restorative power in response to the suffering of the world. As we shall see, critics of *The Matisse Stories* and *The Djinn in the Nightingale's Eye* often reach a similar conclusion.

Charlotte Sturgess's article, 'Life Narratives in A. S. Byatt's *Sugar and Other Stories*', argues that the collection is ultimately about the possibilities and limitations of story-telling. As such, it is implicitly connected to the postmodern concerns we have seen in some of her novels; Sturgess claims that Byatt's fiction 'fabulat[es] our relationship to knowledge by questioning the premises of such knowledge'.[41] Sturgess hints at an autobiographical explanation for this concern with the limits of knowledge as she argues that 'the trauma of origins' in these stories could be a result of Byatt's wartime childhood experiences.[42] 'Sugar' and 'The Next Room' are interpreted as stories that are essentially concerned with the possibilities of finding a personal voice in among the 'tail-ends and unanswered questions of the family history'.[43] In the case of 'The Next Room', Sturgess seems to judge the story as postmodern in her conclusion that 'the ever-intrusive voices of absence challenge a central resolution and closure in the story'.[44] Yet she argues that while Byatt is aware of such theoretical discourses, her stories do not entirely succumb to them. Rather, there is an appeal to the more traditional aspects of story-telling in her collection.

It is interesting to note how Sturgess's account of 'Sugar' has been influenced by the neo-Victorian novels Byatt produced before the appearance of this article. Sturgess claims that in the title story, the 'shadowy outline of Victorian Britain' is discernible and that the family narratives with which the central character contends are grounded in a Victorian sense of 'hierarchy and codes of conduct'.[45] Moreover, she positions Byatt in relation to Victorian literary narratives when she remarks that the figure of the grandfather in 'Sugar' 'retreats into a static literary representation as a Dickensian character'.[46]

Jane Campbell's article in *Studies in Short Fiction* is unusual in focusing its attention on 'Precipice-Encurled'. Her analysis of this story, however, draws out the recurrent interests of Byatt's fiction in the relationship between art and life. Indeed, Campbell claims that the whole collection 'continues [Byatt's] exploration of the struggle of language with things'.[47] Campbell recognizes a positive side to the relationship between language and reality in Byatt's demonstration of 'the fertility of language'.[48] Despite this, she concludes that 'Precipice-Encurled' reveals the ultimate inability of art to capture reality. Campbell reads Joshua's death as a result of his attempt to represent 'the unmediated subject', an attempt to 'reach beyond language'.[49] Campbell implicitly links the story to the process of ventriloquism that was demonstrated in Byatt's subsequent novel, *Possession*. She points out that a reviewer of *Possession* praised 'Precipice-Encurled' for 'its achievement as historical fiction'.[50] Moreover, her assessment of the relationship between the present and the past in this story recalls the critical responses to *Possession*'s relationship to the past that we encountered in Chapter 5. Campbell asserts that 'Precipice-Encurled' 'both openly and covertly – and disturbingly – displays the predatory activity of the imagination as it raids other texts in its fruitless attempts to get to the "thing"'.[51] Here, the 'thing' is specifically the past and the relationship between the present and the past is seen to be a 'predatory' one, based on the type of acquisitiveness that the word 'possession' conjures up. Campbell sees the story as questioning the boundary between fact and fiction and so implicitly connects it to postmodernism. She claims that this 'daringly shows both the impossibility of originality and, conversely, the inevitability, in all writing, of invention and "confection"'.[52] Thus, Byatt's story is seen to reflect self-consciously on the limitations of fiction as well as to reveal implicitly the fictiveness of even historical accounts of the past.

THE MATISSE STORIES (1993)

Reviews

Published in 1993, Byatt's second collection of stories explicitly addresses her interest in the relationship between art and literature. Not only is the collection entitled *The Matisse Stories* but the cover portrays Matisse pictures and each of the three stories is prefaced with a line drawing by Matisse. As we saw in Chapter 3, reviewers and critics of *Still Life* often examined Byatt's incorporation of art into her fiction, and this impulse returns in responses to *The Matisse Stories*.

The review for *The Spectator*, by the novelist and art historian Anita Brookner (born 1928), claims that since these stories are designed for 'the casual reader' it would be 'unfair...to deconstruct' them.[53] This view draws on Matisse's famous observation that art, like a good armchair, should 'please and...be comfortable'.[54] Brookner contends that one of Matisse's greatest achievements was his ability to portray 'an alert but by no means overt sensuality' that resists the imposition of meaning, and is instead 'content to turn in on itself'.[55] By implication, Byatt's collection is judged to have the same aim in its focus on the nature of art and the position of the artist. Brookner's review does not really deal with the individual stories in detail, addressing the concerns of the collection as a whole instead. Yet we are given some relative assessments of the stories; 'The Chinese Lobster' is judged to be a story 'of surprising depth' whereas 'Art Work' is thought to 'succumb to the danger [of] chromatic overdrive'.[56] Brookner concludes that Byatt's writing possesses the '*gravitas* necessary for anyone who attempts to emulate paintings in words'.[57] As we shall see, the relationship between verbal and visual representation is a recurrent feature of critical discussions of this collection.

David Robson's review for *The Sunday Telegraph* explicitly signals this relationship as the central concern of the collection in his title,

'Painting in Prose'. He claims that the 'leisurely tempo' of the stories provides the opportunity for Byatt to demonstrate her 'formidable skills as a word-painter'.[58] He praises Byatt's ability to combine 'ornate' prose with a simplicity of style when needed.[59] Despite identifying art as the central focus of the book and indeed concentrating his discussion on Byatt's style, Robson concludes that ultimately both are less important than the characters, who are 'beautifully and precisely drawn'.[60] He claims that each of the three stories works as an individual piece as well as partaking of a wider unity of theme and style which results in 'a deeply harmonious product'.[61]

Alex Clark's review for *The Times Literary Supplement* identifies a concern with the 'indeterminate and ambiguous nature of representation' as the focal point of this collection.[62] She claims that 'Medusa's Ankles' 'wittily dissects' our notions of beauty both in consumer culture and in the world of art.[63] Byatt draws a parallel between the 'subtle interdependence' of Susannah and her hairdresser and the relationship between the artist and model.[64] 'Art Work' is judged as an example of 'the more consciously erudite mode' that has been alternately condemned and praised in reviews of Byatt's earlier fiction.[65] Although she refrains from overt judgement, Clark's criticisms of the conclusion reveal a negative view of Byatt's style. She states that the resolution derives from Byatt's experimental impulses and as such is 'less satisfying, the emotional release ... is too easy'.[66] Clark is more positive about 'The Chinese Lobster', which she sees as invested with 'wit and an emotional control derived from simplicity and understatement'.[67] As we shall see, Byatt's short stories are often praised for their restraint and control, in direct contrast to the expansiveness that is frequently identified as a negative feature in her novels. For Clark, however, it is not as simple as an opposition between the novel and the short-story forms. She feels that there are still points that feel like a deliberate 'display of writerly erudition' which create an 'oppressive sense' of the reader's inferiority.[68]

In contrast to these generally positive reviews, Geoff Dyer's review for *The Guardian* is almost entirely negative. His main criticism is underlined by serving as the caption to the photograph of Byatt that accompanies the review: 'frowning on snobbery from a vantage point of all-knowing sophistication'.[69] Whereas for Clark this was an occasional fault, for Dyer it is the defining feature of the collection, rendering the stories 'irksome'.[70] Like many other reviewers, Dyer points out the painterly elements of *The Matisse Stories*, focusing on its abundance of colour; yet he claims that it is 'ornamental rather than animate'.[71] Dyer implies that in the opposition between verbal and visual forms of representation explored in this collection, the verbal is found wanting. For him, Matisse's art fails to 'emerge powerfully' from the stories resulting in only a 'thin verbal reproduction'.[72]

The review for *The Independent*, by novelist and poet Michèle Roberts (born 1949), links the collection to Byatt's two previous publications, *Possession* and *Angels and Insects*, claiming that, despite its modern concerns, *The Matisse Stories* 'pay[s] homage' to the realism of the Victorians.[73] She goes on to connect this explicitly to the collection's concern with the relative merits of verbal and visual representation, claiming that these stories 'demand a trust in language'.[74] This idea that language can point to a reality in the world is figured in the 'litanies to colour' these stories incorporate.[75] Roberts's choice of the word 'litanies' reveals the reverential attitude towards language that is often identified as a key feature of Byatt's work. Roberts concludes that in this collection a concern with the relationship between art and the female body is 'struggling up through the shining colour-filled surface of the prose' but that 'it emerges too subtly'.[76] There is a suggestion, then, that Byatt's feminism is not explicit enough for Roberts. Moreover, once again Byatt's style is seen to be hindering the substance of her work. Indeed, 'The Chinese Lobster' is judged to be more a theoretical discussion concerning 'certain anxieties about feminist art practice and art history' than a story.[77]

Bruce Bawer's review for *The New York Times* explicitly positions the collection in relation to *Possession*, claiming that readers will recognize the concern with the role of art. Moreover, he argues that, like *Possession*, *The Matisse Stories* 'deftly juggles an impatience with feminist ideology and a sharp insight into female sensibilities'.[78] Bawer claims that the central tension in all three stories is the conflict between humanity and art and concludes that Byatt's stories ultimately privilege human concerns over art: 'in a world full of beauty and suffering, art matters enormously – but kindness may matter more'.[79]

Criticism

Sarah Fishwick's article on *The Matisse Stories* further explores its feminist concerns, using the position of Matisse in the stories to trace the connections between art, consumer culture and the female characters. Fishwick's article begins by identifying the central focus of the collection as the 'figure of the artist and the practice of artistic creation', linking it to previous Byatt texts, specifically *Still Life* and 'Precipice-Encurled'.[80] She argues that the creators in Byatt's stories should be more accurately seen as '"consumers" of art; protagonists for whom the *appropriation* and *modification* of key Matissean images and motifs play a central role in their artistic practice'.[81] By incorporating references to Matisse, Byatt is examining 'the human subject's interaction with space *through the medium of art*'.[82] Fishwick's discussion of the experience of space is grounded in the ideas of Jean Baudrillard (1929–2007), a theorist of late capitalism and postmodernism. Fishwick quotes at length from Baudrillard's *Le Système des objets* (1968), which argues that in contemporary culture 'the individual does not "consume" objects ... but "dominates, controls and orders them" '.[83] This process is central to the individual's engagement with his physical space as it 'invests material objects with symbolic value, "personalizing" his environment and generating "atmosphere" (*ambiance*)'.[84] Fishwick neatly links this theoretical proposition to the first story in Byatt's collection, 'Medusa's Ankles', through the character of Lucien. She claims that in the 'ironic twist' of Lucien's reaction to Susannah's rage, Byatt reveals the extent to which the individual's experience of space is determined by 'the fickle dictates of fashion mediated by the discourses of consumerism'.[85] Décor is not just used as a vehicle for criticizing consumer culture, however, but is also intimately related to the female protagonist in the story, acting as a 'barometer' for her mental state.[86] This implicitly connects the stories to a concern with the representation of the female body and the position of the middle-aged woman in a culture driven by youth and constant change.

Fishwick deals extensively with the nature of the incorporation of Matisse into Byatt's texts; she identifies both direct verbal references to Matisse and the use of his visual images in what is referred to as the 'peritextual field' around the text itself: the front and back covers have reproductions of Matisse paintings and his line drawings introduce each of the three stories. These 'artistic practices of borrowing and copying' are also reflected in the stories themselves, perhaps most explicitly in the last story, where an art student, Peggy Nollett, defaces Matisse's work as the practical submission for her art degree.[87] Fishwick claims that this prompts a broader consideration of ideas about 'artistic "originality" '.[88] In 'The Chinese Lobster' Byatt presents two different approaches to the process of creating art in the contrasting positions of Professor Diss and Peggy Nollett. While Diss's notion of artistic practice is based on 'respectful imitation and disciplined emulation', Nollett considers art as 'a medium for reworking and challenging artistic conventions and ideological positions'.[89] Interestingly, while both approaches are premised on the practices of '*assimilation* and *copying*' it is only Nollett's approach that Fishwick designates as 'a highly postmodern conception of the creative process'.[90] While Fishwick's discussion of this story seems to present it as a meditation on art, she also signals the importance of the human elements of the story. Although the story does not criticize either approach to art, it implicitly condemns Professor Diss's inability to recognize the pain of the human subject that Peggy Nollett expresses in her work. For Fishwick, this suffering is a response to the position of the female body in art. She claims that Byatt's story reveals 'the intensity of feminine bodily anxieties in the face of the rosy "wellbeing" signified

by many of Matisse's paintings'.[91] Although not explicitly p\
feminist analysis of the stories, Fishwick's discussion repeated\
the interconnections between Byatt's portrayal of art and the p
of women in contemporary culture. Fishwick claims that the fig\
Peggy Nollett disputes Matisse's notion that art should please an_ oe
comfortable. Yet, ultimately, she concludes that for Byatt 'art has the
power to assuage suffering', through its 'capacity to reassure *or* enrage
the human subject'.[92] The consoling power of art returns as an important
question in responses to Byatt's next short-story collection.

THE DJINN IN THE NIGHTINGALE'S EYE (1994)

Published in 1994, Byatt's third short-story collection, *The Djinn in the
Nightingale's Eye* brings together five fairy stories. Readers of Byatt's
novels, however, would have already encountered two of these stories
('The Glass Coffin' and 'Gode's Story') in *Possession: A Romance*. In her
interview with Chevalier, Byatt indicated that her approach to writing
these embedded stories differed from writing 'straight' short stories and
indeed that the experience of reading them differs since, in the case of
the embedded stories, 'it's always of course about a reading experience'.[93]
That is, these stories construct a situation in which both the writer and
the reader are engaged in the process of reading. In a similar instance
of the crossing of the boundaries between text and author, the 1995
edition of *Victorian Poetry* published a letter from Maud Michell-Bailey,
the twentieth-century heroine of *Possession*, which refers to Byatt's
Djinn as 'a self-referring fiction about the life and death of the (female)
body'.[94] Interestingly, whereas Byatt often distances her work from
overtly feminist concerns her fictional creation explicitly draws out
these issues as the central concern in the collection. Indeed, as we shall
see shortly, *Djinn* is most often analysed in terms of its engagement with
feminism.

Unsurprisingly, since it takes up over half of the collection, critical
responses usually focus on the title story 'The Djinn in the Nightingale's
Eye'. The protagonist, Gillian Perholt, is a narratologist who both
analyses story-telling and tells her own stories. Byatt's purpose in *Djinn*
is similar to Gillian's approach in that she is interested in both narrating stories and in critiquing and analysing the conventional forms of
fairytales. This dual impulse between narrative and analysis could be
framed in terms of an opposition between a realistic impulse, the desire
to narrate a story, and a postmodern impulse, the desire to deconstruct
and critique modes of story-telling. While most reviewers and critics agree that 'Djinn' is the best story in the collection, opinion of the
remaining four stories is, as we shall see, more divided.

Reviews

In her review for *Literary Review*, Sarah Smith judges the title story as 'marvellous', a 'showcase' for Byatt's expertise in story-telling.[95] Indeed, she claims that Byatt is 'at her most relaxed and least contrived' in this story, which she sees as at least partly a result of its modern setting.[96] Smith implicitly identifies Gillian with her author when she states that the problem Gillian faces is how to reconcile the fairytale element of stories with the realities of the modern world. For Smith, then, the title story, and indeed the collection as a whole, is ultimately a metafictional tale that explores the nature of stories. Indeed, Smith argues that Byatt uses the figure of the djinn to express her frustration at 'the bland fastidiousness' of contemporary fiction.[97] While Smith recognizes that some elements of the story conform to conventional fairytale expectations, she claims that in Byatt's story they 'are pleasurable and generous'.[98] She goes on to praise Byatt's style more generally claiming that its 'passionate exactitude' and 'emphatic descriptions' render even the most insignificant of the stories (she singles out the two from *Possession*) 'sharp and refreshing'.[99]

While Smith's review focuses on 'Djinn', it does provide brief assessments of the other stories in the collection. As I have already indicated, 'The Glass Coffin' and 'Gode's Story' are judged to be insubstantial stories redeemed only by Byatt's style. 'The Story of the Eldest Princess' is found to be 'original and essentially reassuring' while 'Dragon's Breath' aims at reassurance but is felt to be 'decidedly less successful'.[100] Smith usefully identifies the contexts in which these two stories were produced. 'The Story of the Eldest Princess' was apparently written to fulfil a request for a fairy story about Byatt's own life, while 'Dragon's Breath' was commissioned as part of a project in aid of Sarajevo. As we shall see, 'The Story of the Eldest Princess' is often understood in autobiographical terms, and indeed Smith points out that it addresses Byatt's anxieties about her relationships with her own sisters. The context of 'Dragon's Breath', however, prompts criticism from Smith who sees its message that stories can heal suffering as 'troubling, if not quite offensive' in the context of the Balkans.[101] For Smith, then, the disjunction between the traditional fairytale and the realities of the modern world is not sufficiently resolved in this story.

Jane Shilling's review for *The Sunday Telegraph* differs entirely from Smith's assessment of 'The Glass Coffin' and 'Gode's Story'. While they were a distraction in *Possession*, Shilling claims that in *Djinn* 'they shine with their proper lustre'.[102] Further, she declares 'Gode's Story' as 'the most technically perfect' of the collection.[103] Although Shilling sees 'Dragon's Breath' as 'clever, perceptive, compassionate and beautiful' she seems to concur with Smith in her ultimate conclusion that the story is 'too anxious to make things feel better'.[104] Shilling not only identifies autobiographical elements in 'The Story of the Eldest Princess' but also in the title story. Similarly, David Holloway's review for *The Daily Telegraph* rejected the possibility of viewing Gillian, the protagonist of the title story, as anything other than a reflection of Byatt herself.[105] Interestingly, while Holloway sees a parallel between protagonist and author in terms of their fascination with story-telling, Shilling's comments are more concerned with the physical reality of both Byatt and Gillian. She claims that 'Djinn' is essentially a story about a woman's experience of growing old. She concludes that the story, and by implication the collection as a whole, does not provide consolation but rather is 'merely a diversion ... from which we can learn, or not, as we please'.[106]

Francis Spufford's review for *The Guardian* claims that the collection works as a whole, in which the stories 'stir, then shake, then metamorphose' the expectations of fairytales.[107] Consequently, despite its initial accidental appearance, the collection is designed to present a 'deliberate succession'.[108] He claims that 'Dragon's Breath' works 'within a story's raw material' to examine the purpose of stories.[109] As in some of the other reviews, this story is judged to be less successful than the others are. Spufford claims that Byatt's refusal to name the lava as such, instead of a dragon, comes across as 'tenacious point-making' and so renders the story 'a little dry'.[110] It is fitting that the title story appears last since this is Byatt's most expansive exploration of the fairy story. Indeed, Spufford claims that here the strict formal qualities of the fairy story have been entirely rejected and in its place we encounter a narrative that is 'rich and fluid and risky'.[111] Spufford describes the style of 'Djinn' as 'positively grand' stating that it 'consciously dares charges of heaviness'.[112] As we have seen in the previous chapters, the charge of intellectualism has often been made against Byatt's fiction. For Spufford, though, Byatt's style is 'both insistently carnal and rigorous' in its treatment of ideas.[113] It is this combination of the physical and the intellectual that, for Spufford, brings Byatt's writing to life in this collection.

For Nancy Willard, in her review for *The New York Times*, Byatt's collection neatly marries the oral and written traditions of story-telling. Moreover, her stories blend the traditional fairytale style with contemporary issues, not escaping to the past but rather bringing the magic of the past into the present. Willard claims that the tales are true *wundermärchen*, 'unfettered tales of the marvelous [sic]'; she judges the title story 'a wonder indeed', which presents 'both the theoretical aspects of the fairy tale and the living truth of it'.[114] This assessment implicitly aligns the collection with the postmodern metafictional approach identified in much of Byatt's earlier fiction. Yet Willard claims that Byatt's stories are more than just a postmodern critique of the fairytale genre;

they are much more human in their focus on 'the lives of characters imprisoned by ... plot'.[115] In the case of the title story, the plot in which Gillian is imprisoned is that of the ageing woman in contemporary society. Willard praises Byatt's style, judging the lovemaking scene between the djinn and Gillian 'a gem of exuberant metaphor and linguistic restraint'.[116] This last comment is praise indeed since, as the earlier chapters of the Guide have shown, Byatt's fiction has often been criticized for its linguistic extravagance.

Criticism

As we have seen, reviewers of *Djinn* tended to focus on the title story, viewing it as more substantial than the others in terms of both length and content. This bias continues in critical examinations of the collection, which prioritize the title story over the other four stories.

Annegret Maack's article 'Wonder-Tales Hiding a Truth' (2001) links 'Djinn' to Byatt's earlier novel *Possession* in its concern with questions about the function of story-telling. Given these connections, it is interesting that Maack does not mention the incorporation of two stories from *Possession* into *Djinn*. Maack contends that story-telling is a form of desire, and as such is 'the only way to portray and explain the self'.[117] She argues that the multiple stories Gillian is involved with, as both listener and teller, teach her 'the potential for multiple metaphorical identities'.[118] Maack draws out the connection between wishing and the approach of death, which is significant since prior to her encounter with the djinn, Gillian is haunted by the prospect of her own fate. Maack claims that through telling stories Gillian has learnt that while fate cannot be avoided, stories can provide 'a means to master ... fate'.[119]

Maack argues that the title story is simultaneously a fairy story and 'a metafiction that comments on the rules it follows'.[120] This metafictional aspect would seem to link the story to the postmodern impulses in Byatt's oeuvre. Yet Maack insists that the most postmodern-seeming incident in the story, the conjuring of Boris Becker by the Djinn, is intended as 'proof of magic powers' rather than 'a postmodernist play on ontological levels of signification'.[121] The metafictional commentary on story-telling is most evident in the glass paperweights that Gillian collects. Maack reminds us of the story's description of the paperweights as both 'a medium for seeing and a thing seen'.[122] She takes the analysis a step further, however, identifying the importance of the particular paperweights the djinn gives to Gillian at the end of the tale. The snake and flower encased in the paperweights are understood as 'icons of the cyclic sequence of growth and decay, renewal and ending' and so point self-consciously to the story's refusal of a traditional 'happy-ever-after' ending.[123] Furthermore, Maack argues that in Byatt's system of allusions, the icons of glass, flower and snake represent 'the imagination and ... the activity of writing'.[124] Consequently, the story ends by self-reflexively prompting the reader to consider the nature of story-telling. Despite this, Maack concludes her essay by stressing again Byatt's distance from postmodernist notions about writing and language. She returns to a point made at the outset of the article in order to underline its import-ance for an understanding of Byatt's approach: 'The process of retelling and of reformation in language becomes the active process of cogni-tion that tends to make truth comprehensible for the teller and the listener.'[125] Implicitly, Maack aligns 'The Djinn in the Nightingale's Eye' with the realist project of using language to refer to a reality out-side the world of the story.

Jane Campbell's essay provides an explicitly feminist account of *The Djinn in the Nightingale's Eye*, arguing that the collection presents a feminist critique of the fairytale genre. The stories within the collection not only present 'the "hazards" of women's lives', as traditional fairytales do, but also the 'creative energies' of the female characters.[126] Campbell also hints at the ways in which Byatt's stories challenge the traditional narrative structure of the fairytale. She states that, in rejecting the 'happy-ever-after formula', Byatt pushes the fairy story 'closer to the novel'.[127] This challenging of the formal aspects of fairytales is significant for Campbell's feminist analysis since she believes Byatt's concern is primarily with the position of women in relation to narrative, as both subject and teller.

Campbell divides the collection into two sections, those stories that had appeared in *Possession* and those written for this collection, claiming that the new stories are more overtly 'deconstructing the fairytale'.[128] This sense of a deepening critical response to the fairytale as the collec-tion progresses is reminiscent of Spufford's claim that the order of the stories in the collection is deliberate. Campbell finds, however, that the two stories from *Possession* are reinvigorated by their new context. Of 'The Glass Coffin', she argues that whereas in *Possession* it was explicitly connected to the context of LaMotte's life and art, in *Djinn* its concerns extend to a more general exploration of 'the relationship between nar-rative and female power'.[129] Similarly, 'Gode's Story' takes on a broader significance in its new context; it moves from being a tale about the specific 'entrapment' experienced by women in Victorian Britain to being a general comment on 'the imprisonment of women by the code of chastity'.[130]

Of the original stories, Campbell devotes most attention to the title story. She does, however, tie the other two stories to the feminist pro-ject that she identifies in the collection as a whole. Campbell claims that 'The Story of the Eldest Princess' engages with the quest narratives that are typical of fairytales and questions the plots that are available to women. The eponymous heroine 'violates both the quest plot and the plot of romance – which, for women, usually form one plot'.[131] Instead, she recognizes that the object of the quest is 'narrative freedom' and that in order to achieve this you must reclaim narrative for your own purposes and become the teller of your own tale.[132]

This concern with telling your own tale is explicit in the title story, which Campbell sees as in one sense 'an essay in feminist narratology'.[133] Campbell judges 'Djinn' as the most revolutionary story in its questioning of the fairytale form. The protagonist has 'outlived' the traditional 'marriage plot' and is presented as a 'powerful interpreter of narrative' who is thus in control of creating her own plot.[134] Moreover, she and the djinn become 'cooperative narrators' thus 'obliterating the distinction between the one who wishes and the one who grants the wish'.[135] Furthermore, Campbell claims that 'Djinn' is the only story in the collection that presents a 'satisfying sexual relationship', yet she implicitly criticizes the fact that this can only be imagined with a magical male figure, rather than a human.[136] For Campbell, 'Djinn' is the climax of the collection since it most forcefully demonstrates the 'potential of the female imagination' that has been hinted at in the previous stories.[137] Indeed, the glass paperweights that are such an important metaphor for the creative process in this story also reveal the progression that has occurred between the first and last stories. The collection began with 'the old image of the woman unconscious, enclosed in glass' but by the end presents the image of 'the woman free, active, and an interpreter of glass'.[138] Implicitly, then, Campbell suggests that, in these stories, the female characters come to realize that to avoid entrapment in others' narratives they must understand the power of narratives and use it for their own ends. Campbell suggests that the stories in *Djinn* do not just open up possibilities for the female characters but also provide a space for the reader, in opposition to the 'closed structure and authoritative narration' of the traditional fairy story.[139] Interestingly, despite identifying the feminist concerns of the collection, Campbell concludes that Byatt is most interested in 'the telling itself'.[140] It is this concern with narrative that redeems the title story from the charge of intellectualism that is implicit in Campbell's designation of it as an essay.

ELEMENTALS: STORIES OF FIRE AND ICE (1999)

Reviews

The review for *Literary Review*, by the novelist Jane Gardam (born 1928), connects Byatt's fourth collection of short stories, *Elementals*, to the previous collection, *The Djinn in the Nightingale's Eye*, claiming that they share a thematic concern with 'the necessity of finding our natural element'.[141] More specifically she connects the Eldest Princess from *Djinn* to the heroines of *Elementals* since they 'are concerned with the breaking of patterns'.[142] Gardam briefly summarizes each of the six stories, concluding that while 'Crocodile Tears' is the 'most considerable story', they are all 'deliciously sensuous'.[143] She hints at criticism in her comment that there is 'a touch of the guide-book' in the exploration of Nîmes in 'Crocodile Tears' but excuses it on the grounds that 'it hardly matters, in stories of such benevolence and wisdom'.[144]

Katie Grant's review for *The Spectator* is similarly favourable; she compares the stories to a brooch which both functions as a 'workaday object' and is 'transform[ed] ... into something magical' by the precious stone.[145] This, she argues, is the approach of Byatt. Grant again singles out 'Crocodile Tears' for special attention, praising its skilful combination of the real and fantastical elements. Interestingly, she claims that it is the commitment to realistic detail about place and colour that renders the story 'as mysterious as a fable or a fairy story'.[146] While Grant recognizes that this approach of blending fact and fantasy is not new to the short stories she asserts that they 'seem more memorable' than the novels.[147] One of the distinctions between the two forms is the place of detail and knowledge. Grant claims that *Possession* and *Angels and Insects* 'are as much living encyclopaedias as novels' and that the display of knowledge often detracts from the novels themselves.[148] By contrast, in the short stories, the use of factual detail is perfectly combined with imagination to produce 'a rare balance'.[149] Here again, then, we encounter the view that Byatt's short stories manage to combine the best elements of her novels while avoiding the criticisms often levelled at her intellectual approach.

Alex Clark similarly highlights the benefits that the short-story form provides for Byatt's writing style, suggesting that the 'rigours and economy' of writing short fiction allows 'a paradoxical freedom'.[150] Clark believes that this freedom permits a mischievousness and naughtiness that is usually prevented by Byatt's intellectual style. Of 'Crocodile Tears', Clark asserts that while the resolution is 'logical and satisfactory' it is also 'ironic and wry'.[151] Yet she is not wholly favourable about the collection; indeed she claims that the stories do not represent Byatt's 'most ambitious or considered work'.[152] In particular, she judges the first three stories ('Crocodile Tears', 'Cold' and 'A Lamia in the Cévennes') more favourably than the later three. Her concluding remarks return to a typical criticism of Byatt's style in the suggestion that the stories 'often [rely] on a connoisseurship' which can seem to exclude the reader.[153] Once again, then, we have the charge of intellectual superiority. Yet Clark is keen to stress that she does not intend 'to criticise Byatt's erudition', rather to express a preference for the stories that most display her naughtiness.[154]

This naughtiness is implicitly identified in Erica Wagner's review for *The Times*. She argues that in contrast to the weighty *Babel Tower*, the 'delicate' volume of short stories offers 'lightness, an ability to play'.[155] While Wagner's overall assessment of the volume is positive she does hint at its weaknesses, claiming that the stories are 'beautiful, astonishing, complete and therefore a little isolated'.[156]

Lucy Hughes-Hallett's review for *The Sunday Times* identifies the 'cerebral' elements that have come to be seen as a trademark of Byatt's style, yet she claims that in this collection they are counteracted by a concern with 'the reader's sensual pleasure'.[157] Indeed, she argues that Byatt's writing is not dry but rather 'celebrates the pleasures of the intellect'.[158] Hughes-Hallett singles out 'Cold' as the central story of the collection, comparing it to a musical passage which introduces a theme that will then be subjected to multiple variations. She argues that while this story is conventional in its form, the other stories deconstruct various types of stories and reconstruct them to incorporate other narrative forms. The resulting stories are 'collages that tend to promote disenchantment ... with the practice of tale-telling'.[159] In identifying such a deconstructive impulse in Byatt's approach towards fairytales, Hughes-Hallett implicitly aligns these stories with postmodernism.

Katy Emck's review for *The Times Literary Supplement* identifies vision as a key concern in this collection; not only are the stories full of artists, but their work is 'so minutely described' that we feel we 'are standing before "the thing itself"'.[160] Although this concern with art has been a feature of many of Byatt's novels, Emck asserts that it is most effective in the 'more tightly focused' short stories.[161] She recognizes, however, that even then it is not always successful, claiming that some of the stories in *Elementals* are too concerned with ideas about art to 'deliver the consolations of fiction'.[162] In 'Cold', judged the best story in the collection, this preoccupation with artists is combined with Byatt's recurrent interest in the fairytale. Emck claims that despite its 'feminist, postmodernist knowingness', the story is ultimately 'a celebration of the power of love and art'.[163] In identifying such a commitment to language and art, Emck is implicitly aligning Byatt's stories with realism.

Fernanda Eberstadt's review for *The New York Times* similarly places Byatt within the realist tradition, alongside novelists for whom 'esthetics and moralism fuse'.[164] This approach, along with her interest in fairytales, connects Byatt to Victorian writers. Yet Eberstadt identifies a 'highly conscious duality' in Byatt's oeuvre, which seems to align her more with contemporary writers.[165] Eberstadt's review, like many we have already encountered, prioritizes the first three stories in the collection. In fact, she barely mentions the other half of the collection. Eberstadt praises Byatt's style as 'capacious yet exquisite', singling out the 'acid precision' of 'A Lamia''s opening, which is then quoted at length.[166] The last story is felt to contain the 'repeated message' of the volume as a whole, a message to do with art and its relationship to the world. Artists are implicitly privileged for being 'interested in the world and its multiplicity of forms and forces'.[167] Indeed, this would seem to be Byatt's own approach in the encyclopaedic range that is often noted in her works.

THE LITTLE BLACK BOOK OF STORIES (2003)

Reviews

A. S. Byatt's latest collection, *The Little Black Book of Stories*, is often seen as darker than the previous collections. Helen Dunmore's review for *The Times* claims that the stories 'go beyond melancholy into an altogether grimmer territory'.[168] Yet, there are still familiar elements; Dunmore notes that the stories contain 'very female monsters' and explore 'domestic terror'.[169] Moreover, the characters are again involved in art and Byatt seems to be suggesting the comforting function of art in providing 'some solace'.[170] Yet Dunmore claims that ultimately *Little Black Book* 'has nothing to do with easy balms'; the implication being that it is more concerned with a direct confrontation with reality.[171]

Stephen Abell's review for *The Spectator* similarly views this latest collection as marking a new direction for Byatt. He judges it as 'more edgily modern, more relevant' and so 'far more intriguing' than anticipated.[172] Although he identifies this as a departure from Byatt's previous interest in fairytales, he recognizes that these stories still seek 'to combine the mythic and the modern'.[173] Their commitment to the specific details of emotional and physical states, however, prevents them from becoming mere flights of fancy. This specificity of language is particularly evident in 'A Stone Woman', which Abell singles out for praise. He claims that Byatt's style in this story is 'dauntingly precise and realistic, even as it points to something unnatural and bizarre'.[174] Abell's closing remarks return to the more modern approach of the collection. In contrast to 'The Story of the Eldest Princess', which celebrated the pleasure of telling the story right, he finds *Little Black Book* 'more honestly dissatisfied, impurely accurate'.[175]

Samantha Matthews' review for *The Times Literary Supplement* ties the stories in *Little Black Book* to a concern with physicality in their 'awareness of mortality'.[176] Interestingly, she argues that the collection as a whole follows the pattern of a life. Again, 'A Stone Woman' is singled out for praise as the 'exhilarating centrepiece' of the volume.[177] However, she also finds time to assess two of the other stories. 'The Thing in the Forest' is implicitly characterized as a postmodern story;

Matthews claims that it 'wears its debt to fairytale self-consciously' and that the monster in the story is a postmodern one since it is made up of 'fragments held together by an act of the imagination'.[178] 'Raw Material', however, comes in for harsh criticism; it 'leaves a sour taste', possibly as a result of the self-congratulating ending.[179] As with many responses to the short-story collections, Matthews judges these stories in relation to Byatt's novelistic style. She asserts that while Byatt's novels have earnt her a reputation as an 'intellectual heavyweight', the short stories are 'quite as artful' as the novels, 'but less overtly clever'.[180] While Matthews identifies a few 'disconcerting moments' produced by, presumably, typographic errors, she ultimately overlooks such errors, judging the collection as whole to be a 'sophisticated and powerfully realized work'.[181]

As with Alex Clark's assessment of *Elementals*, Amanda Craig's review for *Literary Review* claims that the short-story form allows Byatt to indulge those elements that are excluded from her novels – 'humour, humility, concision and wit'.[182] It is perhaps for this reason that she predicts that the short stories, rather than the novels, 'are most likely to endure'.[183] 'The Thing in the Forest' is identified as a postmodern story, not only because of the Worm who is seen as 'the incarnation of postmodernism' but also in its self-conscious concern with story-telling, most evident in its 'circular narrative' structure.[184] Interestingly, Craig views 'A Stone Woman' as 'almost a parable' for Byatt's writing: 'It is ponderous to the extent of self-parody, linguistically intoxicated, absurd.'[185] Craig recognizes the combination of realism and the grotesque in the collection claiming that, far from disenchanting the fairytale, the inclusion of the real makes it 'more weird and more wonderful'.[186] Craig hints at a feminist concern in this collection when discussing 'Body Art'. She contends that Byatt's work has always considered two forms of female creation, childbirth and art, as 'intertwined' and that this is perhaps a 'uniquely female preoccupation'.[187]

The review for *The Guardian*, by novelist Ali Smith (born 1962), claims that Byatt's short fiction is characterized by 'a calmness in tone' which contrasts with the 'underlying sense of threatened explosion'.[188] While Smith does not deny these qualities in the novels she suggests they are more prominent in the short stories. For Smith, this latest collection is paradoxical; it not only transgresses the expectations of a Byatt collection, but is also both 'self-consciously dark' and 'surprisingly funny'.[189] Smith singles out 'Raw Material' as the 'funniest and by far the sneakiest' story in the collection, seeing in it a 'double-edged analysis of writing-as-therapy'.[190] Again, 'A Stone Woman' is highlighted as the most significant story in the collection, with Smith identifying it as the 'linchpin'.[191] Indeed, her overall assessment of the collection draws on language relevant to this story; it is 'tough and good, stony in all the best ways, vitally not nice'.[192]

Katie Owen's review for *The Sunday Telegraph* signals the collection's combination of the domestic and the grotesque, claiming that the scene in 'The Thing in the Forest' where the protagonists meet over jam and scones is 'a typical conjunction of the banal and the fantastical'.[193] Owen notes a recurrent 'moral vein' in the collection which is in part conveyed through the fact that the suffering of the stories is usually diffused by a 'hinted-at redemption'.[194] Owen sees the collection's ultimate appeal as lying in its combination of the fantastical with 'emotional truths and domestic realities'; and she claims it is Byatt's 'precise' style which renders the fantastical elements believable.[195]

The review for *The New York Times Book Review*, by novelist Claire Messud (born 1966), identifies the characteristic feature of Byatt's fiction as its intelligence, and sees *The Little Black Book of Stories* as displaying 'all the hallmarks' of Byatt's style.[196] Yet, recognizing that the intellectual aspects of Byatt's work might put off some readers, she is quick to note that the stories in the collection are 'thrilling Gothic tales' as well as 'meditations on art'.[197] Messud points out the dark elements of the collection in its focus on death and argues that, unlike children's stories which are designed to ease our fears, these 'revivify' them.[198] The other aspect of the stories, their position as meditations on art, connects them to the rest of Byatt's oeuvre; all of the stories are concerned with 'spiritual or artistic faith' and the possibility or impossibility of representing the world through art.[199] Messud claims that in 'Body Art' the 'grave and exhilarating fact' of a world beyond art is demonstrated through the birth at the end.[200] 'A Stone Woman' is singled out as being the most allusive of the stories in which all the literary references threaten to 'overburden' it, yet Messud believes this is avoided through Byatt's determination to provide 'a full accounting' of the protagonist's experience.[201] Similarly, Messud interprets 'Raw Material' as an examination of 'the tensions between unmediated and self-conscious fictional pleasures'; indeed, she suggests that the whole collection manages to satisfy both 'primitive readerly desires' and 'our reflective impulses'.[202] Once again, then, we encounter the view that Byatt's fiction manages to incorporate both realist and postmodernist impulses.

The five collections of short stories Byatt has published cover a vast area, not only in terms of the differing periods in which they were produced but also in terms of their approaches. The five fairy stories that comprise *The Djinn in the Nightingale's Eye* initially seem to have very little to do with the three contemporary pieces that make up *The Matisse Stories*. The concerns and issues drawn out in critical responses to these collections, however, connect the short stories to each other and to the rest of Byatt's oeuvre. As the reviews we have discussed show, the positioning of the stories in relation to postmodernism and realism is as problematic as with the novels. Yet, in terms of style, most commentators note a divergence between the Byatt of the novels and the Byatt of the short stories. As we have seen in the preceding chapters, Byatt's novels are often criticized for the density of their allusions and their intellectual leanings. In contrast, the charge of intellectualism is rarely made against the short stories; their style is felt to be more light-hearted and witty than anything found in the novels.

Conclusion

As we saw in the preceding chapter, Byatt's short-story collections have received less critical attention than her novels and are often judged to have a style that is distinct from the intellectualism found there. Despite this, the short stories share many of the interests and preoccupations that were identified in the novels. All the collections demonstrate Byatt's concern with art and the role of the artist. This is most obvious in *The Matisse Stories* but the other collections are also interested in the possibilities provided by art, both visual and verbal. The focus on the nature of story-telling has been identified as a primary concern in both *Sugar* and *Djinn* and is, for some critics, evidence of Byatt's postmodern leanings. Others, such as Maack, however, are keen to distance Byatt from postmodernism and implicitly identify her with the realist tradition of literature. As with the novels, then, Byatt's stories equally occupy an uneasy position in relation to postmodernism and realism. Byatt's work occupies a similarly uneasy position in relation to feminism; the short stories show a concern with feminist issues but, as with the novels, they never quite form a coherent feminist approach.

While these concerns clearly connect the short stories to Byatt's novels, her critical and popular reputation still largely depends on the novels. Although many of the same concerns recur throughout Byatt's novels, it is possible to identify three phases of Byatt's career. The first phase covers Byatt's early fiction, *The Shadow of the Sun*, *The Game* and, although slightly later, *Sugar and Other Stories*. Critical responses to these texts often adopt an autobiographical approach. The second phase comprises the quartet that began with *The Virgin in the Garden* and ended with *A Whistling Woman*. Since these novels span more than 20 years of Byatt's writing career it is not surprising that their approach is not wholly consistent. As we saw in Chapter 8, most critics identify a shift in style and tone between *Still Life* and *Babel Tower*. *Babel Tower* and *A Whistling Woman* are seen to be more postmodernist in their style and thus diverge from the realist project of the first two novels. The third phase of Byatt's career incorporates her most popular and successful work, *Possession*, and her subsequent neo-Victorian texts *Angels and Insects* and *The Biographer's Tale*. Critical accounts of these novels are preoccupied with Byatt's position in relation to Victorian and postmodern literature. Most conclude that these novels combine elements of both and so Byatt should be seen, in Levenson's words, as a 'post-modern Victorian'.[1] This debate over postmodernism and realism is a defining feature of responses to all of Byatt's fiction and will no doubt continue to dominate the critical field. Yet Byatt also establishes connections with other areas of literary tradition; this Guide has particularly drawn out Byatt's engagement with Romanticism and Modernism. These connections have been less fully explored in Byatt's work and so would provide interesting avenues for future criticism.

While many of Byatt's works have received considerable critical attention, ample scope for future research remains. The early novels and short stories have received comparatively little attention to date, yet, as we have seen, they engage with many of the key concerns of Byatt's oeuvre. Given the differences in style, a comparative analysis of Byatt's novelistic output and her short stories could prove particularly interesting.

Since Byatt's reputation primarily derives from the achievements of the quartet and *Possession*, however, critical interest in these projects will certainly continue. The quartet provides a particularly fertile area for extending current criticism, as there is yet to be a sustained analysis that deals with the project as a whole. A consideration of the quartet's relationship to historical fiction and the past it depicts would significantly extend the current critical field on Byatt's oeuvre. Moreover, while the first three novels (*Virgin*, *Still Life* and *Babel Tower*) have received a fair amount of critical attention in their own right, the most recent instalment, *A Whistling Woman*, is yet to prompt a similar critical response. The concerns with the relationship between science and literature and the position of educated women in the 1950s and 1960s will prove particularly fertile areas for analyses of this novel. Despite Byatt's protestations that she is not a feminist writer, feminist analyses of her work have become an important feature of the critical landscape on Byatt. It seems likely that such feminist analysis will continue and could be extended to incorporate her early novels and short stories.

Primarily a novelist of ideas, Byatt writes fictions that explicitly engage with a vast field of intellectual concerns. The current critical impulse to locate Byatt's fiction within its various intellectual climates, whether post-structuralist theory, feminism, the cultural context of 1950s and 1960s Britain, or the latest developments in science, will no doubt continue. Byatt's own critical writings self-consciously reflect upon the concerns and issues treated in her fictions and so criticism of her work must engage with the relationship between her critical and fictional writings.

As a literary critic and former academic, Byatt incorporates an awareness of contemporary critical theories, particularly post-structuralism and postmodernism, into many of her works. These theoretical positions, however, are not necessarily endorsed in Byatt's fictions and in many cases are explicitly criticized. While not wishing to diminish the postmodern elements of Byatt's work, I would suggest that, ultimately, she belongs more to the realist tradition of literature. Underlying all her fiction is a deep commitment to the possibility that language and art can represent the world, despite a surface postmodern scepticism. Byatt's work, then, seems to be characterized by a moralism that has its roots in the realist works of such authors as George Eliot and Iris Murdoch. It is this moral tone, which at times becomes overly didactic, that I would argue distinguishes Byatt's writing from the more playful productions of many of her postmodern contemporaries. Indeed, as we saw in Chapter 4, Byatt's commitment to art and truth has led to her being aligned more with the Modernist project, which 'for all its experiments, took life and art seriously', than with the playful vacuity of postmodernism.[2] Ultimately, Byatt's own designation of her style as 'self-conscious realism' seems to provide the most useful label for understanding the combination of Victorian, Modernist and postmodernist impulses in her fiction.[3]

Notes

INTRODUCTION

1. A. S. Byatt, 'Introduction', *Passions of the Mind: Selected Writings* (New York: Turtle Bay, 1992), p. xiv.
2. Biographical information on A. S. Byatt has been compiled from various sources: *The International WHO's WHO of Women*, Robert J. Elster (ed.), 5th edn (London and New York: Routledge, 2005), p. 121; Pilar Hidalgo 'Byatt, [Dame] A[ntonia] S[usan]', *The Continuum Encyclopaedia of British Literature* (New York and London: Continuum, 2003), pp. 148–9.
3. Richard Todd, *Consuming Fictions: The Booker Prize and Fiction in Britain Today* (London: Bloomsbury, 1996), p. 26; Laura Engel, 'A. S. Byatt (1936–)', in Carol Howard (ed.), *British Writers Supplement IV* (New York: Charles Scribner's Sons, 1997), p. 142.
4. Mervyn Rothstein, 'Best Seller Breaks Rules on Crossing the Atlantic', *The New York Times* (31 January 1991), p. C22.
5. Byatt (1992), p. xiii.
6. Byatt (1992), p. xiii.
7. Quoted in Mira Stout, 'What Possessed A. S. Byatt?', *The New York Times, Magazine* (26 May 1991), p. 14.
8. Susan Heller Anderson, 'Chronicle', *The New York Times* (17 October 1990), p. B5.
9. Quoted in Heller Anderson (1990), p. B5.
10. Quoted in Stout (1991), p. 14.
11. Quoted in John F. Baker, 'A. S. Byatt: Passions of the Mind, Interview', *Publisher's Weekly* 243.21 (20 May 1996), p. 236.
12. See Todd (1996).
13. Byatt (1992), p. xv.
14. Byatt (1992), p. xiv.
15. Byatt (1992), p. xiv.
16. Nicolas Tredell , 'A. S. Byatt', in *Conversations with Critics* (Manchester: Carcanet Press, 1994), p. 66.
17. A. S. Byatt, 'Foreword', *The Shadow of the Sun* (London: Vintage, 1991), p. xii.

CHAPTER ONE

1. A. S. Byatt, 'Foreword', *The Shadow of the Sun* (London: Vintage, 1991), pp. xiii–xiv.
2. Frederic Raphael, 'Girl in a Trap', Review of New Novels, *The Sunday Times, Weekly Review* (12 January 1964), p. 38.
3. Raphael (1964), p. 38.
4. Raphael (1964), p. 38.
5. Forsyth Hardy, 'Fiction', *The Scotsman Week-end Magazine* (18 January 1964), p. 2.
6. Hardy (1964), p. 2.
7. Julian Maynahan, 'Mrs Gaskell up to Date', *The Observer, Weekend Review* (12 January 1964), p. 25.

8. Maynahan (1964), p. 25.
9. 'Living with a Genius', *The Times Literary Supplement* (9 January 1964), p. 21.
10. 'Living with a Genius' (1964), p. 21.
11. 'Living with a Genius' (1964), p. 21.
12. 'Living with a Genius' (1964), p. 21.
13. 'Living with a Genius' (1964), p. 21.
14. 'New Novels', *The Times* (9 January 1964), p. 13.
15. Martin Levin, 'Reader's Report', *The New York Times* (2 August 1964), http://www.nytimes.com/books/99/06/13/specials/byatt-sun.html
16. Irving Wardle, 'Secrets of a Glass Menagerie', New Novels, *The Observer Review* (15 January 1967), p. 26.
17. Wardle (1967), p. 26.
18. Montague Haltrecht, 'Within the Space of the Evening', Fiction of the Week, *The Sunday Times, Weekly Review* (15 January 1967), p. 30.
19. Haltrecht (1967), p. 30.
20. 'New Fiction', *The Times* (12 January 1967), p. 14.
21. 'New Fiction' (1967), p. 14.
22. Robert Nye, 'Chips Off the Modern Block', Books of the Day, *The Guardian* (13 January 1967), p. 7.
23. Nye (1967), p. 7.
24. Nye (1967), p. 7.
25. 'Child's Play', *The Times Literary Supplement* (19 January 1967), p. 41.
26. 'Child's Play' (1967), p. 41.
27. 'Child's Play' (1967), p. 41.
28. 'Child's Play' (1967), p. 41.
29. 'Child's Play' (1967), p. 41.
30. Malcolm Bradbury, 'On from Murdoch', *Encounter* 31.1 (1968), p. 72.
31. Byatt (1991), p. xii.
32. Bradbury (1968), p. 73.
33. Bradbury (1968), p. 74.
34. Bradbury (1968), p. 73.
35. Joanne V. Creighton, 'Sisterly Symbiosis: Margaret Drabble's *The Waterfall* and A. S. Byatt's *The Game*', *Mosaic* 20 (1987), p. 15.
36. Sandra M. Gilbert and Susan Gubar, *The Madwoman in the Attic: The Woman Writer and the Nineteenth-Century Literary Imagination* (New Haven and London: Yale University Press, 1979), pp. 48–9.
37. Creighton (1987), p. 19.
38. Creighton (1987), p. 23.
39. Creighton (1987), p. 24.
40. Guiliana Giobbi, 'Sisters Beware of Sisters: Sisterhood As a Literary Motif in Jane Austen, A. S. Byatt and I. Bossi Fedrigotti', *Journal of European Studies* 22 (1992), p. 242.
41. Giobbi (1992), p. 244.
42. Giobbi (1992), p. 241.
43. Giobbi (1992), p. 247.
44. Giobbi (1992), p. 254.
45. Giobbi (1992), p. 256.
46. Byatt (1991), p. viii.
47. Byatt (1991), pp. x, xi.
48. Byatt (1991), p. xi.
49. Christien Franken, *A. S. Byatt: Art, Authorship, Creativity* (Hampshire: Palgrave, 2001), p. 34.

50. Kuno Schuhmann, 'In Search of Self and Self-Fulfilment: Themes and Strategies in A. S. Byatt's Early Novels', in Alexa Alfer and Michael J. Noble (eds), *Essays on the Fiction of A. S. Byatt: Imagining the Real* (Connecticut: Greenwood, 2001), p. 76.
51. Schuhmann (2001), p. 79.
52. Schuhmann (2001), p. 80.
53. Schuhmann (2001), p. 79.
54. Schuhmann (2001), p. 79.
55. Schuhmann (2001), p. 81.
56. Schuhmann (2001), p. 81.
57. Schuhmann (2001), p. 82.
58. Schuhmann (2001), p. 84.
59. Schuhmann (2001), p. 83.
60. Schuhmann (2001), p. 84.
61. Jane Campbell, 'The Hunger of the Imagination in A. S. Byatt's *The Game*', *Critique* 29 (1988), p. 150.
62. Campbell (1988), p. 149.
63. Campbell (1988), p. 150.
64. Campbell (1988), p. 156.
65. Campbell (1988), p. 147.
66. Campbell (1988), p. 160.
67. Campbell (1988), p. 161.
68. Kathleen Coyne Kelly, *A. S. Byatt* (New York: Twayne, 1996), p. 14.
69. Kelly (1996), p. 18.
70. Kelly (1996), p. 19.
71. Kelly (1996), p. 31.
72. Kelly (1996), p. 31.
73. Kelly (1996), p. 32.
74. Franken (2001), p. xii.
75. Franken (2001), p. 40.
76. Franken (2001), p. 40.
77. Franken (2001), p. 50.
78. Franken (2001), p. 53.
79. Franken (2001), p. 47.
80. Byatt (1991), p. xii.
81. Franken (2001), p. 48.
82. Franken (2001), p. 57.
83. Franken (2001), p. 57.
84. Franken (2001), p. 64.
85. Franken (2001), p. 65.
86. Franken (2001), p. 66.
87. Franken (2001), p. 68.
88. Franken (2001), p. 73.
89. Franken (2001), p. 80.
90. Franken (2001), p. xii.
91. Byatt (1991), p. x.
92. Franken (2001), p. 51.
93. Franken (2001), p. 111.
94. Franken (2001), p. 70.
95. Franken (2001), p. 73.
96. Franken (2001), p. 72.
97. Byatt (1991), p. xiv.

CHAPTER TWO

1. Michael Irwin, 'Growing Up in 1953', *The Times Literary Supplement* (3 November 1978), p. 1277.
2. Irwin (1978), p. 1277.
3. Irwin (1978), p. 1277.
4. Irwin (1978), p. 1277.
5. Irwin (1978), p. 1277.
6. Irwin (1978), p. 1277.
7. Rosemary Dinnage, 'England in the 50's', *The New York Times* (1 April 1979), http://www.nytimes.com/books/99/06/13/specials/byatt-virgin.html
8. Dinnage (1979).
9. Dinnage (1979).
10. Iris Murdoch, 'Force Fields', *New Statesman* (3 November 1978), p. 586.
11. Murdoch (1978), p. 586.
12. Murdoch (1978), p. 586.
13. Murdoch (1978), p. 586.
14. Anthony Thwaite, 'The New Elizabethans', *The Observer, Sunday Plus* (5 November 1978), p. 30.
15. Thwaite (1978), p. 30.
16. Robert Nye, 'Common Room & Kitchen', *The Guardian* (2 November 1978), p. 9.
17. Nye (1978), p. 9.
18. Nye (1978), p. 9.
19. Nye (1978), p. 9.
20. John Naughton, 'Leavisites in Yorkshire', *The Listener* (16 November 1978), pp. 658–9.
21. Naughton (1978), p. 658.
22. Naughton (1978), p. 658.
23. Naughton (1978), p. 659.
24. R. L. Widmann, 'Shades of Brit. Lit.', *The Washington Post* (16 March 1979), p. B2.
25. Widmann (1979), p. B2.
26. Widmann (1979), p. B2.
27. Widmann (1979), p. B2.
28. Widmann (1979), p. B2.
29. 'A. S. Byatt, Interviewed by Juliet A. Dusinberre', in *Women Writers Talking* (New York and London: Holmes and Meirer, 1983), p. 182.
30. 'A. S. Byatt, Interviewed by Juliet A. Dusinberre' (1983), p. 187.
31. 'A. S. Byatt, Interviewed by Juliet A. Dusinberre' (1983), p. 186.
32. 'A. S. Byatt, Interviewed by Juliet A. Dusinberre' (1983), p. 187.
33. 'A. S. Byatt, Interviewed by Juliet A. Dusinberre' (1983), p. 193.
34. 'A. S. Byatt, Interviewed by Juliet A. Dusinberre' (1983), p. 182.
35. 'A. S. Byatt, Interviewed by Juliet A. Dusinberre' (1983), p. 184.
36. 'A. S. Byatt, Interviewed by Juliet A. Dusinberre' (1983), p. 185.
37. Dinnage (1979).
38. D. J. Taylor, 'Reading the 1950s: A. S. Byatt's *The Virgin in the Garden* and *Still Life*', in *After the War: The Novel and England Since 1945* (London: Flamingo, 1994), p. 93.
39. Taylor (1994), p. 92.
40. Taylor (1994), p. 93.
41. Taylor (1994), p. 91.
42. Taylor (1994), p. 102.
43. Taylor (1994), p. 91.
44. Kathleen Coyne Kelly, *A. S. Byatt* (New York: Twayne, 1996), p. 74.

45. Kelly (1996), p. 66.
46. Kelly (1996), p. 67.
47. Kelly (1996), p. 66.
48. Kelly (1996), p. 75.
49. Alexa Alfer, 'Realism and Its Discontents: *The Virgin in the Garden* and *Still Life*', in Alexa Alfer and Michael J. Noble (eds), *Essays on the Fiction of A. S. Byatt: Imagining the Real* (Connecticut: Greenwood, 2001), p. 47.
50. Alfer (2001), p. 48.
51. Alfer (2001), p. 48.
52. Alfer (2001), p. 50.
53. Alfer (2001), p. 50.
54. Alfer (2001), p. 58.
55. Alfer (2001), p. 58.
56. Quoted in Elisabeth Anne Leonard, ' "The Burden of Intolerable Strangeness": Using C. S. Lewis to See beyond Realism in the Fiction of A. S. Byatt', *Extrapolation* 39 (1998), p. 236.
57. Leonard (1998), p. 236.
58. Leonard (1998), p. 239.
59. Leonard (1998), p. 241.
60. Leonard (1998), p. 241.
61. Leonard (1998), p. 242.
62. Leonard (1998), p. 242.
63. Leonard (1998), p. 242.
64. Leonard (1998), p. 245.
65. Leonard (1998), p. 246.
66. Leonard (1998), p. 243.
67. Leonard (1998), p. 247.
68. Leonard (1998), p. 247.
69. Juliet Dusinberre, 'Forms of Reality in A. S. Byatt's *The Virgin in the Garden*', *Critique* 24 (1982), p. 56.
70. Dusinberre (1982), p. 57.
71. Dusinberre (1982), p. 59.
72. Dusinberre (1982), p. 58.
73. Dusinberre (1982), p. 60.
74. Quoted in Dusinberre (1982), p. 61.
75. Dusinberre (1982), p. 61.
76. Dusinberre (1982), p. 57.
77. Kelly (1996), p. 63.
78. Judith Plotz, 'A Modern "Seer Blest": The Visionary Child in *The Virgin in the Garden*', in Alfer and Noble (2001), p. 31.
79. Plotz (2001), p. 32.
80. Plotz (2001), p. 34.
81. Plotz (2001), p. 33.
82. Plotz (2001), p. 34.
83. Plotz (2001), p. 35.
84. Plotz (2001), p. 36.
85. Plotz (2001), p. 36.
86. Plotz (2001), p. 39.
87. Plotz (2001), p. 39.
88. Plotz (2001), p. 43.
89. Plotz (2001), p. 43.
90. Plotz (2001), p. 43.

CHAPTER THREE

1. Patrick Parrinder, 'Thirty Years Ago', *London Review of Books* (18 July 1985), p. 17.
2. Parrinder (1985), p. 17.
3. Parrinder (1985), p. 17.
4. Parrinder (1985), p. 17.
5. Parrinder (1985), p. 17.
6. Lewis Jones, 'What's Wrong with Somerville?', *The Spectator* (20 July 1985), p. 31.
7. Jones (1985), p. 31.
8. Jones (1985), p. 31.
9. Jones (1985), p. 31.
10. Jones (1985), p. 31.
11. Roger Lewis, 'Larger Than Life', *New Statesman* (28 June 1985), p. 29.
12. Lewis (1985), p. 29.
13. Adam Mars-Jones, 'Doubts about the Monument', *The Times Literary Supplement* (28 June 1985), p. 720.
14. Mars-Jones (1985), p. 720.
15. Mars-Jones (1985), p. 720.
16. Mars-Jones (1985), p. 720.
17. Mars-Jones (1985), p. 720.
18. Mars-Jones (1985), p. 720.
19. James Fenton, 'The Tale of Two Sisters', *The Times* (27 June 1985), p. 11.
20. Fenton (1985), p. 11.
21. Fenton (1985), p. 11.
22. Fenton (1985), p. 11.
23. Fenton (1985), p. 11.
24. Peter Kemp, 'Still Life with Books', *The Sunday Times, Review* (30 June 1985), p. 45.
25. Kemp (1985), p. 45.
26. Kemp (1985), p. 45.
27. Paul West, 'Sensations of Being Alive', *The New York Times* (24 November 1985), http://www.nytimes.com/books/99/06/13/specials/byatt-still.html
28. West (1985).
29. West (1985).
30. West (1985).
31. Michael Westlake, 'The Hard Idea of Truth', *PN Review* 15.4 (1989), p. 37.
32. Westlake (1989), p. 33.
33. Westlake (1989), p. 33.
34. Westlake (1989), p. 33.
35. D. J. Taylor, 'Reading the 1950s: A. S. Byatt's *The Virgin in the Garden* and *Still Life*', in *After the War: The Novel and England Since 1945* (London: Flamingo, 1994), p. 90.
36. Michael Worton, 'Of Prisms and Prose: Reading Paintings in A. S. Byatt's Work', in Alexa Alfer and Michael J. Noble (eds), *Essays on the Fiction of A. S. Byatt: Imagining the Real* (Connecticut: Greenwood Press, 2001), p. 16.
37. Worton (2001), p. 16.
38. Worton (2001), p. 16.
39. Worton (2001), p. 17.
40. Worton (2001), pp. 17–18.
41. Worton (2001), p. 21.
42. Worton (2001), p. 23.
43. Worton (2001), p. 24.
44. Worton (2001), p. 28.

45. Sue Sorensen, 'Something of the Eternal: A. S. Byatt and Vincent van Gogh', *Mosaic* 37.1 (2004), p. 65.
46. Sorensen (2004), p. 66.
47. Sorensen (2004), p. 67.
48. Sorensen (2004), p. 75.
49. Sorensen (2004), p. 71.
50. Sorensen (2004), pp. 65, 68.
51. Sorensen (2004), p. 77.
52. Sorensen (2004), p. 65.
53. Sorensen (2004), p. 66.
54. Sorensen (2004), p. 69.
55. Sorensen (2004), p. 70.
56. Taylor (1994), p. 94.
57. Taylor (1994), p. 94.
58. Richard Todd, *A. S. Byatt* (Plymouth: Northcote House, 1997), p. 51.
59. Todd (1997), p. 51.
60. Todd (1997), p. 54.
61. Sue Sorensen, 'Death in the Fiction of A. S. Byatt', *Critique* 43 (2002), p. 115.
62. Sorensen (2002), p. 118.
63. Sorensen (2002), p. 119.
64. Sorensen (2002), p. 120.
65. Sorensen (2002), p. 117.
66. Sorensen (2002), p. 127.
67. Sorensen (2002), p. 127.
68. Sorensen (2002), p. 129.
69. Sorensen (2002), p. 132.
70. Sorensen (2002), p. 117.
71. Tess Cosslett, 'Childbirth from the Woman's Point of View in British Women's Fiction: Enid Bagnold's *The Squire* and A. S. Byatt's *Still Life*', *Tulsa Studies in Women's Literature* 8 (1989), p. 265.
72. Cosslett (1989), p. 277.
73. Cosslett (1989), p. 264.
74. Cosslett (1989), p. 276.
75. Cosslett (1989), p. 279.
76. William Wordsworth, 'Ode: Intimations of Immortality' (1807), l. 194, l. 196, in *The Norton Anthology of English Literature Vol 2*, M. H. Abrams (ed.), 7th edn. (New York and London: Norton, 2000), pp. 287–92.
77. Cosslett (1989), p. 268.
78. Cosslett (1989), p. 277.
79. Cosslett (1989), p. 280.
80. Cosslett (1989), p. 268.
81. Cosslett (1989), p. 268.
82. A. S. Byatt 'Still Life/Nature morte', *Passions of the Mind: Selected Writings* (New York: Turtle Bay, 1992), p. 3.
83. Byatt (1992), p. 5.
84. Byatt (1992), p. 5.
85. Byatt (1992), p. 5.
86. A. S. Byatt, 'Ancestors', *On Histories and Stories: Selected Essays* (London: Chatto & Windus, 2000), p. 79.
87. A. S. Byatt '"Sugar"/"Le Sucre"', *Passions of the Mind: Selected Writings* (New York: Turtle Bay, 1992), p. 17.
88. Byatt (1992), p. 8.

CHAPTER FOUR

1. Richard Todd, *A. S. Byatt* (Plymouth: Northcote House, 1997), p. 1.
2. Quoted in Mervyn Rothstein, 'Best Seller Breaks Rules on Crossing the Atlantic', *The New York Times* (31 January 1991), p. C22.
3. Peter Kemp, 'An Extravaganza of Victoriana', *The Sunday Times* (4 March 1990), p. H6.
4. Kemp (1990), p. H6.
5. Kemp (1990), p. H6.
6. Kemp (1990), p. H6.
7. Richard Jenkyns, 'Disinterring Buried Lives', *The Times Literary Supplement* (2–8 March 1990), p. 213.
8. Jenkyns (1990), p. 213.
9. Jenkyns (1990), p. 213.
10. Jenkyns (1990), p. 213.
11. Jenkyns (1990), p. 214.
12. Danny Karlin, 'Prolonging Her Absence', *London Review of Books* (8 March 1990), p. 17.
13. Karlin (1990), p. 17.
14. Karlin (1990), p. 17.
15. Karlin (1990), p. 18.
16. Karlin (1990), p. 18.
17. Christopher Lehmann-Haupt, 'Books of the Times: When There Was Such a Thing as Romantic Love', *The New York Times Book Review* (25 October 1990), p. C24.
18. Lehmann-Haupt (1990), p. C24.
19. Lehmann-Haupt (1990), p. C24.
20. Lehmann-Haupt (1990), p. C24.
21. Liz Heron, 'Fiction', *The Times Educational Supplement* (6 April 1990), p. 26.
22. Heron (1990), p. 26.
23. Heron (1990), p. 26.
24. Jay Parini, 'Unearthing the Secret Lover', *The New York Times Book Review* (21 October 1990), p. 11.
25. Parini (1990), p. 11.
26. Donna Rifkind, 'Victoria's Secret', *The New Criterion* 9.6 (February 1991), p. 78.
27. Rifkind (1991), p. 78.
28. Rifkind (1991), p. 79.
29. Rifkind (1991), p. 77.
30. Rifkind (1991), p. 80.
31. Jackie Buxton, ' "What's Love Got To Do With It?": Postmodernism and *Possession*', *English Studies in Canada* 22.2 (1996), pp. 199–200.
32. Buxton (1996), p. 206.
33. Linda Hutcheon, ' "The Pastime of Past Time": Fiction, History, Historical Metafiction', in Michael J. Hoffman and Patrick D. Murphy (eds), *Essentials of the Theory of Fiction* (London: Leicester University Press, 1996), p. 474.
34. Buxton (1996), p. 212.
35. Buxton (1996), p. 212.
36. Buxton (1996), p. 212.
37. Buxton (1996), p. 212.
38. Buxton (1996), p. 208.
39. Buxton (1996), p. 217.
40. Buxton (1996), p. 202.
41. Buxton (1996), p. 202.
42. Bo Lundén, *(Re)educating the Reader: Fictional Critiques of Poststructuralism in Banville's Dr Copernicus, Coetzee's Foe, and Byatt's Possession* (Göteborg, Sweden: Acta Universitatis Gothoburgensis, 1999), p. 91.

43. Lundén (1999), p. 130.
44. Lundén (1999), p. 2.
45. Lundén (1999), p. 93.
46. Lundén (1999), p. 130.
47. Lundén (1999), p. 94.
48. Lundén (1999), p. 94.
49. Chris Walsh, 'Postmodernist Readings: *Possession*', in David Alsop and Chris Walsh (eds), *The Practice of Reading: Interpreting the Novel* (London: Macmillan, 1999), p. 164.
50. Walsh (1999), p. 164.
51. Walsh (1999), p. 167.
52. Walsh (1999), p. 168.
53. Walsh (1999), p. 165.
54. Walsh (1999), p. 182.
55. Elisabeth Bronfen, 'Romancing Difference, Courting Coherence: A. S. Byatt's *Possession* as Postmodern Moral Fiction', in Rüdiger Ahrens and Laurenz Volkmann (eds), *Why Literature Matters: Theories and Functions of Literature* (Heidelberg: Carl Winter, 1996), p. 122.
56. Bronfen (1996), p. 120.
57. Bronfen (1996), p. 130.
58. Bronfen (1996), p. 126.
59. Susanne Becker, 'Postmodernism's Happy Ending: *Possession!*', in Beate Neumeier (ed.), *Engendering Realism and Postmodernism: Contemporary Women Writers in Britain* (Amsterdam and New York: Rodopi, 2001), p. 17.
60. Becker (2001), p. 17.
61. Becker (2001), p. 18.
62. Becker (2001), p. 18.
63. Becker (2001), p. 19.
64. Becker (2001), p. 20.
65. Becker (2001), p. 20.
66. Becker (2001), p. 20.
67. Becker (2001), p. 23.
68. Becker (2001), p. 23.
69. Becker (2001), p. 26.
70. Becker (2001), p. 25.
71. Becker (2001), p. 26.
72. Becker (2001), p. 30.
73. Becker (2001), p. 30.
74. Ann Hulbert, 'The Great Ventriloquist: A. S. Byatt's *Possession: A Romance*', in Robert E. Hosmer Jr (ed.), *Contemporary British Women Writers: Texts and Strategies* (London: Macmillan, 1993), p. 59.
75. Dana Shiller, 'The Redemptive Past in the Neo-Victorian Novel', *Studies in the Novel* 29 (1997), p. 547.
76. Shiller (1997), pp. 546–7.
77. Walsh (1999), p. 181.
78. Walsh (1999), p. 167.
79. Buxton (1996), p. 214.
80. Buxton (1996), p. 214.
81. Frederick M. Holmes, 'The Historical Imagination and the Victorian Past: A. S. Byatt's *Possession*', *English Studies in Canada* 20 (1994), p. 322.
82. Henry James, 'The Art of Fiction', in Roger Gard (ed. and intro.), *The Critical Muse: Selected Literary Criticism* (1884. London: Penguin, 1987), p. 190.
83. Frederick M. Holmes, *The Historical Imagination: Postmodernism and the Treatment of the Past in Contemporary British Fiction* (Victoria: University of Victoria Press, 1997), p. 21.

84. A. S. Byatt, 'Introduction', *Passions of the Mind: Selected Writings* (New York: Turtle Bay, 1992), p. xv.
85. Byatt (1992), p. xvi.
86. A. S. Byatt, 'People in Paper Houses: Attitudes to "Realism" and "Experiment" in English Post-war Fiction', *Passions of the Mind: Selected Writings* (New York: Turtle Bay, 1992), p. 155.
87. A. S. Byatt, 'Ancestors', *On Histories and Stories: Selected Essays* (London: Chatto & Windus, 2000), p. 79.
88. Byatt (1992), pp. 147–8.
89. Christien Franken, *A. S. Byatt: Art, Authorship, Creativity* (Hampshire: Palgrave, 2001), p. 83.
90. Franken (2001), p. 86.
91. Franken (2001), pp. 88–9.
92. Franken (2001), p. 92.
93. Franken (2001), p. 101.
94. Franken (2001), p. 94.
95. Franken (2001), p. 105.
96. Deborah Denenholz Morse, 'Crossing Boundaries: The Female Artist and the Sacred Word in A. S. Byatt's *Possession*', in Abby H. P. Werlock (ed.), *British Women Writing Fiction* (Tuscaloosa and London: University of Alabama Press, 2000), p. 150.
97. Denenholz Morse (2000), p. 158.
98. Denenholz Morse (2000), p. 155.

CHAPTER FIVE

1. D. J. Taylor, 'Reading the 1950s: A. S. Byatt's *The Virgin in the Garden* and *Still Life*, in *After the War: The Novel and England Since 1945* (London: Flamingo, 1994), p. 92.
2. Del Ivan Janik, 'No End of History: Evidence from the Contemporary English Novel', *Twentieth Century Literature* 41.2 (1995), p. 161.
3. Janik (1995), p. 161.
4. Janik (1995), p. 160.
5. Janik (1995), p. 161.
6. Janik (1995), p. 163.
7. Janik (1995), p. 161.
8. Janik (1995), p. 163.
9. Janik (1995), p. 162.
10. Janik (1995), p. 160.
11. Janik (1995), p. 164.
12. Janik (1995), p. 165.
13. Janik (1995), p. 162.
14. Frederick M. Holmes, *The Historical Imagination: Postmodernism and the Treatment of the Past in Contemporary British Fiction* (Victoria: University of Victoria Press, 1997), p. 11.
15. Holmes (1997), p. 11.
16. Holmes (1997), p. 12.
17. Holmes (1997), p. 11.
18. Holmes (1997), p. 13.
19. Holmes (1997), p. 86.
20. Holmes (1997), p. 86.
21. Holmes (1997), p. 34.
22. Holmes (1997), p. 86.
23. Holmes (1997), p. 48.
24. Holmes (1997), p. 49.

25. Holmes (1997), p. 24.
26. Holmes (1997), p. 51.
27. Holmes (1997), p. 52.
28. Holmes (1997), p. 52.
29. Jonathan Noakes, 'Interview with A. S. Byatt', in Jonathan Noakes, Margaret Reynolds with Gillian Alban (eds), *Possession: A Romance, Angels and Insects, A Whistling Woman* (London: Vintage, 2003), p. 27.
30. Noakes (2003), p. 27.
31. Dana Shiller, 'The Redemptive Past in the Neo-Victorian Novel', *Studies in the Novel* 29.4 (1997), p. 538.
32. Shiller (1997), p. 539.
33. Shiller (1997), p. 538.
34. Shiller (1997), p. 540.
35. Shiller (1997), p. 539.
36. Shiller (1997), p. 539.
37. Shiller (1997), p. 551.
38. Shiller (1997), p. 551.
39. Shiller (1997), p. 551.
40. Shiller (1997), p. 541.
41. Shiller (1997), p. 542.
42. Shiller (1997), p. 547.
43. Shiller (1997), p. 557.
44. Shiller (1997), p. 557.
45. Suzanne Keen, *Romances of the Archive in Contemporary British Fiction* (2001, Toronto and London: University of Toronto Press, 2003), p. 5.
46. Keen (2003), p. 14.
47. Keen (2003), p. 32.
48. Keen (2003), p. 33.
49. Keen (2003), p. 33.
50. Keen (2003), p. 33.
51. Keen (2003), p. 4.
52. Keen (2003), p. 34.
53. Keen (2003), p. 59.
54. Keen (2003), p. 61.
55. John J. Su, 'Fantasies of (Re)collection: Collecting and Imagination in A. S. Byatt's *Possession: A Romance*', *Contemporary Literature* XLV (2004), p. 684.
56. Su (2004), p. 685.
57. Su (2004), p. 685.
58. Su (2004), p. 686.
59. Su (2004), p. 687.
60. Su (2004), p. 687.
61. Su (2004), p. 688.
62. Su (2004), p. 691.
63. Su (2004), p. 693.
64. Su (2004), p. 700.
65. Su (2004), p. 700.
66. Su (2004), p. 704.
67. Noakes (2003), p. 17.
68. Louise Yelin, 'Cultural Cartography: A. S. Byatt's *Possession* and the Politics of Victorian Studies', *Victorian Newsletter* 81 (1992), p. 39.
69. Yelin (1992), p. 39.
70. Yelin (1992), p. 40.
71. Yelin (1992), p. 38.

72. Yelin (1992), p. 38.
73. Richard Todd, 'The Retrieval of Unheard Voices in British Postmodernist Fiction: A. S. Byatt and Marina Warner', in Theo D'haen and Hans Bertens (eds), *Liminal Postmodernisms: The Postmodern, the (Post-)Colonial, and the (Post-)Feminist* (Amsterdam: Rodopi, 1994), p. 104.
74. Todd (1994), p. 104.
75. Todd (1994), p. 104.
76. Todd (1994), p. 104.
77. Todd (1994), p. 106.
78. Todd (1994), p. 106.
79. Todd (1994), p. 107.
80. Sue Sorensen, 'Taking Possession: Neil LaBute Adapts a Postmodern Romance', *Literature/Film Quarterly* 32 (2004), p. 71.
81. Sorensen (2004), p. 71.
82. Sorensen (2004), p. 71.
83. Sorensen (2004), p. 71.
84. Sorensen (2004), p. 72.
85. Sorensen (2004), p. 74.
86. Sorensen (2004), p. 75.
87. Sorensen (2004), p. 75.
88. Sorensen (2004), p. 75.
89. Sorensen (2004), p. 75.
90. Sorensen (2004), p. 74.
91. Sorensen (2004), pp. 71–2.
92. Sorensen (2004), p. 72.
93. Sorensen (2004), p. 72.
94. Sorensen (2004), p. 72.
95. Sorensen (2004), p. 72.
96. Quoted in Sorensen (2004), p. 72.
97. Noakes (2003), pp. 13–14.
98. Sorensen (2004), p. 76.
99. Sorensen (2004), pp. 71, 72.
100. Sorensen (2004), p. 72.
101. Noakes (2003), p. 28.

CHAPTER SIX

1. Marilyn Butler, 'The Moth and the Medium', *The Times Literary Supplement* (16 October 1992), p. 22.
2. Butler (1992), p. 22.
3. Butler (1992), p. 22.
4. Butler (1992), p. 22.
5. Butler (1992), p. 22.
6. Butler (1992), p. 22.
7. Kathryn Hughes, 'Repossession', *New Statesman* (6 November 1992), p. 49.
8. Hughes (1992), p. 49.
9. Mary Hawthorne, 'Winged Victoriana', *The New Yorker* (21 June 1993), p. 98.
10. Hawthorne (1993), p. 100.
11. Hawthorne (1993), p. 99.
12. Hawthorne (1993), p. 99.
13. Hawthorne (1993), p. 99.
14. Victoria Glendinning, 'Angels and Ministers of Graciousness', *The Times, Saturday Review* (7 November 1992), p. 45.

15. Glendinning (1992), p. 45.
16. Glendinning (1992), p. 45.
17. Walter Kendrick, 'Fiction in Review', *Yale Review* 81.4 (1993), p. 135.
18. Kendrick (1993), p. 135.
19. Kendrick (1993), p. 135.
20. Kendrick (1993), p. 137.
21. John Barrell, 'When Will He Suspect?', *London Review of Books* (19 November 1992), p. 18.
22. Barrell (1992), p. 18.
23. Barrell (1992), p. 18.
24. Barrell (1992), p. 18.
25. Barrell (1992), p. 18.
26. Barrell (1992), p. 19.
27. Michael Levenson, 'The Religion of Fiction', *The New Republic* (2 August 1993), p. 41.
28. Levenson (1993), p. 41.
29. Levenson (1993), p. 41.
30. Levenson (1993), p. 42.
31. Levenson (1993), p. 43.
32. Levenson (1993), p. 43.
33. Sally Shuttleworth, 'Natural History: The Retro-Victorian Novel', in Elinor S. Shaffer (ed.), *The Third Culture: Literature and Science* (New York: Walter de Gruyter, 1998), p. 253.
34. Shuttleworth (1998), p. 253.
35. Shuttleworth (1998), p. 255.
36. Shuttleworth (1998), p. 255.
37. Shuttleworth (1998), p. 256.
38. Shuttleworth (1998), p. 257.
39. Shuttleworth (1998), p. 257.
40. Shuttleworth (1998), p. 258.
41. Shuttleworth (1998), p. 260.
42. Shuttleworth (1998), p. 257.
43. Shuttleworth (1998), p. 253.
44. Shuttleworth (1998), p. 253.
45. A. S. Byatt, *On Histories and Stories: Selected Essays* (London: Chatto & Windus, 2000), p. 79.
46. Shuttleworth (1998), p. 268.
47. Hilary M. Schor, 'Sorting, Morphing, and Mourning: A. S. Byatt Ghostwrites Victorian Fiction', in John Kucich and Dianne F. Sadoff (eds), *Victorian Afterlife: Postmodern Culture Rewrites the Nineteenth Century* (Minneapolis and London: University of Minnesota Press, 2000), p. 234.
48. Schor (2000), p. 235.
49. Schor (2000), p. 237.
50. Schor (2000), p. 235.
51. Schor (2000), p. 236.
52. Schor (2000), p. 237.
53. Schor (2000), p. 237.
54. Schor (2000), p. 244.
55. Schor (2000), p. 240.
56. Schor (2000), p. 240.
57. Schor (2000), p. 247.
58. Schor (2000), p. 237.
59. Susan Poznar, 'Tradition and "Experiment" in Byatt's "The Conjugial Angel"', *Critique* 45.2 (2004), p. 173.
60. Poznar (2004), p. 174.
61. Poznar (2004), p. 176.
62. Poznar (2004), p. 176.

63. Poznar (2004), p. 176.
64. Poznar (2004), p. 181.
65. Poznar (2004), p. 177.
66. Poznar (2004), p. 177.
67. Poznar (2004), p. 178.
68. Poznar (2004), p. 179.
69. Poznar (2004), p. 180.
70. Poznar (2004), p. 180.
71. Poznar (2004), p. 181.
72. Poznar (2004), p. 187.
73. A. S. Byatt, *Angels and Insects*, http://www.asbyatt.com/anglInsct.htm
74. Louisa A. Hadley, 'Spectres of the Past: A. S. Byatt's Victorian Ghost Stories', *Victorians Institute Journal* 31 (2003), p. 92.
75. Hadley (2003), p. 85.
76. Hadley (2003), p. 93.
77. Hadley (2003), p. 93.
78. Hadley (2003), p. 96.
79. Hadley (2003), p. 93.
80. Hadley (2003), p. 93.
81. Hadley (2003), p. 93.
82. Hadley (2003), pp. 93–4.
83. Hadley (2003), p. 97.
84. Hadley (2003), p. 97.
85. Ruth Franklin, 'Inauthentic Fabrics', *The New Republic* (23 April 2001), p. 39.
86. Franklin (2001), p. 37.
87. Franklin (2001), p. 37.
88. Franklin (2001), p. 38.
89. Franklin (2001), p. 38.
90. Franklin (2001), p. 39.
91. Ruth Scurr, 'Underlinings', *London Review of Books* (10 August 2000), p. 38.
92. Scurr (2000), p. 38.
93. Scurr (2000), p. 38.
94. Scurr (2000), p. 38.
95. Scurr (2000), p. 39.
96. Erin O'Connor, 'Book Forum: Reading *The Biographer's Tale*', *Victorian Studies* 44.2 (2002), p. 379.
97. O'Connor (2002), p. 380.
98. O'Connor (2002), p. 380.
99. O'Connor (2002), p. 381.
100. O'Connor (2002), p. 384.
101. Celia Wallhead, 'Metaphors for the Self in A. S. Byatt's *The Biographer's Tale*', *Language and Literature* 12 (2003), pp. 291–2.
102. Wallhead (2003), p. 293.
103. Wallhead (2003), p. 294.
104. Wallhead (2003), p. 294.
105. Wallhead (2003), p. 305.
106. Wallhead (2003), p. 305.

CHAPTER SEVEN

1. Lucy Hughes-Hallet, 'Swinging in the Sixties', *The Sunday Times, Books* (5 May 1996), p. 9.
2. Hughes-Hallet (1996), p. 9.

3. Hughes-Hallet (1996), p. 9.
4. Hughes-Hallet (1996), p. 9.
5. Tom Adair, 'Too Many Tongues Twist the Message', *The Scotsman, Spectrum* (19 May 1996), p. 11.
6. Adair (1996), p. 11.
7. Adair (1996), p. 11.
8. Adair (1996), p. 11.
9. Adair (1996), p. 11.
10. Miranda Seymour, 'An Idea Too Big for Its Plot', *The Financial Times: Weekend FT* (11 May 1996), p. xii.
11. Seymour (1996), p. xii.
12. Seymour (1996), p. xii.
13. D. J. Taylor, 'Reading the 1950s: A. S. Byatt's *The Virgin in the Garden* and *Still Life*', in *After the War: The Novel and England Since 1945* (London: Flamingo, 1994), p. 92.
14. D. J. Taylor, 'My Generation', *Guardian, The Friday Review* (10 May 1996), p. 11.
15. Taylor (1996), p. 11.
16. Taylor (1996), p. 11.
17. Philip Hensher, 'Her Shaping Spirit of Imagination', *The Spectator* (11 May 1996), p. 34.
18. Hensher (1996), p. 35.
19. Hensher (1996), p. 36.
20. Hensher (1996), p. 34.
21. Penelope Lively, 'Truth in Many Tongues', *The Times* (9 May 1996), p. 40.
22. Lively (1996), p. 40.
23. Lively (1996), p. 40.
24. Lively (1996), p. 40.
25. Lorna Sage, 'Frederica's Story', *The Times Literary Supplement* (10 May 1996), p. 24.
26. Sage (1996), p. 24.
27. Hugo Barnacle, 'Has A. S. Byatt Lost the Plot', *The Independent Weekend* (4 May 1996), p. 11.
28. Barnacle (1996), p. 11.
29. Barnacle (1996), p. 11.
30. Barnacle (1996), p. 11.
31. Barnacle (1996), p. 11.
32. Kate Kellaway, 'Tall Stories', *The Observer* (5 May 1996), p. 14.
33. Kellaway (1996), p. 14.
34. Kellaway (1996), p. 14.
35. Kellaway (1996), p. 14.
36. Ann Hulbert, 'Hungry for Books', *New York Times Book Review* (9 June 1996), p. 7.
37. Hulbert (1996), p. 7.
38. Hulbert (1996), p. 7.
39. Celia M. Wallhead, *The Old, The New, and the Metaphor: A Critical Study of the Novels of A. S. Byatt* (London: Minerva Press, 1999), p. xi.
40. Wallhead (1999), p. 145.
41. Wallhead (1999), p. 172.
42. Wallhead (1999), p. 172.
43. Wallhead (1999), p. 159.
44. Wallhead (1999), p. 159.
45. Wallhead (1999), p. xiii.
46. Wallhead (1999), p. 219.
47. Celia Wallhead, 'The Un-utopian Babelic Fallenness of Langage: A. S. Byatt's *Babel Tower*', in A. Gomis and M. Martinez (eds), *Dreams & Realities: Versions of Utopia in English Fiction from Dickens to Byatt*, (Almeria: University of Almeria Press, 1997), p. 133.

48. Wallhead (1997), p. 144.
49. Wallhead (1997), p. 134.
50. Wallhead (1997), p. 144.
51. Wallhead (1997), p. 144.
52. Wallhead (1997), p. 144.
53. Wallhead (1997), p. 133.
54. Wallhead (1997), p. 137.
55. Wallhead (1997), p. 137.
56. Wallhead (1997), p. 137.
57. Wallhead (1997), p. 138.
58. Wallhead (1997), p. 146.
59. Wallhead (1997), p. 146.
60. Wallhead (1997), p. 145.
61. Wallhead (1997), p. 146.
62. Wallhead (1997), p. 142.
63. Wallhead (1997), p. 143.
64. Wallhead (1997), p. 143.
65. Wallhead (1997), p. 143.
66. Wallhead (1997), p. 143.
67. Wallhead (1997), p. 133.
68. Wallhead (1997), p. 139.
69. Wallhead (1997), p. 138.
70. Wallhead (1997), p. 139.
71. Wallhead (1997), p. 148.
72. Wallhead (1997), p. 148.
73. Michael J. Noble, 'A Tower of Tongues: *Babel Tower* and the Art of Memory', in Alexa Alfer and Michael J. Noble (eds), *Essays on the Fiction of A. S. Byatt: Imagining the Real* (Connecticut: Greenwood, 2001), p. 61.
74. Noble (2001), p. 62.
75. Noble (2001), p. 62.
76. Noble (2001), p. 61.
77. Noble (2001), p. 63.
78. Noble (2001), p. 63.
79. Noble (2001), p. 65.
80. Noble (2001), p. 73.
81. Noble (2001), p. 66.
82. Noble (2001), p. 66.
83. Noble (2001), p. 69.

CHAPTER EIGHT

1. Steve Davies, 'Birds of Paradise', *The Independent Magazine* (7 September 2002), p. 24.
2. Davies (2002), p. 24.
3. Davies (2002), p. 24.
4. Davies (2002), p. 24.
5. Davies (2002), p. 24.
6. James Fenton, 'The Tale of Two Sisters', *The Times* (27 June 1985), p. 11.
7. Davies (2002), p. 24.
8. Davies (2002), p. 24.
9. Pamela Norris, 'Foxy Sexuality', *Literary Review* (September 2002), p. 51.
10. Norris (2002), p. 51.
11. Norris (2002), p. 51.
12. Norris (2002), p. 51.

13. Norris (2002), p. 51.
14. Jonathan Noakes, 'Interview with A. S. Byatt', in Jonathan Noakes, Margaret Reynolds with Gillian Alban (eds), *Possession: A Romance, Angels and Insects, A Whistling Woman* (London: Vintage, 2003), p. 32.
15. Noakes (2003), p. 32.
16. Robert MacFarlane, 'A Very Bad Case of Birds on the Brain', *The Observer Review* (15 September 2002), p. 17.
17. MacFarlane (2002), p. 17.
18. MacFarlane (2002), p. 17.
19. MacFarlane (2002), p. 17.
20. MacFarlane (2002), p. 17.
21. MacFarlane (2002), p. 17.
22. MacFarlane (2002), p. 17.
23. George Eliot, 'Silly Novels by Lady Novelists', in A. S. Byatt and Nicholas Warren (eds), *Selected Essays, Poems and Other Writings* (1856. Harmondsworth: Penguin, 1990), p. 140.
24. Lorraine Adams, 'Lady Novelist', *The New Republic* (17 November 2003), p. 38.
25. Adams (2003), p. 38.
26. Adams (2003), p. 38.
27. Adams (2003), p. 38.
28. Adams (2003), p. 38.
29. Adams (2003), p. 38.
30. Adams (2003), p. 38.
31. Amanda Craig, 'When Ideas Get in the Way of Fiction', *The Times, T2* (28 August 2002), p. 20.
32. Craig (2002), p. 20.
33. Craig (2002), p. 20.
34. Craig (2002), p. 20.
35. Craig (2002), p. 20.
36. Craig (2002), p. 20.
37. Craig (2002), p. 20.
38. Daphne Merkin, 'The Novel as Information Superhighway', *The New York Times* (19 January 2003), http://query.nytimes.com/gst/fullpage.html?res=9804E2DC113EF93A A25752C0A9659C8B63
39. Merkin (2003).
40. Merkin (2003).
41. Merkin (2003).
42. Merkin (2003).
43. Merkin (2003).
44. Ruth Scurr, 'The Winter of the Virgin Queen', *The Times Literary Supplement* (30 August 2002), p. 6.
45. Scurr (2002), p. 6.
46. Scurr (2002), p. 6.
47. Scurr (2002), p. 6.
48. Scurr (2002), p. 6.
49. Scurr (2002), p. 6.
50. Allan Massie, 'Satirical Swing through the Sixties with a Modern George Eliot', *The Scotsman, Weekend* (7 September 2002), p. 6.
51. Massie (2002), p. 6.
52. Massie (2002), p. 6.
53. Massie (2002), p. 6.
54. Massie (2002), p. 6.
55. Massie (2002), p. 6.

56. Alice K. Turner, 'Spreading Their Wings', *The Washington Post, Book World* (8 December 2002), p. 3.
57. Turner (2002), p. 3.
58. Turner (2002), p. 3.
59. Turner (2002), p. 3.
60. Turner (2002), p. 3.
61. Ruth Bernard Yeazell, 'Overindulgence', *London Review of Books* (28 November 2002), p. 19.
62. Yeazell (2002), p. 19.
63. Yeazell (2002), p. 20.
64. Yeazell (2002), p. 20.
65. Yeazell (2002), p. 21.
66. Yeazell (2002), p. 20.
67. Alex Clark, 'Trials by Fire', *The Guardian, Review* (7 September 2002), p. 28.
68. Clark (2002), p. 28.
69. Clark (2002), p. 29.
70. Clark (2002), p. 29.
71. Clark (2002), p. 29.
72. Clark (2002), p. 29.
73. Clark (2002), p. 29.
74. Lisa Allardice, 'So Much for Freedom', *The Daily Telegraph* (31 August 2002), p. A5.
75. Allardice (2002), p. A5.
76. Allardice (2002), p. A5.
77. Allardice (2002), p. A5.
78. Allardice (2002), p. A5.
79. D. J. Taylor, 'Farewell to the Virgin in the Garden', *New Statesman* (26 August 2002), p. 34.
80. Taylor (2002), p. 34.
81. Taylor (2002), p. 34.
82. Taylor (2002), p. 34.
83. Taylor (2002), p. 34.
84. Taylor (2002), p. 34.
85. Taylor (2002), p. 34.
86. A. S. Byatt, 'Fiction Informed by Science', *Nature 434* (17 March 2005), p. 295.
87. Byatt (2005), p. 294.
88. Byatt (2005), p. 294.
89. Byatt (2005), p. 294.
90. Byatt (2005), p. 294.
91. Byatt (2005), p. 294.
92. Byatt (2005), p. 296.
93. Byatt (2005), p. 295.
94. Byatt (2005), p. 295.
95. A. S. Byatt, 'Ancestors', *On Histories and Stories: Selected Essays* (London: Chatto & Windus, 2000), p. 79.
96. Byatt (2005), p. 294.
97. Peter Preston, '"I Am in a Novel": Lawrence in Recent British Fiction', in Keith Cushman and Earl G. Ingersoll (eds), *D. H. Lawrence: New Worlds* (London: Associated University Presses, 2003), p. 30.
98. Preston (2003), p. 31.
99. Preston (2003), p. 31.
100. A. S. Byatt, 'Foreword', *The Shadow of the Sun* (London: Vintage, 1991), p. xii.
101. Preston (2003), pp. 38–9.
102. Preston (2003), p. 39.

103. Preston (2003), p. 40.
104. Preston (2003), p. 40.
105. Preston (2003), p. 41.
106. Preston (2003), p. 43.
107. Quoted in Preston (2003), p. 43.
108. Preston (2003), p. 43.
109. Preston (2003), p. 44.
110. Ann Hulbert, 'Hungry for Books', *New York Times Book Review* (9 June 1996), p. 7.
111. Hulbert (1996), p. 7.
112. Allardice (2002), p. A5.
113. Pilar Hidalgo, 'Byatt, [Dame] A[ntonia] S[usan]', *The Continuum Encyclopaedia of British Literature* (New York and London: Continuum, 2003), p. 148.
114. Turner (2002), p. 3.
115. Turner (2002), p. 3.

CHAPTER NINE

1. Jean-Louis Chevalier, 'Entretien Avec A. S. Byatt', *Journal of the Short Story in English* 22 (1994), p. 13.
2. Sabine Durrant, 'Shavings and Splinters', 'Short Stories', *New Statesman* (15 May 1987), p. 30.
3. Durrant (1987), p. 30.
4. Anne Duchêne, 'Ravening Time', *The Times Literary Supplement* (10 April 1987), p. 395.
5. Duchêne (1987), p. 395.
6. Duchêne (1987), p. 395.
7. Duchêne (1987), p. 395.
8. Duchêne (1987), p. 395.
9. Duchêne (1987), p. 395.
10. Duchêne (1987), p. 395.
11. Duchêne (1987), p. 395.
12. Francis Spufford, 'The Mantle of Jehova', *London Review of Books* (25 June 1987), p. 22.
13. Spufford (1987), p. 22.
14. Spufford (1987), p. 23.
15. Spufford (1987), p. 23.
16. Spufford (1987), p. 23.
17. Spufford (1987), p. 23.
18. Spufford (1987), p. 23.
19. Spufford (1987), p. 23.
20. Patricia Craig, 'The Grace of Accuracy', *The Sunday Times, Review* (12 April 1987), p. 58.
21. Craig (1987), p. 58.
22. Craig (1987), p. 58.
23. Elaine Feinstein, 'Solace of Intellect', *The Times* (9 April 1987), p. 13.
24. Feinstein (1987), p. 13.
25. Lynne Sharon Schwartz, 'At Home with the Supernatural', *The New York Times Book Review* (19 July 1987), http://www.nytimes.com/books/99/06/13/specials/byatt-sugar.html
26. Schwartz (1987).
27. Schwartz (1987).
28. Schwartz (1987).
29. Schwartz (1987).
30. Schwartz (1987).

31. Claude Maisonnat, 'The Ghost Written and the Ghost Writer in A. S. Byatt's Story: "The July Ghost"', *Journal of the Short Story in English* 22 (1994), p. 53.
32. Maisonnat (1994), p. 54.
33. Maisonnat (1994), p. 50.
34. Quoted in Maisonnat (1994), p. 50.
35. Maisonnat (1994), p. 50.
36. Maisonnat (1994), p. 49.
37. Maisonnat (1994), p. 60.
38. Maisonnat (1994), p. 60.
39. Maisonnat (1994), p. 61.
40. Maisonnat (1994), p. 61.
41. Charlotte Sturgess, 'Life Narratives in A. S. Byatt's *Sugar and Other Stories*', *Journal of the Short Story in English* 22 (1994), p. 29.
42. Sturgess (1994), p. 32.
43. Sturgess (1994), p. 30.
44. Sturgess (1994), p. 34.
45. Sturgess (1994), p. 31.
46. Sturgess (1994), p. 32.
47. Jane Campbell, '"The Somehow May Be Thishow": Fact, Fiction, and Intertextuality in Antonia Byatt's "Precipice-Encurled"', *Studies in Short Fiction* 28 (1994), p. 115.
48. Campbell (1994), p. 121.
49. Campbell (1994), p. 122.
50. Campbell (1994), p. 117.
51. Campbell (1994), p. 121.
52. Campbell (1994), p. 117.
53. Anita Brookner, 'It's nicer, much nicer, than Nice', *The Spectator* (15 January 1994), p. 28.
54. A. S. Byatt, *The Matisse Stories* (1993. London: Vintage, 1994), p. 122.
55. Brookner (1994), p. 28.
56. Brookner (1994), p. 28.
57. Brookner (1994), p. 29.
58. David Robson, 'Painting in Prose', *The Sunday Telegraph, Books* (9 January 1994), p. 4.
59. Robson (1994), p. 4.
60. Robson (1994), p. 4.
61. Robson (1994), p. 4.
62. Alex Clark, 'Artist and Models', *The Times Literary Supplement* (14 January 1994), p. 21.
63. Clark (1994), p. 21.
64. Clark (1994), p. 21.
65. Clark (1994), p. 21.
66. Clark (1994), p. 21.
67. Clark (1994), p. 21.
68. Clark (1994), p. 21.
69. Geoff Dyer, 'Precious in the Pink', *The Guardian, G2* (11 January 1994), p. 7.
70. Dyer (1994), p. 7.
71. Dyer (1994), p. 7.
72. Dyer (1994), p. 7.
73. Michèle Roberts, 'Matisse: All the Nudes That's Fit to Print', *The Independent, Weekend* (22 January 1994), p. 30.
74. Roberts (1994), p. 30.
75. Roberts (1994), p. 30.
76. Roberts (1994), p. 30.
77. Roberts (1994), p. 30.

78. Bruce Bawer, 'What We Do for Art', *The New York Times Book Review* (30 April 1995), pp. 9–10, p. 9.
79. Bawer (1995), p. 10.
80. Sarah Fishwick, 'Encounters with Matisse: Space, Art, and Intertextuality in A. S. Byatt's *The Matisse Stories* and Marie Redonnet's *Villa Rosa*', *Modern Language Review* 99 (2004), p. 53.
81. Fishwick (2004), p. 53.
82. Fishwick (2004), p. 54.
83. Fishwick (2004), p. 56.
84. Fishwick (2004), p. 56.
85. Fishwick (2004), p. 56.
86. Fishwick (2004), p. 56.
87. Fishwick (2004), p. 54.
88. Fishwick (2004), p. 54.
89. Fishwick (2004), p. 60.
90. Fishwick (2004), pp. 59, 61.
91. Fishwick (2004), p. 62.
92. Fishwick (2004), p. 63.
93. Chevalier (1994), p. 20.
94. Maud Michell-Bailey, 'Letter to the Editor', *Victorian Poetry* 33 (1995), p. 2.
95. Sarah A. Smith, 'Unexpectedly Witty', *Literary Review* (January 1995), p. 9.
96. Smith (1995), p. 10.
97. Smith (1995), p. 9.
98. Smith (1995), p. 9.
99. Smith (1995), p. 10.
100. Smith (1995), p. 10.
101. Smith (1995), p. 10.
102. Jane Shilling, 'The Powerful Magic of the Fairy-Tale', *The Sunday Telegraph, Review* (15 January 1995), p. 10.
103. Shilling (1995), p. 10.
104. Shilling (1995), p. 10.
105. David Holloway, 'Princess and Boris Becker', *The Daily Telegraph, Arts & Books* (7 January 1995), p. 7.
106. Shilling (1995), p. 10.
107. Francis Spufford, 'A Djinn in the Tale', *The Guardian, G2* (17 January 1995), p. 9.
108. Spufford (1995), p. 9.
109. Spufford (1995), p. 9.
110. Spufford (1995), p. 9.
111. Spufford (1995), p. 9.
112. Spufford (1995), p. 9.
113. Spufford (1995), p. 9.
114. Nancy Willard, 'Dreams of Jinni', *The New York Times, Book Review* (9 November 1997), p. 38.
115. Willard (1997), p. 38.
116. Willard (1997), p. 38.
117. Annegret Maack, 'Wonder-Tales Hiding a Truth: Retelling Tales in "The Djinn in the Nightingale's Eye"', in Alexa Alfer and Michael J. Noble (eds), *Essays on the Fiction of A. S. Byatt: Imagining the Real* (Connecticut: Greenwood, 2001), p. 128.
118. Maack (2001), p. 126.
119. Maack (2001), p. 129.
120. Maack (2001), p. 128.
121. Maack (2001), p. 127.
122. Maack (2001), p. 129.

123. Maack (2001), p. 129.
124. Maack (2001), p. 130.
125. Maack (2001), p. 126.
126. Jane Campbell, '"Forever Possibilities and Impossibilities, Of Course": Women and Narrative in *The Djinn in the Nightingale's Eye*', in Alfer and Noble (2001), p. 135.
127. Campbell (2001), p. 135.
128. Campbell (2001), p. 136.
129. Campbell (2001), p. 136.
130. Campbell (2001), p. 136.
131. Campbell (2001), p. 137.
132. Campbell (2001), p. 137.
133. Campbell (2001), p. 139.
134. Campbell (2001), p. 140.
135. Campbell (2001), p. 143.
136. Campbell (2001), p. 145.
137. Campbell (2001), p. 145.
138. Campbell (2001), p. 144.
139. Campbell (2001), p. 144.
140. Campbell (2001), p. 145.
141. Jane Gardam, 'Women Breaking Out', *Literary Review* (November 1998), p. 49.
142. Gardam (1998), p. 49.
143. Gardam (1998), p. 49.
144. Gardam (1998), p. 49.
145. Katie Grant, 'Tricks of the Light', *The Spectator* (14 November 1998), p. 54.
146. Grant (1998), p. 54.
147. Grant (1998), p. 54.
148. Grant (1998), p. 54.
149. Grant (1998), p. 54.
150. Alex Clark, Review of *Elementals: Stories of Fire and Ice*, by A. S. Byatt, *The Guardian, Saturday Review* (5 December 1998), p. 10.
151. Clark (1998), p. 10.
152. Clark (1998), p. 10.
153. Clark (1998), p. 10.
154. Clark (1998), p. 10.
155. Erica Wagner, 'Size Doesn't Matter for Brief Inspiration', *The Times 2* (12 November 1998), p. 42.
156. Wagner (1998), p. 42.
157. Lucy Hughes-Hallett, 'Welcome to the Pleasure Zone', *The Sunday Times, Books* (8 November 1998), p. 13.
158. Hughes-Hallett (1998), p. 13.
159. Hughes-Hallett (1998), p. 13.
160. Katy Emck, 'The Consolations of a Kindly Genie', *The Times Literary Supplement* (13 November 1998), p. 25.
161. Emck (1998), p. 25.
162. Emck (1998), p. 25.
163. Emck (1998), p. 25.
164. Fernanda Eberstadt, 'Running Hot and Cold', *The New York Times* (13 June 1999), http://www.nytimes.com/books/99/06/13/reviews/990613.13eberst.html
165. Eberstadt (1999).
166. Eberstadt (1999).
167. Eberstadt (1999).
168. Helen Dunmore, 'I Am Woman, Hear Me Roar ...', *The Times, Weekend Review* (25 October 2003), p. 13.

169. Dunmore (2003), p. 13.
170. Dunmore (2003), p. 13.
171. Dunmore (2003), p. 13.
172. Stephen Abell, 'Making It a Just So Story', *The Spectator* (29 November 2003), p. 58.
173. Abell (2003), p. 58.
174. Abell (2003), p. 58.
175. Abell (2003), p. 58.
176. Samantha Matthews, 'Monsters, Trolls and Creative Writers', *The Times Literary Supplement* (31 October 2003), p. 21.
177. Matthews (2003), p. 21.
178. Matthews (2003), p. 21.
179. Matthews (2003), p. 22.
180. Matthews (2003), p. 21.
181. Matthews (2003), p. 22.
182. Amanda Craig, 'A Monumental Woman', *Literary Review* (December 2003/January 2004), p. 67.
183. Craig (2003/2004), p. 67.
184. Craig (2003/2004), p. 67.
185. Craig (2003/2004), p. 67.
186. Craig (2003/2004), p. 67.
187. Craig (2003/2004), p. 67.
188. Ali Smith, 'Her Dark Materials', *The Guardian, Review* (6 December 2003), p. 30.
189. Smith (2003), p. 30.
190. Smith (2003), p. 30.
191. Smith (2003), p. 30.
192. Smith (2003), p. 30.
193. Katie Owen, 'Jam, Scones and Horror', *The Sunday Telegraph, Review* (16 November 2003), p. 16.
194. Owen (2003), p. 16.
195. Owen (2003), p. 16.
196. Claire Messud, 'The Beast in the Jungle', *The New York Times Book Review* (9 May 2004), http://query.nytimes.com/gst/fullpage.html?res=9500E6DE173DF93AA3575 6C0A9629C8B63
197. Messud (2004).
198. Messud (2004).
199. Messud (2004).
200. Messud (2004).
201. Messud (2004).
202. Messud (2004).

CONCLUSION

1. Michael Levenson, 'The Religion of Fiction', *The New Republic* (2 August 1993), p.41.
2. Sue Sorensen, 'Taking Possession: Neil LaBute Adapts a Postmodern Romance', *Literature/Film Quarterly* 32 (2004), p. 72.
3. A. S. Byatt, 'Introduction', *Passions of the Mind: Selected Writings* (New York: Turtle Bay, 1992), p. xv.

Bibliography

BIOGRAPHICAL SOURCES

Elster, Robert J. ed. *The International WHO's WHO of Women*, 5th edn (London and New York: Routledge, 2005).

Engel, Laura. 'A. S. Byatt (1936–)', in Carol Howard (ed.), *British Writers Supplement IV* (New York: Charles Scribner's Sons, 1997), pp. 139–56.

Hidalgo, Pilar. 'Byatt, [Dame] A[ntonia] S[usan]', *The Continuum Encyclopaedia of British Literature* (New York and London: Continuum, 2003), pp. 148–9.

BYATT BOOKS

Byatt, A. S. 'Foreword', *The Shadow of the Sun* (London: Vintage, 1991), pp. viii–xvi.

Byatt, A. S. 'Still Life/Nature morte', *Passions of the Mind: Selected Writings* (New York: Turtle Bay, 1992), pp. 3–13.

Byatt, A. S. '"Sugar"/"Le Sucre"', *Passions of the Mind: Selected Writings* (New York: Turtle Bay, 1992), pp. 14–18.

Byatt, A. S. 'Introduction', *Passions of the Mind: Selected Writings* (New York: Turtle Bay, 1992), pp. xiii–xvii.

Byatt, A. S. 'People in Paper Houses: Attitudes to "Realism" and "Experiment" in English Post-war Fiction', *Passions of the Mind: Selected Writings* (New York: Turtle Bay, 1992), pp. 147–68.

Byatt, A. S. *The Matisse Stories* (1993. London: Vintage, 1994).

Byatt, A. S. *On Histories and Stories: Selected Essays* (London: Chatto & Windus, 2000).

Byatt, A. S. *Angels and Insects*, http://www.asbyatt.com/anglInsct.htm

Byatt, A. S. 'Fiction Informed by Science', *Nature* 434 (17 March 2005), pp. 294–7.

Michell-Bailey, Maud. 'Letter to the Editor', *Victorian Poetry* 33 (1995), pp. 1–3.

BYATT INTERVIEWS

'A. S. Byatt, Interviewed by Juliet A. Dusinberre', *Women Writers Talking*, ed., Janet Todd (New York and London: Holmes's and Meirer, 1983), pp. 181–95.

Baker, John F. 'A. S. Byatt: Passions of the Mind, Interview', *Publisher's Weekly* 243.21 (20 May 1996), pp. 235–6.

Chevalier, Jean-Louis. 'Entretien Avec A. S. Byatt', *Journal of the Short Story in English* 22 (1994), pp. 11–27.

Noakes, Jonathan. 'Interview with A. S. Byatt', *Possession: A Romance, Angels and Insects, A Whistling Woman*, eds, Jonathan Noakes, Margaret Reynolds with Gillian Alban (London: Vintage, 2003), pp. 11–32.

Tredell , Nicolas. 'A. S. Byatt', *Conversations with Critics* (Manchester: Carcanet Press, 1994), pp. 58–74.

REVIEWS

THE SHADOW OF THE SUN (1964)

Anon. 'New Novels', *The Times* (9 January 1964), p. 13.
Anon. [Marigold Johnson], 'Living with a Genius', *The Times Literary Supplement* (9 January 1964), p. 21.
Hardy, Forsyth. 'Fiction', *The Scotsman Week-end Magazine* (18 January 1964), p. 2.
Levin, Martin. 'Reader's Report', *The New York Times* (2 August 1964), http://www.nytimes.com/books/99/06/13/specials/byatt-sun.html
Maynahan, Julian. 'Mrs Gaskell Up To Date'. Rev. of New Fiction, *The Observer: Weekend Review* (12 January 1964), p. 25.
Raphael, Frederic. 'Girl in a Trap', Rev. of New Novels, *The Sunday Times: Weekly Review* (12 January 1964), p. 38.

THE GAME (1967)

Anon. 'New Fiction', *The Times* (12 January 1967), p. 14.
Anon. [Mary-Kay Wilmers], 'Child's Play', *The Times Literary Supplement* (19 January 1967), p. 41.
Bradbury, Malcolm. 'On from Murdoch', *Encounter* 31.1 (July 1968), pp. 72–4.
Haltrecht, Montague. 'Within the Space of the Evening', Fiction of the Week, *The Sunday Times: Weekly Review* (15 January 1967), p. 30.
Nye, Robert. 'Chips Off the Modern Block', Books of the Day, *The Guardian* (13 January 1967), p. 7.
Wardle, Irving. 'Secrets of a Glass Menagerie', New Novels, *The Observer Review* (15 January 1967), p. 26.

THE VIRGIN IN THE GARDEN (1978)

Dinnage, Rosemary. 'England in the 50's', *The New York Times* (1 April 1979), http://www.nytimes.com/books/99/06/13/specials/byatt-virgin.html
Irwin, Michael. 'Growing Up in 1953', *The Times Literary Supplement* (3 November 1978), p. 1277.
Murdoch, Iris. 'Force Fields', *New Statesman* (3 November 1978), p. 586.
Naughton, John. 'Leavisites in Yorkshire', *The Listener* (16 Novemebr 1978), pp. 658–9.
Nye, Robert. 'Common Room & Kitchen', *The Guardian* (2 November 1978), p. 9.
Thwaite, Anthony 'The New Elizabethans', *The Observer, Sunday Plus* (5 November 1978), p. 30.
Widmann, R. L. 'Shades of Brit Lit', *The Washington Post* (16 March 1979), p. B2.

STILL LIFE (1985)

Fenton, James. 'The Tale of Two Sisters', *The Times* (27 June 1985), p. 11.
Jones, Lewis. 'What's Wrong with Somerville?', *The Spectator* (20 July 1985), p. 31.
Kemp, Peter. 'Still Life with Books', *The Sunday Times, Review* (30 June 1985), p. 45.
Lewis, Roger. 'Larger Than Life', *New Statesman* (28 June 1985), p. 29.
Mars-Jones, Adam. 'Doubts about the Monument', *The Times Literary Supplement* (28 June 1985), p. 720.

Parrinder, Patrick. 'Thirty Years Ago', *London Review of Books* (18 July 1985), p. 17.
Sage, Lorna. 'How We Live Now', *The Observer, Review* (23 June 1985), p. 22.
West, Paul. 'Sensations of Being Alive', *The New York Times* (24 November 1985), http://www.nytimes.com/books/99/06/13/specials/byatt-still.html
Westlake, Michael. 'The Hard Idea of Truth', *PN Review* 15.4 (1989), pp. 33–7.

SUGAR AND OTHER STORIES (1987)

Craig, Patricia. 'The Grace of Accuracy', *The Sunday Times Review* (12 April 1987), p. 58.
Duchêne, Anne. 'Ravening Time', *The Times Literary Supplement* (10 April 1987), p. 395.
Durrant, Sabine. 'Shavings and Splinters', 'Short Stories', *New Statesman* (15 May 1987), pp. 29–30.
Feinstein, Elaine. 'Solace of Intellect', *The Times* (9 April 1987), p. 13.
Schwartz, Lynne Sharon. 'At Home with the Supernatural', *The New York Times Book Review* (19 July 1987), http://www.nytimes.com/books/99/06/13/specials/byatt-sugar.html
Spufford, Francis. 'The Mantle of Jehova', *London Review of Books* (25 June 1987), pp. 22–3.

POSSESSION: A ROMANCE (1990)

Heller Anderson, Susan. 'Chronicle', *The New York Times* (17 October 1990), p. B5.
Heron, Liz. 'Fiction', *The Times Educational Supplement* (6 April 1990), p. 26.
Jenkyns, Richard. 'Disinterring Buried Lives', *The Times Literary Supplement* (2–8 March 1990), pp. 213–14.
Karlin, Danny. 'Prolonging Her Absence', *London Review of Books* (8 March 1990), pp. 17–18.
Kemp, Peter. 'An Extravaganza of Victoriana', *The Sunday Times* (4 March 1990), p. H6.
Lehmann-Haupt, Christopher. 'Books of The Times: When There Was Such a Thing as Romantic Love', *The New York Times Book Review*, (25 October 1990), p. C24.
Parini, Jay. 'Unearthing the Secret Lover', *The New York Times Book Review* (21 October 1990), p. 91.
Rifkind, Donna. 'Victoria's Secret', *The New Criterion* 9.6 (February 1991), pp. 77–80.
Rothstein, Mervyn. 'Best Seller Breaks Rules on Crossing the Atlantic', *The New York Times* (31 January 1991), pp. C17+.
Stout, Mira. 'What Possessed A. S. Byatt?', *The New York Times, Magazine* (26 May 1991), pp. 121.

ANGELS AND INSECTS (1992)

Barrell, John. 'When Will He Suspect?', *London Review of Books* (19 November 1992), pp. 18–19.
Butler, Marilyn. 'The Moth and the Medium', *The Times Literary Supplement* (16 October 1992), p. 22.
Glendinning, Victoria. 'Angels and Ministers of Graciousness', *The Times, Saturday Review* (7 November 1992), p. 45.
Hawthorne, Mary. 'Winged Victoriana', *The New Yorker* (21 June 1993), pp. 98–100.
Hughes, Kathryn. 'Repossession', *New Statesman* (6 November 1992), pp. 49–50.
Kendrick, Walter. 'Fiction in Review', *Yale Review* 81.4 (1993), pp. 135–7.
Levenson, Michael. 'The Religion of Fiction', *The New Republic* (2 August 1993), pp. 41–4.

THE MATISSE STORIES (1993)

Bawer, Bruce. 'What We Do for Art', *The New York Times Book Review* (30 April 1995), pp. 9–10.

Brookner, Anita. 'It's nicer, much nicer, than Nice', *The Spectator* (15 January 1994), pp. 28–9.

Clark, Alex. 'Artist and Models', *The Times Literary Supplement* (14 January 1994), p. 21.

Dyer, Geoff. 'Precious in the Pink', *The Guardian*, G2 (11 January 1994), p. 7.

Roberts, Michèle. 'Matisse: All the Nudes That's Fit to Print', *The Independent, Weekend* (22 January 1994), p. 30.

Robson, David. 'Painting in Prose', *The Sunday Telegraph*, Books (9 January 1994), p. 4.

THE DJINN IN THE NIGHTINGALE'S EYE (1994)

Holloway, David. 'Princess and Boris Becker', *The Daily Telegraph*, Arts & Books (7 January 1995), p. 7.

Shilling, Jane. 'The Powerful Magic of the Fairy-Tale', *The Sunday Telegraph*, Review (15 January 1995), p. 10.

Smith, Sarah A. 'Unexpectedly Witty', *Literary Review* (January 1995), pp. 9–10.

Spufford, Francis. 'A Djinn in the Tale', *The Guardian*, G2 (17 January 1995), p. 9.

Willard, Nancy. 'Dreams of Jinni', *The New York Times*, Book Review (9 November 1997), p. 38.

BABEL TOWER (1996)

Adair, Tom. 'Too Many Tongues Twist the Message', *The Scotsman, Spectrum* (19 May 1996), p. 11.

Barnacle, Hugo. 'Has A. S. Byatt Lost the Plot', *The Independent Weekend* (4 May 1996), p. 11.

Hensher, Philip. 'Her Shaping Spirit of Imagination', *The Spectator* (11 May 1996), pp. 34–6.

Hughes-Hallet, Lucy. 'Swinging in the Sixties', *The Sunday Times*, Books (5 May 1996), p. 9.

Hulbert, Ann. 'Hungry for Books', *New York Times Book Review* (9 June 1996), p. 7.

Kellaway, Kate. 'Tall Stories', *The Observer* (5 May 1996), p. 14.

Lively, Penelope. 'Truth in Many Tongues', *The Times* (9 May 1996), p. 40.

Sage, Lorna. 'Frederica's Story', *The Times Literary Supplement* (10 May 1996), p. 24.

Seymour, Miranda. 'An Idea Too Big for Its Plot', *The Financial Times, Weekend FT* (11 May 1996), p. xii.

Taylor, D. J. 'My Generation', *The Guardian, The Friday Review* (10 May 1996), p. 11.

ELEMENTALS: STORIES OF FIRE AND ICE (1999)

Clark, Alex. Rev. of *Elementals: Stories of Fire and Ice*, by A. S. Byatt, *The Guardian, Saturday Review* (5 December 1998), p. 10.

Eberstadt, Fernanda. 'Running Hot and Cold', *The New York Times* (13 June 1999), http://www.nytimes.com/books/99/06/13/reviews/990613.13eberst.html

Emck, Katy. 'The Consolations of a Kindly Genie', *The Times Literary Supplement* (13 November 1998), p. 25.

Gardam, Jane. 'Women Breaking Out', *Literary Review* (November 1998), p. 49.

Grant, Katie. 'Tricks of the Light', *The Spectator* (14 November 1998), p. 54.

Hughes-Hallett, Lucy. 'Welcome to the Pleasure Zone', *The Sunday Times, Books* (8 November 1998), p. 13.
Wagner, Erica. 'Size Doesn't Matter for Brief Inspiration', *The Times 2* (12 November 1998), p. 42.

THE BIOGRAPHER'S TALE (2000)

Franklin, Ruth. 'Inauthentic Fabrics', *The New Republic* (23 April 2001), pp. 37–40.
O'Connor, Erin. 'Book Forum: Reading *The Biographer's Tale*', *Victorian Studies* 44 (2002), pp. 379–87.
Scurr, Ruth. 'Underlinings', *London Review of Books* (10 August 2000), pp. 38–9.

A WHISTLING WOMAN (2002)

Adams, Lorraine. 'Lady Novelist', *The New Republic* (17 November 2003), pp. 37–41.
Allardice, Lisa. 'So Much for Freedom', *The Daily Telegraph* (31 August 2002), p. A5.
Clark, Alex. 'Trials by Fire', *The Guardian, Review* (7 September 2002), pp. 28–9.
Craig, Amanda. 'When Ideas Get in the Way of Fiction', *The Times, T2* (28 August 2002), p. 20.
Davies, Steve. 'Birds of Paradise', *The Independent Magazine* (7 September 2002), p. 24.
MacFarlane, Robert. 'A Very Bad Case of Birds on the Brain', *The Observer Review* (15 September 2002), p. 17
Massie, Allan. 'Satirical Swing through the Sixties with a Modern George Eliot', *The Scotsman, Weekend* (7 September 2002), p. 6.
Merkin, Daphne. 'The Novel as Information Superhighway', *The New York Times* (19 January 2003), http://query.nytimes.com/gst/fullpage.html?res=9804E2DC113EF93AA25752C0A9659C8B63
Norris, Pamela. 'Foxy Sexuality', *Literary Review* (September 2002), pp. 51–2.
Scurr, Ruth. 'The Winter of the Virgin Queen', *The Times Literary Supplement* (30 August 2002), p. 6.
Taylor, D. J. 'Farewell to the Virgin in the Garden', *New Statesman* (26 August 2002), pp. 34–5.
Turner, Alice K. 'Spreading Their Wings', *The Washington Post, Book World* (8 December 2002), p. 3.
Yeazell, Ruth Bernard. 'Overindulgence', *London Review of Books* (28 November 2002), pp. 19–21.

THE LITTLE BLACK BOOK OF STORIES (2003)

Abell, Stephen. 'Making It a Just So Story', *The Spectator* (29 November 2003), p. 58.
Craig, Amanda. 'A Monumental Woman', *Literary Review* (December 2003/January 2004), pp. 67–8.
Dunmore, Helen. 'I Am Woman, Hear Me Roar...', *The Times, Weekend Review* (25 October 2003), p. 13.
Matthews, Samantha. 'Monsters, Trolls and Creative Writers', *The Times Literary Supplement* (31 October 2003), pp. 21–2.
Messud, Claire. 'The Beast in the Jungle', *The New York Times, Book Review* (9 May 2004), http://query.nytimes.com/gst/fullpage.html?res=9500E6DE173DF93AA35756C0A9629C8B63
Owen, Katie. 'Jam, Scones and Horror', *The Sunday Telegraph, Review* (16 November 2003), p. 16.
Smith, Ali. 'Her Dark Materials', *The Guardian, Review* (6 December 2003), p. 30.

CRITICISM

THE GAME (1967)

Campbell, Jane. 'The Hunger of the Imagination in A. S. Byatt's *The Game*', *Critique* 29 (1988), pp. 147–62.
Creighton, Joanne V. 'Sisterly Symbiosis: Margaret Drabble's *The Waterfall* and A. S. Byatt's *The Game*', *Mosaic* 20 (1987), pp. 15–29.
Giobbi, Guiliana. 'Sisters Beware of Sisters: Sisterhood As a Literary Motif in Jane Austen, A. S. Byatt and I. Bossi Fedrigotti', *Journal of European Studies* 22 (1992), pp. 241–58.

THE VIRGIN IN THE GARDEN (1978)

Dusinberre, Juliet. 'Forms of Reality in A. S. Byatt's *The Virgin in the Garden*', *Critique* 24 (1982), pp. 55–62.
Leonard, Elisabeth Anne. '"The Burden of Intolerable Strangeness": Using C. S. Lewis to See beyond Realism in the Fiction of A. S. Byatt', *Extrapolation* 39 (1998), pp. 236–48.
Plotz, Judith. 'A Modern "Seer Blest": The Visionary Child in The Virgin in the Garden', *Essays on the Fiction of A. S. Byatt: Imagining the Real*, eds, Alexa Alfer and Michael J. Noble (Connecticut: Greenwood Press, 2001), pp. 31–45.

STILL LIFE (1985)

Cosslett, Tess. 'Childbirth from the Woman's Point of View in British Women's Fiction: Enid Bagnold's *The Squire* and A. S. Byatt's *Still Life*', *Tulsa Studies in Women's Literature* 8 (1989), pp. 263–86.
Sorensen, Sue. 'Something of the Eternal: A. S. Byatt and Vincent van Gogh', *Mosaic* 37 (2004), pp. 63–81.

SUGAR AND OTHER STORIES (1987)

Campbell, Jane. '"The Somehow May be Thishow": Fact, Fiction, and Intertextuality in Antonia Byatt's "Precipice-Encurled"', *Studies in Short Fiction* 28 (1991), pp. 115–23.
Maisonnat, Claude. 'The Ghost Written and the Ghost Writer in A. S. Byatt's Story: "The July Ghost"', *Journal of the Short Story in English* 22 (1994), pp. 49–62.
Sturgess, Charlotte. 'Life Narratives in A. S. Byatt's *Sugar and Other Stories*', *Journal of the Short Story in English* 22 (1994), pp. 29–35.

POSSESSION: A ROMANCE (1990)

Becker, Susanne. 'Postmodernism's Happy Ending: *Possession*!', *Engendering Realism and Postmodernism: Contemporary Women Writers in Britain*, ed., Beate Neumeier (Amsterdam and New York: Rodopi, 2001), pp. 17–30.
Bronfen, Elisabeth. 'Romancing Difference, Courting Coherence: A. S. Byatt's *Possession* as Postmodern Moral Fiction', *Why Literature Matters: Theories and Functions of Literature*, eds, Rüdiger Ahrens and Laurenz Volkmann (Heidelberg: Carl Winter, 1996), pp. 117–34.
Buxton, Jackie. '"What's Love Got to Do with It?": Postmodernism and *Possession*', *English Studies in Canada* 22 (1996), pp. 199–219.

Denenholz Morse, Deborah. 'Crossing Boundaries: The Female Artist and the Sacred Word in A. S. Byatt's *Possession*', *British Women Writing Fiction*, ed., Abby H. P. Werlock (Tuscaloosa and London: University of Alabama Press, 2000), pp. 148–74.

Holmes, Frederick M. 'The Historical Imagination and the Victorian Past: A. S. Byatt's *Possession*', *English Studies in Canada* 20 (1994), pp. 319–34.

Holmes, Frederick M. *The Historical Imagination: Postmodernism and the Treatment of the Past in Contemporary British Fiction* (Victoria: University of Victoria Press, 1997).

Hulbert, Ann. 'The Great Ventriloquist: A. S. Byatt's *Possession: A Romance*', *Contemporary British Women Writers: Texts and Strategies*, ed., Robert E. Hosmer Jr. (London: Macmillan, 1993), pp. 55–64.

Janik, Del Ivan. 'No End of History: Evidence from the Contemporary English Novel', *Twentieth Century Literature* 41 (1995), pp. 160–89.

Keen, Suzanne. *Romances of the Archive in Contemporary British Fiction* (2001. Toronto, London: University of Toronto Press, 2003).

Lundén, Bo. *(Re)educating the Reader: Fictional Critiques of Poststructuralism in Banville's* Dr Copernicus, *Coetzee's* Foe, *and Byatt's* Possession (Göteborg Sweden: Acta Universitatis Gothoburgensis, 1999).

Shiller, Dana . 'The Redemptive Past in the Neo-Victorian Novel', *Studies in the Novel* 29 (1997), pp. 538–60.

Sorensen, Sue. 'Taking Possession: Neil LaBute Adapts a Postmodern Romance', *Literature/Film Quarterly* 32 (2004), pp. 71–7.

Su, John J. 'Fantasies of (Re)collection: Collecting and Imagination in A. S. Byatt's *Possession: A Romance*', *Contemporary Literature* XLV (2004), pp. 684–712.

Todd, Richard. 'The Retrieval of Unheard Voices in British Postmodernist Fiction: A. S. Byatt and Marina Warner', *Liminal Postmodernisms: The Postmodern, the (Post-)Colonial, and the (Post-)Feminist*, eds, Theo D'haen and Hans Bertens (Amsterdam: Rodopi, 1994), pp. 99–114.

Todd, Richard. *Consuming Fictions: the Booker Prize and Fiction in Britain Today* (London: Bloomsbury, 1996).

Walsh, Chris. 'Postmodernist Readings: *Possession*', *The Practice of Reading: Interpreting the Novel*, eds, David Alsop and Chris Walsh (London: Macmillan, 1999), pp. 163–83.

Yelin, Louise. 'Cultural Cartography: A. S. Byatt's *Possession* and the Politics of Victorian Studies', *Victorian Newsletter* 81 (1992), pp. 38–41.

ANGELS AND INSECTS (1992)

Poznar, Susan. 'Tradition and "Experiment" in Byatt's "The Conjugial Angel"', *Critique* 45 (2004), pp. 173–89.

Schor, Hilary M. 'Sorting, Morphing, and Mourning: A. S. Byatt Ghostwrites Victorian Fiction', *Victorian Afterlife: Postmodern Culture rewrites the Nineteenth Century*, eds, John Kucich and Dianne F. Sadoff (Minneapolis and London: University of Minnesota Press, 2000), pp. 234–51.

Shuttleworth, Sally. 'Natural History: The Retro-Victorian Novel', *The Third Culture: Literature and Science*, ed., Elinor S. Shaffer (New York: Walter de Gruyter, 1998), pp. 253–68.

THE MATISSE STORIES (1993)

Fishwick, Sarah. 'Encounters with Matisse: Space, Art, and Intertextuality in A. S. Byatt's *The Matisse Stories* and Marie Redonnet's *Villa Rosa*', *Modern Language Review* 99 (2004), pp. 52–64.

Index